THE
CHURCH
IN
GOD

THE
CHURCH
IN
GOD

Expository Values in Thessalonians

BY

HAROLD J. OCKENGA

FLEMING H. REVELL COMPANY

Contents

Preface

IN MAKING AN EXPOSITION OF THESE EPISTLES ONE GOES OUT on a limb because of the predominance of the teaching concerning the Second Coming and the modern divisions concerning it.

Yet the Thessalonian epistles were the first writings of the New Testament and Paul intended that they be understood, and that by a Greek audience. Hence, we must not read into this things we habitually do. Take it, interpret it in the light of itself, and accept that teaching at face value. It is primitive Christian doctrine, faith, and life. Let it speak for itself.

For me, a premillennialist and one brought up in the dispensational school, it has been difficult to refrain from reading into this what I have been taught about the seventieth week of Daniel, the distinction between the coming for the saints (παρουσία) and the appearance (ἐπιφάνεια) or the revelation (ἀποκάλυψις) in judgment, the two resurrections, the day of Christ, and the day of the Lord, etc. Close scrutiny will find, however, that these things simply are not here in the epistles. We must let the epistles speak for themselves.

I have found no work setting forth a full exposition of these epistles in homiletic form. That seems strange, since they probably were the first writings of the New Testament. In fact, I myself have preached through the entire New Testament in nineteen years of expository ministry at Park

Street Church, leaving these epistles for the last. Now I wish I had dealt with them earlier in my ministry.

Here I set them forth exactly as they were preached to my patient and encouraging congregation and radio audience.

Harold John Ockenga

Boston, Massachusetts

THE
CHURCH
IN
GOD

I

The Birth of a Church

*For our gospel came not unto you in word only, but also in
power, and in the Holy Ghost, and in much assurance. . . .*
                                    —I THESSALONIANS 1:5A

IN WRITING THE FIRST EPISTLE TO THE THESSALONIANS, ST.
Paul was reliving the experience of founding a church in the
first century. Paul was living at Corinth (Acts 18:1,3) near
the end of his second missionary journey. Timothy had just
returned from a mission of consolation and instruction to the
infant Thessalonian Church and had brought news of its condition to the Apostle. The good tidings of their faith, their
love of St. Paul, and their desire to see him greatly cheered
the Apostle, who had been passing through one of the seasons
of great distress which marked his career (I Thess. 3:6,7).
As a result, the encouraged Apostle preached the Word with
great liberty at Corinth, and almost simultaneously sat down
to write the Epistle to the Thessalonians in which he thanks
God for their faith, love, and hope, demonstrating that they
were established in the faith which they had so eagerly received.

This church was as important to St. Paul as a newborn
baby is to the parents of the child; in fact, he compares himself to a nurse cherishing her own children and to a father
affectionately disposed to his child. It was as important to

him as the launching of a great ocean-going liner is to the
builder thereof, or as the completion of a cathedral is to its
architect. Recently, I stood in the Salisbury Cathedral, mar-
veling at the wonders of its architecture and the graceful lines
of the pillars which support so tremendous a load of cement,
stone, and iron in the more than four-hundred-foot tower,
which has stood for seven hundred fifty years. In the year
1205 A.D., Elias of Durham conceived and began to execute
the building of this great cathedral. Fifty years later he was
able to look on the completed edifice which has been called
"the most glorious building in the world." The feelings which
Elias of Durham experienced toward his architectural creation, St. Paul must have experienced over the Thessalonian
Church. His reliving of that experience of the founding of
the church and his affection and his tender references to it
in his epistle have survived to quicken all succeeding generations of Christians.

This epistle is the first writing of St. Paul which is contained in our Bible and it is possibly the first of all of our
New Testament writings. The only possible exceptions are
the Epistle of James and the Gospel of Matthew. It brings us
back to within the time somewhere between 49 and 53 A.D.
or a little less than twenty years after the crucifixion and the
resurrection of Christ.[1] This brings us in close touch with
the doctrine and life of the primitive church. The teachings
of St. Paul are not presented as something new, but as something accepted by the primitive church.

The authenticity of this book is accepted by all scholars
since the time of F. C. Baur. Its contents correspond accu-
rately with historical facts and constitute an amplification of
the record of the founding of this church given to us in Acts
17:1-8.

In Thessalonians we find illustrated the method and message of apostolic evangelistic work which resulted in a new
church. The results of this preaching were phenomenal. In

the course of a few weeks the church was founded, established, and developed into vigorous life. No wonder St. Paul
could write, "Our gospel came not unto you in word only,
but also in power, and in the Holy Ghost, and in much
assurance . . ." (I Thess. 1:5).

The founding of the Thessalonian Church is a prime example of the way the apostles came into a community and
sowed the seed which ultimately fructified in a Christian
civilization. Thessalonica was a heathen city on the Gulf of
Thermaikos so situated as to be a natural center of commerce
in addition to possessing hot springs used for medicinal
purposes.[2] In 315 B.C. Cassander, one of the generals of Alexander the Great, rebuilt this city and named it after Thessalonica, a sister of Alexander. When the Romans divided
Macedonia into a tetrarchy, Thessalonica became the chief
city of the second province. It was located on the Roman
road called the "Via Egnatia" leading southwesterly from
Philippi on the Northern Aegean to the Adriatic and thence
to Rome.[3] The value of its natural location has been demonstrated by the fact that Salonika is still an important city of
modern Greece and was the prize of much fighting in World
War II.

Here the mystery religions thrived, namely, the Eleusinian
and the cult of the Kabeiroi. The latter was second only to
the Eleusinian Mysteries and, as Lightfoot suggests, it may
have included foul orgies in connection with the worship.
"The pagan attitude to sex relations was extremely tolerant—
and in some religious societies, sacramental fornication was a
part of the worship,"[4] for it was supposed to lead the par-
ticipant into mystical union with the deity.

The city itself was a free city ruled over by politarchs who
were elected by the people.[5]

Into this heathen community of moral indifference, materialism, and false religion came the gospel to create a holy
Christian community of born-again ones, a colony from

heaven, a called-out people. The community at first must have been small, but it was exceedingly important and influential, for not only common people, but some of the leading personages of the city believed the gospel (Acts 17:4). A great multitude of Greeks also embraced the faith and a strong church was founded.

Hope to transform the new heathenism of our day must also rest in the Christian message. Heathenism today may not be as raw and open as it was in Paul's day, but it is as totally secular and it is becoming more and more similar to the materialism and immorality of the Hellenism of that first century. The new heathenism is as totally divorced from God as was the old heathenism. If the gospel flourished in such an environment, it can flourish again under the power of God.

The phases of this little church's experience in relation to the world are here detailed in the epistle. It describes the birth of the church, the growth of the church, the testimony of the church, the detractions of the church, the church and anti-Semitism, the sufferings of the church, the Lord's coming for His church, prayer for the church, and the holiness of the church. It is to these subjects that we will address ourselves in the studies which are ahead.

We do so with the basic conviction that these epistles have a tremendous contribution to make to the modern church when they are understood and when their meaning is appropriated. Our text describes the birth of that church— "Our gospel came not unto you in word only, but also in power, and in the Holy Ghost, and in much assurance. . . ." Here we see the entrance of the gospel into Thessalonica, the experience of the gospel by the Thessalonians, and the effect of the gospel preaching on the Thessalonians.

I. *The Entrance of the Gospel to Thessalonica*

Paul said, ". . . our gospel came . . ." (I Thess. 1:5). He also referred to their knowledge of "what manner of men we were among you" (*Ibid.*), and ". . . our entrance in unto you . . ." (I Thess. 2:1). The fact that the gospel had entrance to the Thessalonians is the important thing for it is the event which transformed that city and constituted it a habitation of the church of God.

When did this occur? We have already said that it was on the second missionary journey. Godet, in his *Studies on the Epistles*, describes the events which preceded this in the life of St. Paul. Paul must have been above thirty years of age when he was converted on the Damascus Road or he would not have been entrusted with so important a mission by the Sanhedrin. Following that conversion, he sojourned for three years in Arabia, clarifying his own thinking and making his beginnings in preaching. Then he returned to Jerusalem for a few days before leaving for Tarsus. It is interesting to note that Paul was called to be an apostle to the Gentiles and that undoubtedly at Tarsus, which was then the rival of Athens in culture, he prepared for that mission to the Gentiles. This was finally ended by the coming of Barnabas, summoning him to Antioch to assist in the revival which was taking place among the Gentile community of that city. Somewhere around the year 45 Paul and Barnabas were ordained as missionaries and set apart to the great call of God. The first journey through Cyprus, Pamphylia, and lower Asia Minor probably took several years. After this they participated in the Jerusalem Council to clarify the content of the gospel. Almost immediately after that, Paul began his second missionary journey accompanied by Silas, a Hebrew Christian, which took him through Galatia, where he added Timothy to his party, then westward to Troas, where apparently Luke joined his party. From there the little group, in answer to the Macedonian call, went to Philippi certainly not later than the autumn of 52 A.D. Here their ministry was ended by a severe beating, an imprisonment, and finally a deliverance with an invitation to leave the city. They made their way in a southwesterly direction along the Via Egnatia through Amphipolis and Apollonia until they came to Thessalonica. Here they made their way to the synagogue of the Jews and began to preach the gospel— "Opening and alleging (out of the scriptures), that Christ must needs have suffered, and risen again from the dead; and that this Jesus . . . is Christ" (Acts 17: 3). Paul declares that he preached the gospel unto them in much agony (I Thess. 2:2), so that he evidently came, still lame from the severe treatment he had suffered at Philippi, showing unhealed cuts on his face and his head and with torn, much-mended clothing, approximately in the spring of the year 53 A.D.

For three Sabbath days Paul entered the synagogue of the Jews and reasoned with them out of the Scriptures. As far as the Scripture implies, this is the length of his stay in Thessalonica, but it seems that a longer time is necessary to permit some of the Jews to become converted, the chief women of the city to become followers of the gospel, and proselytes and heathen to be turned from their idols to the living God.[6] On the other hand, Paul's reference to the power with which the gospel entered may imply that the time was very brief and not much longer than that which is referred to in connection with the synagogue. What a campaign of evangelism this comprised! One can easily see the crowds thronging the synagogue, the excitement caused by the new doctrine, the visitors at Paul's lodgings in the home of Jason, the final repudiation of the doctrine by the Jews, the withdrawal of Paul to preach in some public place, and the subsequent riot which drove him from the city. The very success of the mission is the reason why the Jews opposed the Apostle. Luke says they were ". . . moved with envy . . ." (Acts 17:5). Much of the derogatory criticism and overt opposition of materialists or even of some so-called religious leaders to the work of the gospel is due to its popularity when it is preached in power. In this same manner the gospel has been going into communities all over the world ever since the days of St. Paul. Missionaries have faced similar obstacles and yet have established churches in most of the nations, tribes, and peoples of the world.

How did this gospel come to Thessalonica? The point of contact for the apostles was the synagogue. Here the monotheistic Jews worshiped. Here the proselytes from heathendom worshiped. Here the God-fearers, who were disgusted with the immorality and obscenity of idolatry, came to be instructed in our more elevated form of religion. This was the natural point of contact for the religious people of those days. Paul was a Rabbi and would be accepted in the synagogue as a teacher, thus giving him an opportunity to preach. As a result of his declaration of the gospel and his reasoning among them from the Scriptures, there always were some who believed and some who rejected. Here they are described as ". . . having received the word in much affliction, with joy of the Holy Ghost" (I Thess. 1:6). Their affliction arose from those who rejected; their joy arose from daily receiving the gospel and experiencing the work which the Holy Ghost did in their hearts. Thus both Paul's opportunity and his opposition stem from the same direction, namely, the synagogue. Our points of contact in preaching the gospel today are utterly different, but we must seize upon them as faithfully as St. Paul did upon his.

In referring to Paul's condition as he entered Thessalonica, he draws on the testimony of the opposition, namely, the Jews, for "they themselves shew of us what manner of entering in we had unto you . . ." (I Thess. 1:9). He came in physical pain due to the beating which he had received at Philippi. He came in mental tension which was due to the opposition at Philippi and again at Thessalonica. He came in social uneasiness because of the conflict of the gospel with the customs of that day.

Paul's plan of attack was first to present the gospel to the

Jews from their own Scriptures, then to declare the glad
tidings unto the Gentiles, and then to teach from house to
house. This constituted the accepted means of making the
gospel known in that day. Our mode of reaching the religious
and non-religious people of our own day with the gospel may
be a bit different due to printing, radio, and amplification, but
the essential method is still the same, namely, preaching. Let
no man think lightly of preaching or ask for a moratorium on
preaching for it is by preaching that God is pleased to save
those who believe.

What did Paul preach when the gospel entered Thessalonica? Much is made of the fact that St. Paul had not yet
developed his theology when he wrote the Book of Thessalonians and that he did not present a systematic treatise on
doctrine. We are told that this epistle is more practical, more
personal, that there is little doctrine in it, but how untrue that
is when one actually reads the epistle and ascertains for himself what Paul preached. The gospel which Paul preached at
Thessalonica is recapitulated in the epistle itself. Moreover,
St. Paul had already preached for fifteen years and was more
than halfway through his whole ministry at this point. Are we
to believe, then, that he had not yet received his gospel? Are
we to believe that he had not yet developed his theology? A
close scrutiny of this Book will find that St. Paul declared the
doctrine of the Trinity, greeting the church which is in God
the Father and in the Lord Jesus Christ and declaring the
ministry of the Holy Spirit (I Thess. 1:1,5). He many times
calls Jesus Lord in the epistle and in one place he prays unto
Christ and to God the Father requesting direction of his way
(I Thess. 3:11). Paul unequivocally declares the work of the
Holy Spirit in ministering the truth, he acknowledges their
election of God (I Thess. 1:4), he points out the fact of their
conversion or turning from idols to God (I Thess. 1:9), he
warns them about the wrath of God to come upon the Jews
and upon all men (I Thess. 2:16), he describes the tribulation

of the church (I Thess. 3:3), he exhorts to holiness (I Thess. 5:23), he expounds the second coming and the resurrection both of Christ and of the believers (I Thess. 4:13-17), he points out the necessity of practical work in order to live, of prayer and of perseverance. If this is an undeveloped gospel it at least is a sufficient gospel to transform the lives of men.

This gospel is the only adequate reason for such missionary work and for such sacrificial living as is found in the life of Paul, in the life of Silas, and in the life of Timothy. What else could explain the things through which they passed?

That gospel is sufficient now to change the lives of heathen into Christians, of homes from debased dwelling places to habitations of love, of communities from cesspools of iniquity to testimonies of righteousness. Let the gospel be preached and believed and the transformation will come.

II. *The Experience of the Gospel*

Paul says, "Our gospel came not unto you in word only, but also in *power*, and in the *Holy Ghost*, and in *much assurance* . . ." (Thess. 1:5). It is good to note what gospel preaching is not. It is not declaring the truth in word only. Lightfoot says that the passage may be paraphrased thus, "Our preaching was not mere declamation, a hollow and heartless rhetoric: in it there was earnestness and power. Yet this is not enough. There may be a power which is not from above, a fearful earnestness which is not inspired by God. Not such was ours, for we preached in the Holy Spirit. Still even the holiest influences may be transitory, the noblest inspirations may waver from lack of faith. Far otherwise was it with us, for we preached in a deep conviction of the truth of our message, in a perfect assurance of the ultimate triumph of our cause." [7] The apostles did not preach a word of eloquence, of fact, of truth alone, but of life, of salvation and of grace. They came unto them not with words of man's wisdom, but in the demonstration and power of the Holy

Ghost (I Cor. 2:2). The gospel is not the wisdom of men. If we treat it as human reasoning and logic rather than divine revelation, it will be of no value. In Galatians (Gal. 1:8), Paul even invokes the judgment of God upon those who preach any other gospel than that which has been preached. Listening to such a gospel which does not come in the power of the Holy Ghost, one can only call it "words! words! words!" Instead of the divine presence and working in preaching, there is nothing but futility with such presentation.

If the gospel is not in word only, then in what does it consist? St. Paul emphasizes in Romans 1:16, I Corinthians 1:24, and in this text that the gospel is the power of God unto salvation. The time element in the sojourn and the ministry at Thessalonica gives evidence that it is the power of God. In a few weeks a supernatural work was done which surpasses parallel.[8] The question with all preaching today should be, Are people getting saved? Are they being transformed? Is the church being edified? Are heathen being reached? If not, the gospel is in word only. In Thessalonica great changes were wrought in the people. The power of which Paul speaks was not the power to do miracles in order that the gospel might be attested, but the power to transform their lives from that of immoral fornicators and adulterers to pure, holy, and clean lives, from dishonest to honest persons, from rioters to those who walk in quietness and sobriety. Let that be the test of our preaching today. The fruit will reveal whether it is dry ethical essaying or whether it consists of words of flaming fire.

Gospel preaching is that attended by the Holy Ghost. What is Holy Ghost preaching? Certainly not mere zeal, enthusiasm, and fervor alone, although when the Holy Ghost lays hold upon a man he will be on fire and he will speak with fervor and enthusiasm. Holy Ghost preaching, however, is preaching attended by the Holy Ghost's blessing and work. That work begins in regeneration. The work of the Holy Ghost is to recreate the natures of people and bring them into the kingdom of God. One thing for which I prayed in my last ministry in Westminster Chapel, London, was that there would be fruit, and how I rejoiced when men such as an air force officer, a Cook's Travel Agency director, a London policeman, a man in the diplomatic service, a Swiss commercial man came and confessed faith in Jesus Christ as a result of the preaching. That was the work of the Holy Ghost. It is the Holy Ghost's work to convict of sin, to burden men's consciences for breaking the law, and to lead them to confess Christ as their Saviour. It is the Holy Ghost's work to sanctify the believers, bringing them to a complete break with sin and a transformation in their living. They must be made Christlike by the work of the Holy Spirit so as to bear fruit in their living.

Gospel preaching is with much assurance. The bane of much Christianity is its inanity, its uncertainty, its hesitancy rather than its certainty, boldness, and security. St. Paul preached with real conviction, but it is not this kind of conviction which is described as full assurance. Full assurance was the doctrine of the Wesleyan revival. It proclaimed that the people could know when they were saved and that they were saved. Assurance is a biblical doctrine—the doctrine that the Spirit of God bears witness with our spirits that we are the children of God (Rom. 8:16). This assurance ought to be the experience of every believer. It is Holy Ghost preaching when it produces assurance in the lives of men and women that they are forgiven of their sin, are children of God, and have eternal life.

What does such gospel preaching do? It brings a revival. It brought a revival in Thessalonica and it will bring a revival today. Whenever you get that type of preaching, something happens. Real conversions occur and real controversy ensues.

That preaching makes certain men miserable because they love their sins and they will try to attack the preacher and try to refute that which he preaches. What happened at Thessalonica can happen again. We ought to expect it with true gospel preaching. This is the standard which is lifted up in the primitive church and by it we should judge our work today. Where then do we stand in this experience? Do we know the power of the gospel to save and to deliver? Do we know the work of the Holy Ghost in convicting, converting, and comforting? Do we have the assurance that our sins are forgiven and that we are children of God? May the Lord help us to be satisfied with no less.

III. *The Effect of Gospel Preaching on the Thessalonians*

"And ye became followers of us, and of the Lord, having received the word in much affliction, with joy of the Holy Ghost" (I Thess. 1:6). Paul knew immediately that the influence of himself, of Silvanus, and of Timothy on these converts was great. They became imitators or followers of them. You may not think so but those who believe and hear the gospel immediately begin to imitate those who declare the gospel. Many figures are used by St. Paul to represent this influence and they describe the tenderness with which he considered his Thessalonian converts. On one occasion he describes himself as a father longing for his children, on another as a nurse cherishing her own, on another as an orphan deprived of his parents because he is away from them. Thus running from one figure of speech to another, St. Paul attempts to show the people his affection, his interest, his care, his longing for them. Mindful then of this influence, Paul keeps these converts constantly before his thinking. So must we. We cannot live unto ourselves. We must remember that people are constantly reading us as epistles of God, that they will be established in the faith because of what they see in us, or they will be caused to stumble because of what they see in us. Let, therefore, our conduct be governed by our brother's needs.

But Paul hastens on stating that they also were imitators of the Lord. In I Corinthians 11:1 he says, "Be ye followers of me, even as I also am of Christ." That is undoubtedly the meaning here. They imitated St. Paul but only insofar as Paul was an imitator of Christ. From the messenger of salvation, the convert must have his eyes ultimately fixed upon Christ. This means maturity in the faith. It does not occur immediately, but it must come or such a convert will have his faith built upon false foundations. Though we may see Christ in the messenger of the gospel, yet our eyes must be lifted above that messenger and fastened upon the Lord Himself.

It is fatal to such converts if the messenger fails to represent Christ. Paul walked so closely that he could urge them to imitate him as he also imitated Christ. He could look back upon his sojourn in Thessalonica and remember that there was nothing which would disparage the character of Christ or the content of the gospel in what he did. The power of Christian example is inestimable.

How futile are the words of a Christian if his example belies them. Then the gospel comes only in word—not in power, in the Holy Ghost and in much assurance. Consistency, thou art a jewel!

The immediate influence of the apostles was thereby enlarged for St. Paul says, ". . . ye were ensamples to all . . ." (I Thess. 1:7). The order is first Christ, then we, then you, then all. So the outreach of the gospel is like a pebble dropped in a pool until the ripples are felt on the final edge of the lake in larger and larger circumferences. No one ever lives or dies to himself, and the sooner a Christian learns that the better it is. On and on go the influences of the Holy Ghost in Christian experience through the world.

Thus a church was born and through it an endless power

of good was set in motion in the world. In the multiplication of such churches in such communities there was laid the foundation of Christian civilization. Let that work be repeated in every community which hears the gospel and wherever we can send the gospel, and God will attend that gospel with power, with the Holy Ghost and with much assurance.

II

The Growth of a Church

*We give thanks to God always for you all, making mention
of you in our prayers; remembering without ceasing your
work of faith, and labour of love, and patience of hope in
our Lord Jesus Christ, in the sight of God and our Father;
knowing, brethren beloved, your election of God.*

—I THESSALONIANS 1:2-4

THE EPISTLE OPENS WITH THE INVOCATION OF GRACE UPON THE
infant church of Thessalonica. The concept of grace was the
predominant thought in the ministry of John Henry Jowett.
His biographer, Arthur Porritt, says, "To Jowett, redeeming
grace was the fulcrum of the evangelical message . . . In a
hundred sermons he proclaimed it. All his wealth of imagery
and illustration was lavished upon this theme." Jowett himself
said, "There is no word I have wrestled so much with as
grace. It is like expressing a great American forest by a word.
No phrase can express the meaning of grace . . . Grace is
more than mercy. It is more than tender mercy. It is more
than a multitude of tender mercies. Grace is more than love.
It is more than the innocent love. Grace is holy love, but it is
holy love in spontaneous movement going out in eager quest
toward the unholy and the unlovely, that by the ministry of

its own sacrifice it might redeem the unholy and the unlovely
into its own strength and beauty. The grace of God is holy
love on the move to thee and me, and to the like of thee and
me. It is God unmerited, undeserved, going out towards the
children of men, that He might win them to the glory and the
brightness of His own likeness . . . Grace moved to the cross
to set the bondman free and to proclaim an amnesty to all
mankind. At the cross the grim monarchies of sin and death
die the unutterable death of the Son of God. It is all of
grace." [1]

Grace is from God the Father and from the Lord Jesus
Christ, not from the apostles, even though the reference to the
Father and to Christ is omitted from the best manuscripts. The
thought is still carried over from the introductory sentence.
Grace may be attributed equally to the Father and to the Son.
The plan of redemption may have originated with the Father's
love and wisdom, but it was by no means confined to the Father. Grace flows from Christ as well as from the Father. We
read, "And the Word was . . . full of grace . . ." (John 1:14).
The activity of the Trinity in behalf of men in creation, in
redemption, in providence, and in answer to prayer is all of
grace. There are no rights on the side of man. It is never a bit
earned, but it is all given. It even anticipates all asking on the
part of man. All benefits to the church and to the souls of
men stem from the grace of God. Paul illustrates this by saying, ". . . Grace be unto you, and peace . . ." (I Thess. 1:1).
There could never be peace unto men without it being devised
by divine grace. The grace which produced the cross is the
grace which brought peace to men. We ". . . are made nigh
by the blood of Christ. For he is our peace, who hath made
both one . . . so making peace" (Eph. 2:13-15). Hence holiness, fellowship, sonship, and eternal life are all of grace. It
is impossible to wish a church or a man a greater blessing than
the grace of God.

Greetings in grace from the triumvirate of fellow workers

were extended to these Thessalonian Christians. Only the fact that they had received God's grace in the gospel and lived in the grace of God made these men feel their debt to communicate the gospel to the Thessalonians under the circumstances in which they did. They were debtors to the Greeks (Rom. 1:14). Though they were now absent from the Thessalonian Church, they continued their interest in it. I have often felt, as a pastor, that I made a mistake in so abruptly breaking off relationships to my previous church, which I had served for five and one-half years. Under the mistaken notion that I ought to leave the field free for my successor, I refused to have much intercourse with the members and friends of that church by means of mail and personal visit. Had I to do it over again, I would not have pursued that course any more than St. Paul withdrew all interest in the Thessalonian Church when he left that community.

The first in the triumvirate was Paul. It is impossible to estimate the meaning of that great name to these new Christians and to the churches ever since this epistle was written. The name Paul conveys strength, stability, comfort, courage, conviction. It is a name with which to conjure, for Paul was a vessel of the truth in divine revelation, he was a powerful opponent of error, he was a general in the art of strategy, and he was a man sent from God. Those who were connected with Paul were on the rock on which Paul stood, namely, Christ.

From time to time God has privileged me to be used in sending young men into the ministry. Recently a letter came stating the source of strength and comfort which my own evangelical position has been to a young man now in a pulpit of great prominence. I pray God that stability and strength will always be mine so that those who have been led into the ministry because of my own influence will find comfort and courage in it.

The second member of the triumvirate was Silvanus or

Silas, as he is called in other parts of the Bible.[2] Silas along
with Judas was marked by the Jerusalem Council as
". . . chief men among the brethren" (Acts 15:22). Hence,
before Silas ever became connected with St. Paul, he was a
leader in his own right in the Christian community. He was
chosen by Paul and accepted the invitation to make the second
missionary journey after the unfortunate division between
Barnabas and Paul over taking Mark with them on this
journey. Thus Silas shared the hardships, the sufferings (Acts
16:25), the responsibility, the preaching, and the personal
work of St. Paul on this long and arduous missionary journey.
Like Paul, he was a Roman citizen (Acts 16:38). Such companions in labor are a great boon. Christ adopted the method of
sending out His disciples two by two and it has always proved
a good psychology. Man is not made to be alone. When Paul
was alone, he was discouraged and dejected, but when his
companions in travel were with him, he waxed bold and
strong in the faith. This was true when Silas and Timothy
joined him at Corinth (Acts 18:5). Silas had been performing
a Macedonian ministry after his Thessalonian experience, and
he joined up with Timothy to reach the Apostle at Corinth,
there to undertake his last mutual work with St. Paul. There-
inafter he seems to have become connected with Peter and
was the bearer of his first epistle (I Pet. 5:12).

Timothy, the third member of the triumvirate, was Paul's
dear son in the faith (I Tim. 1:2; II Tim. 1:2). No relationship in the New Testament is comparable to that of Paul and
Timothy. From the time that Paul called him to be his associate in the gospel (Acts 16:1-3), they enjoyed the relationship
of father and son—intimate, loving, and unbroken—to the
end. Paul's second epistle to Timothy is a living monument of
that intimate relationship, of Paul's longing to see him, and of
his last advice given to one whom he thought he might never
see again. It is the Christian faith which creates such fellowship and friendship, and those who give their lives to Christ

receive in return one hundredfold. I count as my personal friends many of the greatest living leaders of the church, who are likewise loyal to the faith of Jesus Christ. Our knowledge of Timothy's character drawn from the Scripture shows him to be the opposite of St. Paul. He was reticent, youthful, diffident, submissive, and cheerful and thus his presence was of inestimable value to St. Paul in all of his journeying. It was Timothy who brought the news from Thessalonica and thus gave Paul the material cause of this epistle. He had been thinking and praying about his church for a long time, but when he learned from Timothy the good news of their stability in the face of affliction and also received a report of their problems, he felt obligated to defend his own person and way of life before his detractors and to present a series of teaching concerning their way of life, dealing with practical problems.

The growth of the Thessalonian Church was dependent upon the grace of God. The hostility of its environment to this gospel and to the infant church was very evident. The heathen had no use for purity, for honesty, for self-sacrifice and service. Their lives were beamed to the exact opposite of these. So these Christian folk would be misfits among them. Moreover, the Jews had rejected this message in fulfillment of the prophetic blindness which was already coming upon them. Their opposition to the gospel was unremitting.

Here was a helpless church without teachers, without written Bible, without past experience, and without knowledge. No wonder Paul was concerned about their continuance in the faith. No wonder he prayed for them constantly.

How interesting is it to note that this infant church was established by faith in the second coming of Christ joined with other truths. This truth is the most emphasized truth in the first epistle to the Thessalonians and it is confirmed by the fact that his opponents charged him with doing ". . . contrary to the decrees of Caesar, saying that there is another

king, one Jesus" (Acts 17:7). Those who think that the
second coming should never be held out in teaching and
preaching before young Christians are refuted by the overwhelming emphasis of this epistle and of this practice by St.
Paul. Fasten your faith on Christ crucified as the Saviour and
on Christ coming as King, and you will be secure in your
faith, you will grow as did the Thessalonian Church. What
were the factors in this growth in grace?

I. *Prayer*

Paul said, "We give thanks to God always for you all,
making mention of you in our prayers; remembering without
ceasing your work . . ." (I Thess. 1:2,3). The apostles mag-
nified God for the work of grace done in Thessalonica. They
said, "We give thanks to God always for you. . . ." The
experience of awakening through the reception of the Word
of God at Thessalonica by the heathen, by the God-fearers,
by the proselytes, and by the Jews was enough to enrich their
faith forever. They remembered that the gospel came not in
word only but in power, in the Holy Ghost, and in much
assurance. For this experience they could always thank God.
Several such experiences I too have known under the blessing
and grace of God. One was the Mid-Century Evangelistic
Campaign when the Lord did so graciously a great work in
Massachusetts and in New England. Another was at St. John,
New Brunswick, where a whole series of churches could not
contain the people who wanted to hear the gospel and where
scores and scores accepted Christ in a few days. What God
has done once, He can do again. As St. Paul did, help me to
remember and to be thankful, O Lord.

This experience was a great encouragement to St. Paul in
Athens and in Corinth. We cannot doubt that when Paul
came to Corinth he was discouraged, for he came in trembling
and in weakness and in fear. There are those who feel that
his experience at Athens was a monumental failure. We can-

not share that convicition for there were converts and from Athens came one of Paul's closest followers, yet it was the memory of this wonderful Thessalonian revival that sustained him in the midst of his difficult work at Corinth. Let past blessings excite faith for future ones. This is the value of keeping a prayer list. As you mark the answers to your previous prayers, you have faith to ask God for greater things to come.

The expression of thanksgiving or gratulation is basic to Paul. In all his epistles it is only omitted in Galatians and in the pastoral epistles. Otherwise they all begin with thanksgiving. Let the Christian learn this habit—to be thankful to his family, to his fellow workers in his speech, and to God in his prayers. Here is the secret of unanswered prayer (Phil. 4:6).

In Paul's prayer he made mention of individuals and of details. He said, "Making mention of you in our prayers." The expression is used continuously by St. Paul in reference to his praying (Eph. 1:16; Philemon 4, Rom. 1:9). It suggests the specific nature of Paul's praying. He who prays in generalities does not pray at all. Prayer which is effective is praying about specific objectives. If one prays in general for all missionaries and names none, he usually knows the condition of none. If one uses nebulous phrases in praying about persons and work, he may expect nebulous results. Paul undoubtedly carried Jason and the members of his household to the throne of grace very often because of the danger in which they were on account of his ministry. He brought many of those Thessalonians to God by name and in accordance with their needs. The references of St. Paul to individual persons in his epistles show that practice. What about the needy members of your family? Or your community? Or your circle of friends? Have you brought them by name to the Lord?

Paul also made the practice of speaking to God. He says he

made mention of them. Some men of prayer found it essential
to pray while they were kneeling, others while they were
lying on their faces, but talk to Him they did. I know a man
of God who also is well known to you all who usually begins
on his knees, and before he finishes in prayer will have walked
up and down the room and finally have fallen upon his face
before God. At Wesley's home on City Road, London, one
may see the room where he slept for the last eighteen years of
his life. Opening off that room to the east is a little closet with
a fireplace and a window. In it is a table and a chair and a
candlestick. Here it was where John Wesley prayed an hour
each morning for his churches, his local preachers, his converts, his sermons, and all the phases of the Wesleyan Revival.
When the sun came up in the east, John Wesley was on his
knees in prayer.

Spiritual aspiration for individuals ought to be expressed
to God. Their deepening, their growth in the faith, their en-
largement of vision will come by prayer because someone has
released spiritual power in them. If you want your preacher
to be a better preacher, a deeper preacher, a more spiritual
preacher, pray for him, and if we preachers want our people
to grow in grace, we ought to pray for them, not neglecting
to bring them by name to the throne.

Memory is exercised in such prayer. Paul says, "Remembering without ceasing . . ." (I Thess. 1:3). The word "un-
ceasing" or unremitting modifies "making mention," [3] as also
it does in Romans 1:9. The conclusion which we reach is that
the spiritual development of this church is dependent upon
the continuous prayer of Paul. The greatest need in our
churches today is prayer warriors, that is those who practice
the ministry of intercession. God grant us men and women of
prayer and of faith and the ministers and officers of the
church can do wonders.

The union of this activity of prayer with the memory of
their good works brought a stimulus to Paul as he prayed.

He was remembering their ". . . work of faith, and labour of love, and patience of hope . . ." (I Thess. 1:3). They brought forth fruit meet for repentance while Paul was there and the fresh thought of that stimulated him to pray more concerning them. Let us unbind our memories! Let us unlock the closets in which we have shut up past experiences! Jesus said, ". . . this do in remembrance of me" (Luke II 19). Everyone wants to be remembered and memory is a wonderful aid to prayer and good works. When an aged parent becomes feebleminded and irresponsible, many a child who has locked up the closet of memory puts such a parent away, whereas he who will remember the works of love, of provision, of faith, and of sacrifice made by that parent will be led into good works in caring for him.

II. *Progress*

The object of Paul's memory was their ". . . work of faith, and labour of love, and patience of hope . . ." (I Thess. 1:3). This triad of Christian graces is common to the epistles of St. Paul. To the Colossians he wrote, "We heard of your faith in Christ Jesus, and of the love which ye have to all the saints, for the hope which is laid up for you in heaven . . ." (Col. 1:4,5). To the Galatians he wrote, "We through the Spirit wait for the hope of righteousness by faith . . . faith which worketh by love" (Gal. 5:5,6). To the Corinthians Paul wrote, "Now abideth faith, hope, charity, these three; but the greatest of these is charity" (I Cor. 13:13). The sequence of these graces is natural. First comes faith the source of all Christian virtues, second comes love the sustaining principle of the Christian life, and third comes hope the beacon which guides us to the life to come.[4] The virtues of work, labor, and patience are connected with the graces as effects are to causes or as results to sources.

Work, labor, and patience are not synonymous, but are progressively distinguished in their meaning. Christ said to the

Ephesians, "I know thy works, and thy labour, and thy patience . . ." (Rev. 2:2). These virtues rise in an ascending scale as proof of their steadfastness and devotion. Lightfoot says of Colossians 1:4,5, "Faith rests on the past; love works on the present; hope looks to the future." [5] Let us therefore look at these three virtues of the Christian life.

Paul is thankful for their work of faith. Faith is the source and the root of all good works. The entire Scripture emphasizes the necessity of such works as evidence of saving faith. James said, "Thou hast faith, and I have works: shew me thy faith without thy works, and I will shew thee my faith by my works" (James 2:18). The tree must have not only the trunk and branches, but a root system which compares in size to the trunk and the branches. Faith is the root; works are the fruit.

Faith was the means of the salvation or justification of these Thessalonians, as it is with all Christians. Paul's epistles to the Romans and to the Galatians were written as an exposition of the doctrine of justification by faith. That faith is a trust in Christ's finished work on the cross, without which no one knows even the basic fundamentals of a Christian experience. With alacrity the Thessalonians had received and obeyed the gospel and theirs was not a profession alone. They immediately began to bring forth fruits of repentance and faith. Faith then is man's response to God's grace and love.

Faith without such works is dead. It cannot save. There are four different kinds of faith mentioned in the Scripture. There is historical faith, which is an intellectual assent to the truths of the gospel without a personal committal to them. The demons believe the gospel and they tremble, but they are not saved (James 2:19). There is a temporary faith, which is based on the emotions, which receives with gladness the word, but since it has no depth in understanding and in life, it soon withers away under the scorching sun of persecution and tribulation (Matt. 13:6). There is a miraculous faith, namely, the kind which is seated in the will and may perform miracles

but does not transform the human heart. Such was Judas'
faith. Then there is saving faith, which is based upon the
heart and involves the whole man—mind, heart, and will—
so that he has committed himself in complete trust to Jesus
Christ as Saviour. This is the kind of faith which produces
works of righteousness.

Next in the ascending scale of virtues is the labor of love.
Labor actually means toil, fatiguing work, exhausting service.
Christians have been noted for taking upon themselves such
redemptive labors which are exhausting. Probably two of the
best illustrations of this who are known to any of us are Mrs.
Julia Lake Kellersberger and her husband, Dr. Eugene Kellersberger, who have the responsibility of the American
Leprosy Mission which is attempting to reach over 10,000,000
lepers with the gospel of Jesus Christ. Their love, their com-
passion, their humility, and their fervency in living entirely
for others demonstrates this truth. A characteristic of Christians has been this incessant labor to enlighten, to ennoble, to
purify, and to aid humanity. Such moral superiority to other
religions should in itself commend the Christian gospel to us.
Let it not be thought that God will be unmindful of such
labors of love which are expended toward His people. He
surely will compensate His servants for them (Heb. 6:10).

The motive of such exhaustive, sacrificial, self-denying
service is love. First, it is love for Christ. Paul states that
motive when he says, "For the love of Christ constraineth us;
because we thus judge, that if one died for all, then were all
dead: and that he died for all, that they which live should not
henceforth live unto themselves, but unto him which died for
them, and rose again" (II Cor. 5:14,15). Second, it is love
for our fellow men. One cannot be separated from the other,
for it is only as we see Christ in our fellow men that we can
love them and want to perform this kind of labor for them.
Notable is it that when Christ rebuked the Ephesian Church,
it was because they had lost their first love, namely, this moti-

vating affection so that their works became mere mechanical
service (Rev. 2:2-4). It is love which moves the Christian
religion, beginning with God in the redemptive plan, continuing in Christ, who laid down His life for us, and ending
in the believer with a manifestation of a selfless life of service.

Faith then is manifested in love. Paul says, ". . . faith
which worketh by love" (Gal. 5:6). It is the love which Jesus
demonstrated to the men and women of His time. Faith
without that love is nothing (I Cor. 13:1-3). What Paul in
I Corinthians the thirteenth chapter states as the highest grace,
he here places in the ascending scale as leading to the eternal
hope, for the purpose which he had in writing is different
from the purpose he had in the hymn of love. The Corinthians stood in need of charity and he emphasized that there.
Here he proclaims the natural order, which is progressive
from faith to love to hope. Love grows out of the faith that
God loves us and that love of God brings us hope.

The third virtue is the patience of hope. This hope is an
eschatological hope, as the whole epistle of I Thessalonians
reveals and as the explanatory phrase ". . . in our Lord Jesus
Christ . . ." (I Thess. 1:3) reveals. The hope rests in the
coming of Christ, with both His rewards and His retributions.
Thus the hope is defined for us as the blessed hope of His
coming in glory and in His kingdom. In the fifth chapter
Paul repeats it by saying, "Let us, who are of the day, be
sober, putting on the breastplate of faith and love; and for an
helmet, the hope of salvation. For God hath not appointed us
to wrath, but to obtain salvation by our Lord Jesus Christ"
(I Thess. 5:8,9). Paul adds another appositional phrase which
modifies hope with the words, ". . . in the sight of God and
our Father" (I Thess. 1:3). God's presence as supreme ruler,
as judge, and as tender father is fulfilled in the judgment of
Christ's coming. All judgment of God is committed to the
Son. God Himself judgeth nothing. In this epistle, that blessed

hope is ever before the Apostle and the people as the answer to their sufferings and as their comfort in tribulation.

The consequence of this hope is patience in suffering, in tribulation, in misunderstanding, in inequality, and in injustice. Paul bore witness that the Christians were appointed to tribulation and that, as they know, these tribulations would come to pass (I Thess. 3:4), but with this hope one may abide his time, he may endure indignity, or humiliation, or injustice with equanimity. Let the storms blow and the waves beat, the ship will move on.

The Christian who has this hope is able to commit his cause to Christ who judgeth righteously and will avenge. He is able to make place for wrath, he is able to believe that vengeance belongeth unto the Lord, he is able to heap coals of fire upon his enemy. The Christian's hope is an eternal hope, an other-worldly outlook in the unending vista. Therefore he is able to endure in hope.

III. *Predestination*

Paul adds, "Knowing, brethren beloved, your election of God" (I Thess. 1:4). Literally it should be translated, "Knowing, brethren beloved of God, your election." Election is a troublesome word. It comes from a Greek word *ekloge* meaning "the act of choosing out, electing to privilege by divine grace." It represents God's choosing of the Thessalonians to be recipients of the blessings of salvation.

In speaking of election, we must make a differentiation between it and foreordination. Foreordination refers to God's establishing whatsoever comes to pass. It is His sovereign control of all events. Predestination is God's predetermining of the eternal destiny of the saved and of the lost in accordance with the good pleasure of His will. Election means God's predestination of those in Christ to be sons, to be saved, and to show forth the glory of His mercy and grace. Reprobation means God's predestining of those outside of Christ to eternal condemnation and punishment.

The doctrine of election is clearly taught in the Bible. The II Thessalonian epistle says, ". . . God hath from the beginning chosen you to salvation through sanctification of the Spirit and belief of the truth" (II Thess. 2:13). Paul wrote to the Romans, "For whom he did foreknow, he also did predestinate to be conformed to the image of his Son . . ." (Rom. 8:29). To the Ephesians he wrote, ". . . he hath chosen us in him before the foundation of the world . . . having predestinated us unto the adoption of children by Jesus Christ to himself, according to the good pleasure of his will" (Eph. 1:4,5). Peter wrote to the dispersion addressing them as "Elect according to the foreknowledge of God the Father . . ." (I Pet. 1:2). Men have stumbled over the confusion between responsibility and freedom in reference to salvation. They have failed to take into account God's eternal nature which transcends time, also His omniscience which embraces future events. These become helps in our understanding of election. Certainly men are conscious of the experience of election. Some men believe and some do not. How wonderful it was that a mere handful in this great heathen city believed unto salvation and became the church of Jesus Christ.

Evidence of their election was clear for Paul referred to his knowledge of it. How did Paul know they were elect? Did God reveal it to him? Can we know the division which passes through every group? Can we know "I am of the elect?" James Denney said, "Election has often been taught as if the one thing that could never be known about anybody was whether he was or was not elect." [6] Paul's knowledge of their election came from what he had seen among them and what he had heard about them. They had responded affirmatively and quickly to the Word as it was preached, for it came to them in power, in the Holy Ghost, and in much assurance. They had also brought forth the fruit of faith in works of faith, labors of love, and patience of hope. Thus it is that we know the elect in any time and age. Thus you may know that you are elect, and thus you may recognize the chosen of God.

History declares that some nations, some cities, some people are elect or chosen of God. Thus Paul was forbidden to go into Bithynia when he desired to go (Acts 16:6,9) and was called to Europe instead. Thus the Thessalonians, the Romans, the Europeans, the English, and the Americans were chosen. Why? The answer is an inscrutable mystery of divine grace. No answer advanced is quite sufficient to solve this mystery.

The explanation of election is suggested in the statement, ". . . brethren, beloved . . . of God" (I Thess. 1:4). The reason advanced as a clue is the love of God. Their being chosen did not originate with them but with God. It was God's love in action. They are beloved of God. Therefore He has chosen them. The initiative is of divine grace. Election is inseparably connected with the love of God. That fact ought to make us trust God's election and not question it. A love which gave Christ and spared Him not so that we might be saved is enough for me.

The relation of these individuals as brethren derives from this divine love. Since they were loved by God and were one in Christ, they should be loved as brethren in the Lord. The word brother may have lost its significance for us today, but once it was the epitome of Christian affection in the family of God.

Rest then in the unmerited love of divine grace extended to you in Christ. As you have heard the gospel, as you have experienced its power and assurance, and as you have brought forth fruit, know by these facts that you are children of God's eternal love.

Grace! Grace! All is of grace! Others preached the word of the gospel to us. Others prayed for us. Others have prompted us. So we have grown in faith, in love and in hope as the elect of God. Let the glory go to the unfathomable grace of God.

III

The Testimony of a Church

Ye were ensamples to all that believe in Macedonia and Achaia.

—I THESSALONIANS 1:7

HAVING A TESTIMONY IS THE SUBJECT OF THIS SCRIPTURE. Individuals have testimonies. When holding an evangelistic campaign in Augusta, Georgia, I met a cattleman who is the leader in a local Bible study group. At dinner he gave me his testimony. He said he had been a very worldly man, a heavy drinker, and quite profane, but during the meetings of Dr. Mordecai Hamm, his wife was converted. Several other people in his strata of society were likewise converted, and one day when he was at an auction, one of his fellow cattlemen jokingly said to him, "John, when are you going to get yourself a testimony?" He replied, "Pretty soon," and then he could not throw off the conviction that came upon him because he did not have a testimony. After wrestling with his problem for some time, he went home, gathered up all the liquor that was in his house (for it was in the days of prohibition), and drove down to the river into which he threw it. Then he went back, attended the special meetings and became a Christian. He has been living faithfully ever since, bearing a good testimony for Jesus Christ.

Churches also have testimonies. There are some churches in America which are great orthodox centers from which the gospel sounds forth and from which it is defended most ably. I refer for instance to the First Presbyterian Church of Pittsburgh, Pennsylvania. There are other churches which are noted for their youth work. I refer particularly to the First Presbyterian Church of Hollywood or the University Church of Seattle. Other churches are great evangelistic centers. I refer to the First Baptist Church of Dallas, the Moody Church of Chicago, the Church of the Open Door of Los Angeles, and the Calvary Baptist Church of New York. Other churches are known for their missionary work. I refer to the People's Church of Toronto, and I trust that Park Street Church is noted not only for its missions and evangelism and youth work and othodoxy, but also as a revivalistic center.

The testimony of the church at Thessalonica was a good one. Paul calls it an ensample which literally is a *typos* or a die which has taken an impression and can pass that impression on. The word might be translated a model church. This Thessalonian church was a church zealous of work, of labor, and of patience. It was a church which imitated the Lord Jesus Christ. Hence it was a church that had a great testimony. In studying this church, let us look at the content of its testimony, the characteristics of its testimony and the consequences of its testimony.

I. *The Content of Its Testimony*

Paul declared that people were speaking of "how ye turned to God from idols to serve the living and true God; and to wait for his Son from heaven." This comprised the essence of the testimony of these Thessalonians.

They turned to God from idols. They had been in heathen bondage, that is, in idolatry. Here Paul literally denounces idols as a figment of the imagination, but he recognizes the reality of demonism behind the idols. In doing so, he takes his place with Jeremiah and Isaiah, who scathingly denounced and mocked the use of idols in their worship. Such idolatry is anti-moral and it is also impersonal because of the multiplicity of gods and, therefore, the impossibility of there being any unifying force back of them.

Nevertheless, demonism of idolatry is very real.[1] The demon is represented by the idol, and the obscenity of the worship is inspired by the demon. Demonic worship exercises full control of a man's passions. This is not gone forever. There is a new heathenism today and the demons are again taking over. Conditions are being repeated which are very similar to those of the ancient heathen world.

This letter should be read in the light of Paul's sermon given on the Areopagus bordering the Parthenon in Athens. Some people grow very sentimental over the mythology of ancient Greece. Paul denounced it with all the condemnation which it was possible for him to speak because of the way in which it had degraded the people and kept them in ignorance of the true God. He declared, "The times of this ignorance God winked at; but now commendeth all men everywhere to repent: because he hath appointed a day, in which he will judge the world in righteousness . . ." (Acts 17:30,31).

Therefore these Thessalonians broke with idolatry. They turned to God. This is the essence of conversion, and it presupposes the response to the gospel, the belief in Christ, and justification by faith. With these believers, the centrality of Christ was established with the urgency of a decision.[2] They turned, they converted, they believed.

They embraced God in faith and obedience. Conversion must always be Godward. In Paul's missionary sermons recorded in Acts, he preached repentance toward God and faith in the Lord Jesus Christ. This embrace of God changed their whole outlook. The new life begins and ends with God for St. Paul. Paul had a deep God-consciousness. He believed in the election by God in the person of Jesus Christ (I Thess. 1:4; II Thess. 2:13). This God-consciousness must be restored to men today if we are going to have true conversion.

The second phase in their testimony was that they turned to serve the living God. They took on divine bondage or servitude. This was a new bondage in contrast to the slavery which they had had to idolatry and to evil. The bondage of God is perfect freedom. It is the state of not being torn between two forces. To be a Christian is to be perfectly free to do the will of God, to enjoy that for which we are made. The hymn writer puts it thus:

> My glorious Victor, Prince divine,
> Clasp these surrendered hands in Thine.
> At length my will is all Thine own,
> Glad vassal of a Saviour's throne.

> My Master, lead me to Thy door:
> Pierce this now willing ear once more:
> Thy bonds are freedom; let me stay
> With Thee to toil, endure, obey.
>   . . . H. C. C. Moule

To take on the service of the Lord is to have a new lord—one who is living and true. God is not an invention, or a vain imagination, or a fantasy, or a projected passion personified. He is a living God. He is not a dead idol which is made out of a log, one end of which a man burns for the purpose of warming himself and from the other end of which he makes himself an idol and bows down and worships it. But God is active in creation, in redemption, and in world affairs. He is a God who speaks, a God who delivers, a God who sustains, a God who guides. Moreover, we may know this true and living God. One translation of the word true is real. God, according to this passage of Scripture, is real. Is He real to you? Do you know Him in the person of the Lord Jesus Christ and in the truth revealed in the Scripture? Let us not have a nebulous viewpoint of God, but serve the living and true God.

This resulted in a new experience, namely, a bondage of freedom instead of a bondage of terror. It is the paradox of faith that freedom comes in servitude. It is a slavery of love, an impulsion of desire, a something that is never known in serving the heathen gods. Their servitude is cruel and brutal, but this is freedom and love.

The third phase of their testimony is that they tried to live in view of Christ's coming. J. B. Phillips[3] translates this epistle in the following way: ". . . and how your whole lives now look forward to the coming of his Son from Heaven . . ." (I Thess. 1:9,10). Such an anticipation of the second coming of Christ is a transforming experience. He who has this hope purifies himself and only does what he would want Christ to find him doing when He comes. Such a hope is a great motive to holiness, to evangelism, and to service. Fifty years ago Dr. Kellogg pointed out that those who were most engaged in evangelizing the world through missions were those who believed in the premillenial coming of our Lord Jesus Christ. "He that is unjust, let him be unjust still: and he which is filthy, let him be filthy still: and he that is righteous, let him be righteous still: and he that is holy, let him be holy still. And, behold, I come quickly; and my reward is with me, to give every man according as his work shall be" (Rev. 22:11, 12). This truth of the second coming must be kept in the forefront of all preaching. The earliest churches were conscious of living in the end times. The eschatological hope was present in the church from the beginning.[4] Were these in the early church mistaken? Did Christ and Paul teach the doctrine of the second coming or was it attributed to them later? Three facts throw light upon this discussion.

First, Christ came. This is indisputable and it is a fact which bears meaning to the world through the redemption wrought out by Christ.

Second, Christ is coming again. That coming is not His coming in our conversion, or His coming when we die, or His coming when the Holy Spirit came, or His coming in the judgment on Jerusalem or on any of the nations, but it refers to His coming personally, gloriously, catastrophically at the end time.

Third, Christ is present. This is suggested in the very word coming—*parousia*—which not only means coming, but present. It is also suggested in the word *maranatha* which means the Lord is at hand. We repudiate the Barthian removal of the second coming out of time. Neil says, "The true assessment of the primitive expectation of the Second Coming is not to dismiss it as a hope that was never realized but that may be some day, but to recognize that it is not an event in time at all." [5] We believe that it is in time but that there is a truth in the teaching that Christian life is essentially eschatological, that the Lord is always at hand and comes to every generation, and we pass the judgment of doomsday upon ourselves every living moment. In our zeal for the second coming as a personal event, we must not overlook this constant presence of Christ.

The trouble with the old churches of Christendom is that they have lost this incentive. Since the second coming of Christ as an historic event has been deferred, postmillenialism has become the viewpoint of most old-line denominations. As a result, they have substituted social programs for personal evangelism. In the percentage that they have lost the blessed hope of the second coming, they have become dead in their works of faith, labors of love, and patience of hope. They need the advice of Bishop Lightfoot, "Live a holy life, that you may be prepared to meet your Lord." [6]

II. *The Characteristics of a Testimony*

A testimony is new. At Thessalonica something happened, something was achieved, something interesting occurred. Paul describes it: ". . . having received the word in much affliction, with joy of the Holy Ghost" (I Thess. 1:6). They had affliction all right. It began with a riot and it continued through the persecutions long after Paul left. The pertinacity with which the Jews followed Paul to Berea and attempted to stir up opposition to him there demonstrates the attitude they would have taken toward the converts of St. Paul in Thessalonica. These Christians endured the opposition, the antipathy, the hatred, and the violence of their fellow countrymen. Trouble with those who refuse the gospel is almost inevitable if the Word of God is preached in power. There have been those who have been stirred to a white heat of anger by a few questions which I have raised concerning their conduct in the various departments of the government of this state, but at least they know we are watching what they are doing with our funds and our property.

In the affliction of the Thessalonians, they had the joy of the Holy Ghost. This joy proceeds from the Spirit. He produces it as one of His fruits or graces. Olshausen says that this joy is "opposed to natural, sensual, joy, which cannot, of course, consist with the *thilpis* (tribulation)." [7] Joy in tribulation is the Christian paradox. Paul gloried in it. Peter declared that Christians should glory in it. The disciples followed Christ ". . . who for the joy that was set before him endured the cross . . ." (Heb. 12:2). Luther said, "If Christ wore a crown of thorns, why should His followers expect only a crown of roses?" [8] The Thessalonians imitated Paul and Christ in displaying victorious mastery over outward circumstances.

A change had taken place in the people. The displaying of

the characteristic tokens of a Christian life proved that they had been chosen of God. What the transformation of the drunkard in a small town does, the transformation of these Thessalonian Christians did in their city. The devil gets active. When John Bunyan was a drunken, profane, violent young man in the village of Elstow, he attracted little attention, but when he became converted, transformed in life, holy in conduct, and lived and preached according to the gospel, he stirred considerable interest and was ultimately placed in the jail at Bedford, where he languished for twelve years.

Another characteristic of a testimony is that it is known by others. Paul said, "For from you sounded out the word of the Lord . . ." (I Thess. 1:8). The Word of the Lord is God's revelation. It is the word that God has spoken, but the content of it is the gospel of salvation which has "the Lord for its origin, center and end." [9] It is evident that Paul suggests that their enemies spread it abroad in an attempt to discredit Paul. They told what ". . . manner of entering in we had unto you . . ." (I Thess. 1:9), probably emphasizing their bedraggled appearance as a result of the beating and shameful treatment they had received at Philippi. Yet even this news proved to be good news, for people were interested everywhere in what had happened at Philippi and at Thessalonica. Thus Paul did not have to tell people what had happened, for they already knew as he passed along the Ignatian Way.

Moreover, the preaching of the Thessalonians spread it abroad. Immediately they became evangelists and missionaries. Some argue for an early date of the Epistle to the Thessalonians based upon their zeal in spreading the Word to Macedonia. This is an inevitable effect of being saved. When one is a true Christian, he wants others to hear the gospel. In my own case, one of the conditions of my salvation was that I would be willing to tell others what had satisfied my life if the Lord truly saved me. When I made that decision, I was saved and I have never doubted it for thirty years. It is impossible to be saved and to keep to oneself the experience which he has had. We begin to long for others to be saved.

Their deeds also spread it abroad. Paul said, ". . . in every place your faith to God-ward is spread abroad . . ." (I Thess. 1:8). Their faith was not their creed, but it was their extraordinary deeds of faith, love, and hope. It was by these deeds of consecration and service that people knew what had happened in Thessalonica. They immediately became ambitious to evangelize Macedonia and Achaia. The businessmen who were centered at Thessalonica began to publish abroad what had happened, as they went forth in their travels. They launched a program for their whole area.

This testimony was noised abroad without any great effort. Paul said, ". . . we need not to speak anything" (*Ibid.*). The people already knew what had taken place there. Such a testimony rises from deeds, not from self-seeking or boasting. Paul did not boast in the Thessalonian Church or herald this church abroad. The knowledge of it came from their own works. That is the best advertising of any church. Only this week, I had three requests from different magazines to write articles upon our missionary program and I received one minister who wanted to know how we did it. Nobody had to go forth and sell such an idea to them. They see that the work is being done and the deeds speak for themselves. The triumph of confirmation of the gospel comes in the works of faith which Christians do.

III. *The Consequences of a Testimony*

Paul describes these Christians as ". . . ensamples to all that believe in Macedonia and Achaia" (I Thess. 1:7). The influence of the Thessalonian Church spread far beyond their own city throughout Greece, in fact, it may even have spread to Rome, for Paul had just received Aquila and Priscilla from Rome and he began to live with them in Corinth, and it may well be that the riot and the resulting church and its work had already been reported in Rome. If a church is strong, it will strengthen other churches. If it is weak, it will discourage other churches. In spiritual things one church may nerve a number of churches to do greater things. It may stimulate them to defend the faith, to educate people in the Word of God, to evangelize their own areas, to send a testimony to the ends of the earth in missions, and to contend for civic righteousness. It is impossible to measure the influence of a a testimony of a church. In his inspired hyperbole Paul says, ". . . in every place your faith to God-ward is spread abroad . . ." (I Thess. 1:8).

The impact of this testimony is suggested in the meaning of the words "sounded out." It is a word used nowhere else for the gospel. It is compared to the blast of a trumpet, to the peal of thunder. In the Septuagint this word is used in Psalm 19 to describe the testimony of God which has gone forth in the glory of nature throughout the whole world. Such was the proclamation of the word by their lives and by their lips. It made a mighty impact upon the heathen community which saw their work, their labor, their patience, their assur-ance, and their hope.

Such the church ought always to be. It should not be moribund, indulgent, careless, but vigilant, awake, aroused, and working. In the fifth chapter of this same epistle, Paul declared that we are not to be as those who sleep, as those who drink in the night, but to be as those who are of the day, who are sober, who put on the breastplate of faith and love and have for an helmet the hope of salvation. From every one of us a witness should sound forth. The church should be the means of God's voice being heard throughout the world's confusion and bewilderment. If the church does not give God's message, who will? This must be done through the witness of its members and through the prophetic voice of the pulpit. A clear, certain sound of grace, of judgment, of character and ethics, of life and work must be given. Men want this authoritative guidance. They want to receive the note of alarm, of direction, of courage, of understanding. The church then must be the one to call to action or there will never be any battle for righteousness.

Such God will do through us if we will respond as did the Thessalonians. Such testimony is of God, of His Spirit, of His breath in us. Alexander MacLaren declares that it is God who sounds on the church as a trumpet so that His breath brings forth the clarion note of direction to the church.[10]

The imitation of Christ results in bringing others to imitate Him. The testimony of the Thessalonian Church was the result of Paul's effect upon them. His manner of life, his doctrine, his selflessness, his purity made a tremendous impact upon them and brought them to a saving faith in Jesus Christ. Their effect upon Macedonia, Achaia, and even upon Rome was equally influential. They were able to lead others in the way. Whenever Christians imitate Christ, being truly regenerate, they further the propagation of the gospel, even though they do it in the presence of persecution by unbelievers.

Here then is the great example of the truth. ". . . ye shall be witnesses unto me . . ." (Acts 1:8). The Thessalonians became that immediately. They were true, effective, powerful witnesses through the testimony of faith, life, and deeds. When God has such testimonies in the church today, the gospel will again sound forth to the ends of the earth and will stimulate others to emulate the action.

IV

Jesus, the Great Deliverer

Jesus . . . delivered us from the wrath to come.
—I THESSALONIANS 1:10

Wrath and grace comprise the message of the primitive Christian evangelists. To the heathen community engaged in idolatry and resultant irresponsibility and immorality, the primary emphasis of the New Testament evangelists was the wrath and judgment of God. By fear of such judgment, the moral sense of men was awakened. The habitual practice of sin so dulls the conscience that some alarm must be sounded to awaken men. The truth calculated to do this awakening in the days of St. Paul and now is the wrath of God.

The historical record of humanity is that wherever God is rejected, deterioration rapidly occurs. Paul describes the process in Romans 1:19-32. "Even as they did not like to retain God in their knowledge, God gave them over to a reprobate mind . . ." (Rom. 1:28). The Greeks constitute an excellent illustration of this truth of the deterioration of humanity without God. In the days preceding the golden era of grace, the emphasis was upon being, upon truth, and upon God. But preceding the days of Greece's decay and destruction, the emphasis was upon man, leading into relativism, skepticism, and humanism.

Human morality is somewhat dependent upon environment, that is upon what other people do. Hence, in a heathen environment such as that of decadent Greece, these people had to be shocked out of their moral apathy by facing the truth of immanent judgment. Paul confronted them with the fact of God's wrath, and, as a result, the whole moral sensibility of their lives was aroused.

The message at Thessalonica must have been very similar to the message Paul gave at Athens. The evangelist preached that the living God in whom they had their being revealed Himself by raising Jesus from the dead and by quickening those who believed in Jesus. These people had had no immediate experience or evidence of the resurrection except as the Holy Spirit quickened the believers, which quickening was an earnest of His final work. A more ample presentation of the content of Paul's missionary message on judgment and wrath is given to us in Romans 1:18-2:16. There he distinctly tells how the wrath of God is revealed against people, how God gives these people up, how God reserves them for judgment of the great day, and how they treasure up for themselves wrath and righteous indignation against the day of wrath and the revelation of the righteous judgment of God. The reference in Thessalonians to the wrath of God without further explanation implies a rather full exposition of this teaching when St. Paul was present with them. He must have emphasized the wrath and judgment of God as one of the cardinal doctrines of his message.

The means of moving these pagans to repentance and faith was both negative and positive. They feared the wrath and judgment of God. They hoped for participation in the salvation wrought through His Son. Though fear may be in reproach as a motive for action in our day, it is still basic to Christian theology. We have a great gospel of deliverance, but we also have a terrible alternative in the wrath of God, resulting in hell.

To the Christian community rescued from idolatry and facing persecution, the primary emphasis was that of the grace of God. Paul opened the Thessalonian Epistle with the words, "Grace be unto you." Just as wrath is God's holiness in motion against sin, unrighteousness and ungodliness, bringing it into judgment, so grace is God's love in motion through Calvary bringing forgiveness, life, peace, and joy to the godly. As wrath holds jurisdiction over the unbeliever, so grace holds jurisdiction in the believer's experience and releases favor, mercy, love, kindness, and fellowship of God in us and from us to each other. The juxtaposition of grace and wrath in this chapter reminds us of the diverse potentialities of life and of the pressing need for a decision as to which principle will operate in our experience. We stand either under wrath or grace, but never between the two. St. Paul describes himself as being alternately in one and then the other. ". . . we all had our conversation in times past in the lusts of our flesh, fulfilling the desires of the flesh and of the mind; and were by nature the children of wrath, even as others. But God, who is rich in mercy, for his great love wherewith he loved us . . . hath quickened us together with Christ . . ." (Eph. 2:3-5). Rescue from wrath is now available as it was for St. Paul and for the Thessalonians, but it will not always be so.

To all people, Jesus is the touchstone of wrath or of grace. He makes the difference whether we are delivered from wrath or not. He is the source of all grace, for ". . . grace . . . came by Jesus Christ" (John 1:17). About Him and His work of deliverance we would now think.

I. *The Christology of the Deliverer*

Paul implies much in his statement, "to wait for his Son from heaven, whom he raised from the dead, even Jesus . . ." (I Thess. 1:10). Here the historical Jesus is identified with

God's Son from heaven. This identity is unquestionable in the gospel history. On several occasions Jesus was acknowledged by God Himself as His Son. He said, ". . . This is my beloved Son, in whom I am well pleased" (Matt. 3:17; 17:5). The teaching is plain that Jesus is God's Son. "In the beginning was the Word, and the Word was with God, and the Word was God . . . No man hath seen God at any time; the only begotten Son, which is in the bosom of the Father, he hath declared him" (John 1:1,18). When Jesus met the blind man whom He had healed, He said unto him, "Dost thou believe on the Son of God? He answered and said, Who is he, Lord, that I might believe on him? And Jesus said unto him, Thou hast both seen him, and it is he that talketh with thee" (John 9:35-37). The gospels reveal to us that Christ had two natures, that He was true humanity and true deity. The epistles amply confirm this by declaring that God was in Christ, and though Christ was in the form of God, He emptied Himself (Phil. 2:5-9). We will never fully comprehend the extent of the self-emptying of Christ, but we are sure from Scripture teaching that He retained the essential elements of His deity while He was here on earth.

This identity of the historical Jesus with God's Son is unacceptable to various movements. One is rationalism. To the rationalist, Jesus must be all man or all God, but He cannot be both. For this reason, the Kenoticist tends in the direction of Unitarianism, for when one empties Christ of His attributes, it is hard to stop until he has mere man. Another is naturalism. The naturalist holds that it is impossible for an incarnation of God in human flesh by a virgin birth because of his presuppositions. Therefore, the dual nature of Christ is excluded. Another is Unitarianism. The Unitarian believes that Jesus was only a man like other men but developed His religious consciousness of God until He was a unique personality.

The identity of the historical Jesus with the Son of God is

indispensable to His being our deliverer. He could very well be an example or a teacher or a religious leader or a reformer if He were merely Jesus of Nazareth, but He could never be the redeemer of sinful men without also being God incarnate. Only His deity could make His sacrifice on the cross sufficient for the salvation of all men. Paul here emphasized that Jesus was God's Son from heaven.

The next point of emphasis in Paul's Christology was the reality of the death of Jesus Christ, God's Son. He said, ". . . his Son . . . whom he raised from the dead . . ." (I Thess. 1:10). The historical, incarnate Son had a temporal beginning and a temporal ending. That death of Jesus on the cross was no illusion but was real. The eternal Son took death into Himself as His permanent experience. The horror of the crucifixion of the Son of God must have been set forth by Paul in his preaching at Thessalonica exactly as it was at Corinth and at Galatia (I Cor. 1:19-23; Gal. 3:1). The hope of the Thessalonians and of us for deliverance is inevitably connected with the death of the Son of God.

The third point of Paul's Christology was the certainty of the resurrection of Jesus Christ, God's Son. This doctrine received primary emphasis. It was used by Paul to argue the inevitability of judgment. He declared, "Because he hath appointed a day, in the which he will judge the world in righteousness by that man whom he hath ordained; whereof he hath given assurance unto all men, in that he hath raised him from the dead" (Acts 17:31). This is the most important message of Christianity. Hence, it was first in all the declarations of the gospel. Paul said, "I delivered unto you first of all that which I also received, how that Christ died for our sins according to the scriptures; and that he was buried, and that he rose again the third day according to the scriptures" (I Cor. 15:3,4). The resurrection is taken by St. Paul to be the decisive proof that Jesus of Nazareth was the Son of God (Rom. 1:4).

The proof of the resurrection was habitually given by St. Paul, due no doubt to the fact that unbelievers called it "an idle tale." The resurrection was the foundation of Paul's faith. Before his experience on the Damascus Road, he knew all the doctrines about Jesus Christ, but he did not believe that He was the Son of God (II Cor. 5:16). Once, however, he saw the resurrected Christ and was convinced that Jesus of Nazareth was the Son of God, he began preaching those doctrines. The fact of the resurrection substantiated all the gospel facts.

The preaching of this doctrine of the resurrection is the impartation of hope to human hearts, of comfort to those in bereavement, of power for Christian living. The resurrection life is the victorious life and it is this resurrection power which we must come to know.

The fourth emphasis in Paul's Christology was the expectancy of the second coming of the Son of God, even of Jesus. He said, "Ye . . . wait for his Son from heaven . . ." (I Thess. 1:10). When Jesus ascended from earth, He went to a definite place called heaven. Since He had a body, that body had to go to some place. The Scripture describes Him as seated at the right hand of the Father in glory, and it tells us that like as He was taken up, He shall so come again. Paul had so emphasized the return of Jesus that the Thessalonians lived their lives in the light of this hope. There can be no difficulty in showing that the Bible makes this a cardinal doctrine of the Christian faith. It declares that He is going to come with clouds, that He will be accompanied by His angels, that He will sit in judgment upon all men, that He will establish His kingdom. This second coming of Jesus is usually associated with the resurrection. Nevertheless, this cataclysmic event is not the source of fear to Christians, but the source of infinite comfort. This struggle of good and evil, of light and darkness, of God and the devil will not go on forever. Jesus will be the victor. The name of Jesus means Saviour or deliverer, and such is Jesus. He is able to deliver,

II. *The Consequences from which Delivered*

Paul speaks of "the wrath to come" (*Ibid.*). What do we mean by wrath? The Greek word *orge* denotes an internal motion, especially that of plants and fruits swelling with juice. It describes a movement or agitation of the soul. In the Bible, wrath or indignation expresses this word. It is different from the other Greek word *thumos* which means passion, heat, anger, in that *orge* denotes "indignation which has arisen gradually and become more settled." [1] The *orge* attributed to God in the New Testament is that in God which stands opposed to man's disobedience, obduracy, and sin and manifests itself in punishing the same. *Orge* actually is the holiness of God in motion toward man's sin, necessitating the inevitability of punishment in a moral universe. C. H. Dodd has shown that it always had the meaning of "an inevitable process of cause and effect in a moral universe." [2] Since we live in a moral universe, wrath follows sin as effects follow causes.

On whom shall this wrath descend? Those under God's wrath are the ungodly (Rom. 1:18). The ungodly are people without God (Eph. 2:12), and they are not like God. They are wicked, profane, selfish, envious, irreverent, and without a sense of values.

Wrath is manifested against the unrighteous, that is, those who lack the imputed righteousness of Christ. The unrighteousness does not refer necessarily to the perjurer, the murderer, or the thief, but to the one who "believeth not" and on whom ". . . the wrath of God abideth . . ." (John 3:36).

The wrath of God rests upon the disobedient, those who would hold the truth in unrighteousness, those who believe not the gospel (II Thess. 1:9). They having heard and known the gospel reject it. They suppress the truth and thus they are already under God's wrath and will be brought into judgment.

But when will this wrath come upon people? Paul says it is ". . . wrath to come" (I Thess. 1:10). The phrase "to come" means "which is now approaching," for it is in the present tense. Thus it is present wrath. Lightfoot says, "It may refer either to the present and continuous dispensation or to the future and final judgment." [3] The present tense of wrath is the moral order of the universe working in the life of an individual. In other epistles we read, ". . . because of these things cometh the wrath of God upon the children of disobedience" (Eph. 5:6; Col. 3:6). Thus a man may be living under the wrath of God now and literally be a child of wrath.

Wrath, however, will be manifested at the second coming. We read of the day of His wrath and of the wrath of the Lamb and of the fierceness and wrath of Almighty God. This wrath will never fall upon believers who have been rescued from the wrath of God and who will be caught up together with Christ in the rapture before that wrath is manifested. The tribulation on earth will be the time of God's wrath over men. Zephaniah describes it by saying, ". . . I may assemble the kingdoms, to pour upon them mine indignation, even all my fierce anger: for all the earth shall be devoured with the fire of my jealousy" (Zeph. 3:8).

The final manifestation of wrath is described as ". . . the wrath to come" (Matt. 3:7; Rom. 2:5,8; 5:9). Hence, the moral indignation of God against sin results in the eternal condemnation of souls which is called the wrath of God.

III. *The Cross by which We Are Delivered*

Paul speaks of Jesus "which delivered us" (I Thess. 1:10). The measure of God's wrath is the cross. The necessity of the death of God's Son to satisfy offended justice is one means of understanding the intensity of wrath. Had there been any other way for man to be forgiven, it would have been found. For the Son of God coming from heaven to die such a horrible, ignominious, painful death can only be justified by necessity, and that necessity arose out of the wrath of God based upon His holiness and justice.

Consider the nature of the sufferings of Christ. We must never dwell upon nor overemphasize the physical sufferings because others too have faced death in very painful ways. But the spiritual sufferings of Christ were unique. Therein He experienced God-forsakenness, the judgment of hell, the wrath of God, the punishment for the guilt of sin and by means of this He placated God's wrath. The cross reconciled God, removing His wrath. A misunderstanding of God's wrath and an identification of it with an ebullition of anger would be to deprecate the nature of God. But when wrath is understood as inevitable action in a moral universe, actions which placate that wrath are of a very high ethical and moral nature. There was nothing else which could remove the wrath of God against man except a satisfaction given by His own Son.

> There was no other good enough
> To pay the price of sin,
> He only could unlock the gates
> Of heaven, and let us in.

The manifestation of wrath on Calvary brings into play the various points of emphasis which have resulted in theories of atonement. There was the exhibition of punishment of sin in a moral universe. Sin is never overlooked. It is essential that the governor of the universe should demonstrate the punishment of sin. Thereby Calvary exhibits God's righteous government of the universe. This is the essence of the governmental view of the atonement and there is a measure of truth in it.

Calvary presented the example of forgiving love in that God Himself met the demands of holiness and offered grace through the sufferings of Calvary. This is declared to be a moral influence which changes the thinking and feelings and actions of men. There is a measure of truth in it.

Calvary, however, is declared in Scripture to be the means of the expiation for sin through Christ's taking our place as a substitute and assuming our punishment as well as our guilt. This is called a vicarious satisfaction and this is the heart of the biblical teaching of atonement in that it removed the wrath of God.

The cross, therefore, became the means of reconciliation between God and man, of the removal of wrath. Thus Bunyan depicts Pilgrim as losing the burden of his guilt at the foot of the cross in his journey from the City of Destruction to the Celestial City. Thus St. Paul knowing he was saved by the cross declared, "God forbid that I should glory, save in the cross of our Lord Jesus Christ . . ." (Gal. 6:14). Thus those who believed that Jesus died for them on the cross to rescue them from this present evil world find that they are delivered from sin and wrath which rests upon the sinner.

IV. *Conversion through which We Are Delivered*

Paul referred to the Thessalonians having ". . . turned to God from idols . . ." (I Thess. 1:9). The believers at Thessalonica who converted were delivered. Having heard of Jesus, His person and His work, they turned from idols to God as God was revealed to them in Christ. Therein they experienced heaven's favor instead of heaven's frown. They received peace instead of enmity, justification instead of condemnation. They were delivered. By a hearty reliance upon Christ, they found their deliverance, their salvation, their rescue. The testimony which they possessed and the joy they received resulted from this conversion.

By conversion, we mean the change of one's attitude toward God, toward life, toward Christ, and toward Christian truth. By it we mean a contrition or a godly sorrow over sin and what it has done to God and man, thus resulting in wrath. By it we mean a confession of our sinfulness to God and by it we mean a committal of our destiny to Jesus Christ, the great deliverer. This then is conversion.

The burden rests upon those who hear of Jesus to flee from the wrath to come, to escape by the one established and appointed means, and to be rescued from impending doom. Thus each one of us must also respond. To be a disobedient person is to bring wrath upon ourselves.

Christ loved us and gave Himself for us that He might fulfill His work of deliverance. Thus He is called the Saviour or deliverer. Of Him we say:

> Jesus, the great Emancipator,
> Now and forever
> He shall be mine.

V

Detractors of the Church

For our exhortation was not of deceit, nor of uncleanness, nor in guile.

—I THESSALONIANS 2:3

THE TEXT REVEALS THE ATTACKS WHICH WERE BEING MADE upon the ministry of St. Paul and of his fellow workers. When Timothy returned from his visit to Thessalonica, he not only brought good news about their steadfastness in the faith, their zeal in good works, labors of love and patience of hope, their commendable testimony, and their concern for St. Paul, but he also brought the report of calumnies which were being spread abroad against St. Paul. The source of these calumnies was the Jews, the fellow countrymen of St. Paul. Those who should have accepted his message because they already believed in God nevertheless rejected the gospel and opposed St. Paul. The report in the Book of Acts suggests that they resisted the gospel because of envy. Matthew tells us that they killed the Lord Jesus because of envy. What a terrible motive envy is and what horrible things it leads us to commit! Paul says of the Jews that they ". . . both killed the Lord Jesus, and their own prophets, and have persecuted us; and they please not God, and are contrary to all men: forbidding us to speak to the Gentiles that they might be saved, to fill up their sins alway: for the wrath is come upon them to the uttermost" (I Thess. 2:15,16).

The nature of the calumnies is suggested by the report of them given to us in the second chapter of the Thessalonian Epistle. First they declared that Paul was deluded. They included him in the whole crop of wandering stargazers, minstrels, magicians, astrologers, popular philosophers, charlatans, and religious quacks of that day. The first century was an age in which religious cults were rife, just as is the twentieth century. Such an accusation could easily arouse suspicion and prejudice against St. Paul. It was a cruel accusation. They said that he was mentally unbalanced and spiritually dishonest. This is the same kind of attack which the naturalists make against all believers in biblical Christianity today. With a wave of the hand and a flip of the tongue, they declare that we too are among those superstitious folk who follow every new cult.

The second accusation was that Paul was impure. This readily could be affirmed of the heathen, whether at Corinth, at Thessalonica, at Ephesus, at Antioch or in any other center of that day. Moral impurity was a constant temptation to all men because it was condoned in the religious practices of the hour. At least one thousand prostitutes were connected with the temple at Corinth and this kind of sexual looseness was very general. The Jews had kept themselves on a very high level of morality, but now they accused St. Paul and the Christians of being a sect given to immorality. This charge was to arise on other occasions, especially when the Christians met in the catacombs of Rome, which lent an air of mystery to their worship, but it was a groundless accusation.

Thirdly, they accused St. Paul of being a deceiver. They said he was a charlatan seeking to profit by these poor deluded followers. They affirmed that he was traveling in ease and enjoying himself at the expense of his converts. They affirmed that he had thrown over the faith of his fathers for selfish ends. He was described as providing for his future by means of the offerings from these believers.

The effects of these attacks were quickly seen. St. Paul was hurt by them. He had a sensitive spirit and was grieved and wounded when people made false accusations against him. Men engaged in Christian work need to pray for a forehead of brass and a backbone of iron, as God offered to give to Jeremiah, in order to face the criticisms of their day. These accusations also hurt Paul's influence on his converts. In spite of the falsity of the charges, some people believe them and the charges linger with them in order to do some harm. Paul had to say, "For yourselves, brethren, know our entrance in unto you, that it was not in vain (i.e. no failure)" (I Thess. 2:1). Every servant of the Lord who is falsely accused is hurt by it, and such accusations may have a deleterious effect upon those who know not the truth, thereby the work may be hindered. Paul answered them directly. He said, "Our exhortation was not of deceit, nor of uncleanness, nor in guile" (I Thess. 2:3). He affirmed that they were not impostors, and that the best proof of their sincerity was the success of their mission, that the gospel had come in power, in the Holy Ghost, and in much assurance. This success was due to his manner of life, his message of life, and his motivation of life.

I. *His Manner of Life*

Thrice Paul referred to his manner of life saying, ". . . ye know what manner of men we were among you for your sake" (I Thess. 1:5). "For they themselves shew of us what manner of entering in we had unto you . . ." (I Thess. 1:9). "For yourselves, brethren, know our entrance in unto you, that it was not in vain" (I Thess. 2:1). Paul referred to his appeal to them before God, to his affection for them under God, and to his action with them for God.

That Paul was free from insincerity, from covetousness and

self-seeking was witnessed by their knowledge and by God
Himself. In verse 5 he declares, "as ye know" and "God as
witness." In verse 10 he says, "ye are witnesses, and God also."
It is a wonderful thing for a man to be able to stand before
his congregation and before God with a clean and clear conscience and to say, "God is my witness." Paul was clear from
all insincerity. He said, "Neither at any time used we flatter-
ing words." Insincerity was the mark of false teachers, of
deceivers, of quacks. They flatter, they praise, and they use
obsequiousness in order to worm themselves into the affections of the people. Not so with St. Paul. St. Paul recognized
the good characteristics of his congregations and almost every
epistle opens with a word of praise and thanksgiving. But
there is a difference between sincere recognition and insincere
flattery. Better is it to avoid all praise than to praise people
insincerely.

Paul was free from covetousness. He said, "Neither at any
time used we . . . a cloak of covetousness . . ." (I Thess.
2:5). A cloak of covetousness is a figure of speech describing
making a good front or appearance to cover up one's taking
advantage of others. It includes more than covetousness of
material things. It actually refers to selfishness of any kind.
Religious leaders who use their religion as a cloak of covetousness in order to feather their own nests or in order to
advance their own material standing or in order to achieve
influence politically are guilty of this kind of insincerity and
covetousness.

Paul was free from self-seeking. He said, "Nor of men
sought we glory, neither of you, nor yet of others . . ." (I
Thess. 2:6). Paul was no ambitious, power-hungry, glory-
seeking individual. His sermons never were on the front page
of the paper on Monday morning. He never sought to have
his picture before the people constantly. These self-seeking
apostles may be contrasted with a true apostle who never
asserts himself nor rests upon his dignity as an apostle for

personal advantage. Paul did what he did for the glory of God, and we are amazed at the courage which he displayed when, having been scourged in one city, he went immediately on to another one to face opposition there in spite of his own horror of physical suffering. In these first and sixth verses Paul showed them that he was no deceiver.

Next Paul appeals to his affection for them under God. He said, "So being affectionately desirous of you, we were willing to have imparted unto you, not the gospel of God only, but also our own souls, because ye were dear unto us" (I Thess. 2:8). Paul compares himself to a mother gently nourishing, cherishing, and providing for her children. No more tender display of love could be given than that of a mother for her own. She exercises care, nurture, provision, protection, and true love. Thus Paul and his associates tenderly put these converts first. He said, "Ye were beloved to us" (Ibid.). He contrasted the imparting of the gospel to them, which cost him nothing for he received it gratuitously, and the imparting of his own soul to them. Paul and his companions considered themselves expendable for these converts. Here is the true relationship of a pastor and his people. He also combined this deep tenderness with the parental responsibility of a father, saying, "As ye know how we exhorted and comforted and charged every one of you, as a father doth his children" (I Thess. 2:11). Without that tenderness all our service is void. "Though I speak with the tongues of men and of angels, and have not love, I am become as sounding brass, or a tinkling cymbal. And though I have the gift of prophecy, and understand all mysteries, and all knowledge; and though I have all faith, so that I could remove mountains, and have not love, I am nothing" (I Cor. 13:1,2). Love truly sanctifies service, and Paul could appeal to his tender affection toward them.

Paul reminds them of his actions with them for God. He said, "For ye remember, brethren, our labour and travail:

for labouring night and day, because we would not be chargeable unto any of you, we preached unto you the gospel of
God" (I Thess. 2:9). When with them, he had exercised
physical labor and toil. He had toiled to support himself and
possibly his companions so as not to be chargeable to them.
This constituted a severe burden to Paul, so that he worked
in the daytime and he preached publicly and from house to
house at night. St. Paul teaches clearly that the laborer is
worthy of his hire, that he who ministers of the things of God
shall live of the things of God, that every preacher has a right
to expect physical and material support. Yet Paul was willing
to forego this right in order to win these people to Jesus
Christ. Undoubtedly, there were many in Thessalonica who
were amply able to support him and his companions, and yet
he would not accept their gifts in order that he might more
adequately and unblameably preach the gospel to them.

He reminds them of his personal purity. He said, "Ye are
witnesses, and God also, how holily and justly and unblameably we behaved ourselves among you that believe" (I Thess.
2:10). Holily should be translated purely and refers to his
life, which was sanctioned by the law of God. He and his
friends were no licentious offenders. They were truly pure.
Justly may be translated righteously and refers to a proper
relationship in conduct before men. Blameless refers to being
without defect. Thus it was that these disciples walked in the
presence of the Thessalonians.

He reminds them of his paternal interest. He said, ". . . we
exhorted and comforted and charged every one of you, as a
father doth his children" (I Thess. 2:11). He exercised a
father's relationship in authority as well as love. He was a
father to them in God. As a father, he exhorted the wavering,
he encouraged the tested, he charged the tempted, he adapted
his attitude toward their needs in order to establish them in
Christ. All this was to lead them to walk worthy of God, who
had called them into His kingdom and glory.

Thus also we may judge ourselves and be judged by others today. We must have a manner of life which is acceptable to God and righteous before men.

II. *His Message of Life*

Now we must revert to the fourth verse of this second chapter of I Thessalonians in which St. Paul says, "But as we were allowed of God to be put in trust with the gospel, even so we speak. . . ." The message preached by these apostles was committed to them by God, which in itself was an attestation of their character. The manifestation of such a trust is hardly harmonious with a questionable character. It is possible for a man to preach the gospel and to be a rogue, but it is not probable. The men who successfully preach God's grace and the gospel of Christ so that their preaching is not a failure (I Thess. 2:1), and so that the gospel comes in power, in the Holy Ghost, and in much assurance cannot be deceivers, for God is witnessing to the truth which converts and establishes the convert.

The message which Paul preached was the message of the gospel. He speaks of being "entrusted with the gospel." Paul's gospel was the gospel of the sinfulness, the depravity, and the inability of man. This is the truth which natural men hate, whether it was in Paul's day or in the twentieth century. Men want to think of themselves as innately good, as being able to save themselves, as being justified by works in the sight of God. Then Paul also preached the satisfaction of the cross. His was a gospel of a divine redeemer, of the Lamb of God who taketh away the sin of the world, of an atonement made by substitution of the Son of God for the human race. This is spoken of as the offence of the cross. It is a stumbling block unto the Jews and it is foolishness to the Gentiles. He who preaches such a gospel does not seek to be popular with his fellow men. Paul's gospel also included the surety of the resurrection. Trace his preaching in his epistles or in the sermons recorded in the Book of Acts. In every case the great polemic doctrine is that of the resurrection and of the coming judgment. This at Athens was called an idle tale, but it was Paul's gospel. And it is our gospel too.

This message had to be carried to others. Paul said, ". . . even so we speak . . ." (I Thess. 2:4). He has a burden to get the word of life out. Thus he was courageous to go from Philippi to Thessalonica to preach in spite of all opposition. This is what multiplies missionary societies, gospel broadcasts, evangelistic campaigns, personal calling campaigns, and every effort to win people to Jesus Christ. How otherwise could we explain these servants of the Lord who push on and on at self-sacrifice in order to win men to Jesus Christ. By being saved, one feels the responsibility of leading others to Christ. Thus preaching, witnessing, and sending forth the gospel become natural to the saved man. The conclusion of those who hear and are saved is "How beautiful . . . are the feet of him that bringeth good tidings . . ." (Isa. 52:7).

III. *His Motivation of Life*

Then Paul adds, ". . . not as pleasing men, but God, which trieth our hearts" (I Thess. 2:4). Literally he refers to God, who tests and learns by experience what is in our hearts. God can attest us because He has tested us.

It is a great fact that God tests our hearts. The Psalmist says, "Thou hast proved mine heart; thou hast visited me in the night; thou has tried me, and shalt find nothing; I am purposed that my mouth shall not transgress" (Psa. 17:3). The heart means the real self, the inner man, the core of our being; not the emotions, or the will, or the mind, but the man himself. The cry of a true Christian heart ought to be, "Search me, O God, and know my heart: try me, and know my thoughts: and see if there be any wicked way in me, and lead me in the way everlasting" (Psa. 139:23,24). The heart of every man is known by God. He is called the knower of all hearts (Acts 1:24). We may say of Him, ". . . Thou God seest me . . ." (Gen. 16:13). Nevertheless, God tests us in order to reveal what is within us. That is why when Abraham had gone through his greatest test and the hand of the angel had prevented him from offering up the seed of the promise as a sacrifice on Mount Moriah, God said, ". . . now I know that thou fearest God . . ." (Gen. 22:12). God knew because He had revealed Abraham's faith by a test. Brother, God will test you. He will test me. He will test us all. This is a great fact of Christian experience.

This fact constitutes the great force impelling us to purity, to holiness, and to consistency. We stand or we fall to God alone. We cannot hide anything from God. It is inconceivable then that God would bless us while we have wicked hearts. Our highest aim ought to be to please God. Thus St. Paul declared, "We are confident, I say, and willing rather to be absent from the body, and to be present with the Lord. Wherefore we labour, that, whether present or absent, we may be accepted of him. For we must all appear before the judgment seat of Christ; that every one may receive the things done in his body, according to that he hath done, whether it be good or bad" (II Cor. 5:8-10).

This great faith vindicates one's life and ministry. Trust God as just, true and sovereign, as having control of all things, and commit your cause unto Him. All goodness, service, and sacrifice will then be rewarded by Him whom we serve. Our grace of life, our peace, our confidence is derived from this great faith . . . that God knows and tests our hearts.

Thus Paul could leave his detractors to God. He remembered the Lord's warning, "Touch not mine anointed . . ." (Psa. 105:15). Thus David would not so much as touch the hem of Saul's garment without being smitten in conscience, lest he had put a finger upon the Lord's anointed, and thus the Amalekite who put Saul to death was executed by David because he too had touched the Lord's anointed.

Paul also remembered the promise, ". . . Vengeance is mine, I will repay, saith the Lord" (Rom. 12:19). Therefore Paul made place for the wrath of God. He did not fight his own battles. He stepped aside. He believed that God would deal with these detractors of the gospel. Paul also practiced the precept of the Lord. He was willing to heap coals of fire upon his enemy's head by doing good to those who persecuted him, to pray for those who despitefully used him, and to bless those who cursed him. Thus he became the child of his Father in heaven, and thus also you will demonstrate and exhibit before men that you are the children of your Father in heaven.

VI

Worthy of the Great Name

As ye know how we exhorted and comforted and charged every one of you, as a father doth his children, that ye would walk worthy of God, who hath called you unto his kingdom and glory.

—I THESSALONIANS 2:11,12

CHRISTIANITY IS DESCRIBED IN THE BIBLE AS "THE WAY" AND the life of a Christian is described as a "walk" in this way. Paul's purpose in going to Damascus which resulted in his conversion was ". . . that if he found any of this way . . ." (Acts 9:2), he might bring them bound to Jerusalem. Thrice in this epistle to the Thessalonians Paul speaks of the Christian walk. He says, ". . . walk worthy of God . . ." (I Thess. 2:12), ". . . ye ought to walk and to please God . . ." (I Thess. 4:1), and ". . . walk honestly toward them that are without . . ." (I Thess. 4:12). Thus on three occasions Paul emphasized this Christian walk. The Christian way and the Christian walk are figures of speech to describe our inward character and our outward conduct.

The Bible description of this walk is both negative and positive. The unbeliever walked ". . . after the flesh . . ." (II Pet. 2:10). The wicked are described as walking ". . . after their own ungodly lusts" (Jude 18), as sensual, not hav-

73

ing the spirit (Rom. 8:9), as walking ". . . in lasciviousness, lusts, excess of wine, revellings, banquetings, and abominable idolatries" (I Pet. 4:3), as walking ". . . according to the course of this world, according to the prince of the power of the air, the spirit that now worketh in the children of disobedience . . . fulfilling the desires of the flesh and of the mind . . ." (Eph. 2:2,3). Unbelief and sin are summarized in the Scripture as walking in man's own way. (Acts 14:16.)

In a positive way, the Bible describes the believer as walking in newness of life (Rom. 6:4). He is a new creature and begins a new life when he becomes a believer. The contrast of the new walk with the old walk is clearly drawn (Rom. 8:1). The Christian walk is as an imitator of the Lord (I John 2:6), it is in Christ (Col. 2:6), and it is with Christ (Rev. 3:4). These phrases describe the inner life and conduct of a believer.

The believer may revert to walking in the old way and thus need the exhortation, encouragement, and admonition of a father in the faith to walk worthily, as is given in our text. Evidently, the Thessalonians were walking disorderly (II Thess. 3:11). They had ceased work in anticipation of the glorious coming of Christ, they had succumbed to the temptation of fornication, and they had grown discouraged. At times the apostles themselves had not walked uprightly and were to be blamed. Thus Peter acted out of character at Antioch (Gal. 2:11-13). The universal temptation is for believers to relapse into the old way of life. A Christian who has been an alcoholic needs constantly to be on guard; a believer who once was profane needs to guard his lips; a licentious man who has been converted must take care to avoid the temptations to the flesh. Our text leads us to examine the worthy walk to which Paul exhorted the believers.

I. *The Walk Is in Faith*

In Romans 4:12, we are told that we are to walk ". . . in the steps of that faith of our father Abraham." The phrase "the steps of that faith" is beautiful and could be used as a topic for a series of sermons. Abraham was called the father of the faithful and was the progenitor of all who are justified by faith, "Even as Abraham believed God, and it was accounted to him for righteousness. Know ye therefore that they which are of faith, the same are the children of Abraham. And the scripture, foreseeing that God would justify the heathen through faith, preached before the gospel unto Abraham, saying, In thee shall all nations be blessed. So then they which be of faith are blessed with faithful Abraham" (Gal. 3:6-9; 3:29). A study of Abraham's life will reveal that he commenced his walk of faith in hesitancy. It was not until he was seventy-five years old that he overcame that hesitancy and went out, not knowing whither he was going, but simply obeying the word of God. Once initiated, the life of faith was the life of discipline in which the Lord permitted testings, trials, obstacles, great disappointments, deferments of hope to come into his life, so that through the struggle and the long weary hours of conflict his faith would be developed. Finally, he received the reward of faith and Abraham stands forever as the great example of a man who walked by faith. His constituency represents a far larger group than the mere physical descendants of Isaac and Jacob. All believers of all nations and all times are the descendants of Abraham spiritually.

As soon as we talk about faith, someone will ask, "How can you get a faith like that? Is faith a given something bestowed gratuitously, or is it achieved, something developed? How can a man live a life of faith in a world like this, where temporal things are pressing him from all sides? How shall we believe in a moral universe when aggression pays such dividends as it has to Russia, to China? How shall we believe in honesty when so much dishonesty thrives? Is the believer the one who has faith bestowed upon him?"

If justification, regeneration, and eternal life are contingent upon faith, how are we going to get that faith? Faith is the arm with which we receive the gift of salvation, but what if we have no faith? That is a very important question. We must get faith the same way Abraham got his faith.

Faith is action in accordance with the truth to which we give assent intellectually. One must have a philosophy of things. He must have some conception about God, about the world, about self, about morality, about sin. A man may be a materialist, he may deny that there is a God, but he must have some thought about God. He may say that matter is ultimate. He may think that his relationships to men are based upon expediency and that all moral standards are relative, but he has a philosophy. When a man has a philosophy, he acts in accordance with that philosophy, and, in that sense, he is a man of faith, though he be a materialist, an idealist, or a theist. Objective faith is the truth to which a man gives assent. Consideration of the Christian revelation in competition with other systems brings such conviction or assent. Either Christian truth is self-authenticating or it is not. Without it, there can be no faith. When one has the conviction that the Christian revelation is true, one acts. This is faith. Such faith does not exist until action accompanies the assent. Thus the mind and will are intricately involved in faith.

Three steps of faith can be enumerated. First is the hearing and receiving of the Word. Abraham heard the Word of God while he was in Ur of Chaldees. His faith was the result of long wrestling with theoretical and moral problems of his time. Faith is not born without travail. Abraham passed through the struggle, broke with his environment, separated from his family, and went out not knowing whither he went. When you hear God's word about law, righteousness, holiness, and obedience, you must make a decision as to whether you will submit to it or not. This involves repentance or the change of one's mind.

The second step is obeying God's Word. For Abraham this meant a change in his mode of life. He tore out his roots and moved away from Ur of Chaldees in obedience to the divine Word. This is called conversion. If any man is going to be a man of faith and walk with God, he must break with his past and begin a new life. He must be converted. Such conversion is essential to the way of faith.

The third step is to choose in accordance with God's Word and not by sight. Many decisions of Abraham were made on such principles of faith. When separation from Lot came, Abraham chose the barren hills of Judea instead of the fertile plain of Jericho. When he possessed not so much as a foot of Canaan land, he believed that the entire land was to be given to him by God. In spite of all evidence to the contrary, he believed that he would have a seed to be his heir and successor. In all this Abraham was conforming to God's Word. Thus our daily choices must be made in the light of the eternal truth. We must walk in the steps of faith as did the heroes of the faith listed in Hebrews 11.

II. *The Walk Is in the Spirit*

Paul said, ". . . walk in the Spirit, and ye shall not fulfill the lust of the flesh" (Gal. 5:16), and "There is therefore now no condemnation to them which are in Christ Jesus, who walk not after the flesh, but after the Spirit" (Rom. 8:1). The Spirit is of life. Paul declared, "For the law of the Spirit of life in Christ Jesus hath made me free from the law of sin and death" (Rom. 8:2). Regeneration is wrought by the Holy Spirit. When a man repents and believes, God gives to him the Holy Spirit. This is the third Person of the Trinity constituting life, power, and strength that work in man which an unbeliever knows not. It is compared to a resurrection from the dead (Eph. 2:1; Rom. 8:11; Eph. 1:19). The renewal of the life of an individual is brought about by this spiritual quickening. The motives, intentions, purposes, and dispositions of the mind are made new. What formerly we hated, we now love. Instead of sin and death working in us, life is work-

ing in us. We are renewed in the spirit of our minds (Titus
3:5; Eph. 4:23). The life which man lost in the fall is restored
and eternal life, the life of God, is conferred upon him in and
through the Holy Spirit. This is the glory to which we are
called according to the text.

The Spirit in which we walk is the Spirit of love. Paul said,
"And walk in love, as Christ also hath loved us, and hath
given himself for us an offering and a sacrifice to God for a
sweetsmelling savour" (Eph. 5:2), and "the fruit of the Spirit
is love . . ." (Gal. 5:22). It is possible to imitate and copy
these elements in the divine nature such as righteousness and
love, but it is hard work. Much more natural is the renewal of
the human mind by the gift of the Spirit who is able to transform us into the image of the Lord Jesus Christ (II Cor.
3:18). That love was portrayed in Christ who is our pattern.
We are to love ". . . as Christ also hath loved us . . ." (Eph.
5:2). If the touchstone of love, tenderness, and kindness is
not there, we cannot love. All contending for the truth, witnessing, and warning must be in love. The experience of the
believer should include perfect love. John says, "Herein is our
love made perfect, that we may have boldness in the day of
judgment: because as he is, so are we in this world. There is
no fear in love; but perfect love casteth out fear . . ." (I
John 4:17,18). Even John Wesley thought that the only
Christian perfection possible was perfection in love. Paul exhorts us to be thus minded and to walk by this rule (Phil.
3:15,16).

The Spirit in which we are to walk is the Spirit of wisdom.
"Walk in wisdom toward them that are without, redeeming
the time" (Col. 4:5). Here is grace shown to others, those
'without.' This wisdom is Christian conduct. "The wisdom
that is from above is first pure, then peaceable, gentle, and
easy to be intreated, full of mercy and good fruits, without
partiality, and without hypocrisy" (James 3:17). That wisdom is the gift of the Holy Spirit. When Stephen was full of

the Holy Spirit, he was also full of wisdom (Acts 6:10). Thus when he preached to the Libertines, they could not withstand the wisdom with which he spake. The wisdom in which a believer ought to walk is that which redeems the time, which reaches as many as possible with the gospel, and which bears the most fruit for the Lord Jesus Christ.

III. *The Walk Is in Good Works*

Paul declared, "For we are his workmanship, created in Christ Jesus unto good works, which God hath before ordained that we should walk in them" (Eph. 2:10). The purpose of election, calling, and conversion is to produce these good works in which we are to walk. The text declares that we are "called" unto this standard.

Let us therefore walk according to His commandment (II John 6). The believer has received no new commandment. The moral standards of his life are the standards of the Ten Commandments, which have never been changed. This plumb line of righteousness, this criterion of holiness is originally found in the Ten Commandments and in their interpretation found in the Sermon on the Mount. Here we learn what a Christian man should do, all of which is quite contrary to the world's view.

The walk is honestly toward them which are without (I Thess. 4:12). Paul said, "Let us walk honestly, as in the day; not in rioting and drunkenness . . . But put ye on the Lord Jesus Christ . . ." (Rom. 13:13,14). The continued exhortations of St. Paul to believers reveals that honesty is basic and essential to Christians. It seems redundant to mention this, but the oft repetition of it in the epistles of St. Paul reveals its essential nature. We ought to expect honesty to be found in a believer by intuition. The Scripture makes it plain that God, who knows the heart, expects such honesty. There is necessity then for self-examination if we are to be worthy of our high calling.

This walk is to be well pleasing to God. Paul says, ". . . as ye have received of us how ye ought to walk, and to please God, so ye would abound more and more" (I Thess. 4:1). He also declared, "Wherefore we labour, that, whether present or absent, we may be accepted of him" (II Cor. 5:9). These Thessalonians were instructed by St. Paul to walk ethically by way of separating from idols and from all sin. It is apparent that they were walking this way and he encouraged them to continue. The intention in all action of a Christian should be to please God before whom we stand or fall, for we must some day answer for the deeds done in the body (Rom. 14:1-18). The highest aim of Christian living is to please God. Inventory of personal practices in the light of this divine standard for our works would elevate Christian living.

The text declares that we are to ". . . walk worthy of God, who hath called you unto his kingdom and glory" (I Thess. 2:12). The walk in the light produces worthiness in character. We who walk in the light as given shall always have new light in which to walk, for then the blood will cleanse and the light of the world will be bestowed (John 8:12; Eph. 5:8; Matt. 5:16; I John 1:9). Since we bear His name, let us walk worthy of the name of God.

VII

The Church and the Word of God

*For this cause also thank we God without ceasing, because,
when ye received the word of God which ye heard of us,
ye received it not as the word of men, but as it is in truth,
the word of God, which effectually worketh also in you that
believe.*

—I THESSALONIANS 2:13

St. Paul here emphasized the place of the Word of God
in the ministry of the church.

Notice in the second verse of this chapter Paul speaks of
their preaching the gospel in "much contention." In the
fourth verse he again speaks of being "put in trust with the
gospel." God had entrusted them with the gospel and they
believed it. Again in the eighth verse he speaks of being willing not only to impart the gospel to them, but also his own
soul. And in the ninth verse he declares, ". . . we preached
unto you the gospel of God."

St. Paul equates the gospel of God with the Word of God
and says in our text, "For this cause also thank we God without ceasing, because, when ye received the word of God
which ye heard of us, ye received it not as the word of men,
but as it is in truth, the word of God." Here the gospel which

he preached unto them is called the Word of God and he sounds a note of thanksgiving because they received it in its true form and in its true authority as God's Word.

There is a constant emphasis in Paul's writings on thanksgiving and praise. Without ceasing he thanked God for every work the Lord did, for every blessing He gave, for all hearts which He opened, for all prayers which were answered. This ought to be a Christian attribute. Here Paul illustrated what he taught in Philippians 4:6, ". . . in every thing by prayer and supplication with thanksgiving let your requests be made known unto God." The ground of further answers to prayer is gratitude for those already received. The thanksgiving season should come not only once a year, but every day of the year. How can we ever be thankful enough for the spiritual blessings which have come upon our church? Think of the people who have been saved, the young men and women who have been called to the mission field, the outreach of our educational program, the granting of the privilege of broadcasting the gospel by radio for so many decades, the beauty of the church building in which we work, the fellowship of the gospel which we enjoy—for all these things we must thank God.

Paul lifted up his praise to God because he knew that God is the source of every blessing. "Every good gift and every perfect gift is from above, and cometh down from the Father of lights . . ." (James 1:17). In no sense did Paul depend upon himself as sufficient for all things, but he felt he was communicating unto men the word that came from God, the content of the gospel, which was the means of their reconciliation with God and of their eternal salvation. He had a sense of a directed, ordered, controlled universe in which events did not happen from fortuitous caprice but had their source in God. Therefore, if the Jews at Thessalonica heard the Word, if the Gentiles embraced the gospel, and if the proselytes received his message as God's message, he knew all this was due to God's goodness and he gives the praise unto God.

The unforgettable experience at Thessalonica which now occupied the Apostle's mind and was the material cause of his burst of gratitude was quite in contrast with what happened to him later at Athens where, for the most part, his message was rejected and he established no church. From the time he preached at Athens until the time that Timothy returned from Thessalonica, bearing the good word of the continued prosperity of the Thessalonian Church, the Apostle was deeply burdened concerning this church. The report of Timothy that they had so seriously received his preaching as the Word of God and had given it obedience was the occasion of this burst of praise on the part of the Apostle and the statement of a magnificent truth.

I. *The Word of Revelation*

The cause of Paul's thanksgiving was that they ". . . received the word of God which ye heard of us . . . not as the word of men, but as . . . the word of God . . ." (I Thess. 2:13). Paul employs a technical term to describe the acceptance of the contents of the gospel. He uses the word *paralambano* and means the receiving of that which is delivered over. Connected with it is another technical word which means to hand over or to deliver. When the express man delivers a package at your home, you sign a slip and he delivers the package over to you. Thus you receive it and he hands it over. In a relay race, a runner usually has a small token which he passes to the next member of his relay team, having completed his own course. As he hands over the token, the word is used which is used here for the delivering over of the contents of the gospel. As the second runner receives it, the same technical word could be used for his reception that is used for the reception of the gospel.

This reveals that the gospel deals with a body of doctrine which is handed over. Paul did not originate this nor did the disciples. In I Corinthians he says, "For I have received of the Lord that which also I delivered unto you . . ." (I Cor. 11:23), or "for I delivered unto you . . . that which I also received . . ." (I Cor. 15:3). He also declares that he received his gospel from the Lord not from men (Gal. 1:12). The mark of a faithful apostle was his willingness to hand down the body of truth which is called the gospel of God and is synonymous with the Word of God.

The duty of the church is to conserve and to transmit this body of truth unto the next generation. Today it is infinitely easier than it was when it was an oral word not yet committed unto writing. Now we have it inscripturated in the Bible so that each generation may learn that body of doctrine from the Book itself. Nevertheless, we have the duty to conserve this body of truth called the gospel.

The truth which Paul handed down is emphasized in the first Epistle to the Thessalonians, where Paul declares what he had preached unto them. This epistle contains all the major doctrines. A more clear treatise was later written by Paul in the Epistle to the Romans, but the very doctrines are in the Thessalonian Epistle in incipient form. Paul speaks of the doctrine of God versus idols, of Christ as the great deliverer, of election unto salvation, of conversion, of holiness, of prayer, of the second coming, of the resurrection, of the Holy Spirit's ministry, of the righteous testimony of a believer, of the responsibilities of church members, of the means of grace.

The body of doctrine up until the writing of this epistle had been communicated in unwritten form by the apostles. It was a body of truth committed to and taught by the apostles. The unity of the apostolic doctrine found its source in the resurrection ministry of our Lord Jesus, who tarried for forty days after His resurrection to instruct them in things pertaining to the Kingdom of God. Immediately following that we read, "they continued stedfastly in the apostles' doctrine . . ." (Acts 2:42). As the epistles of the New Testament were written, this oral doctrine became in-scripturated.

What is the relation of the spoken to the written word? Some affirm that the Word of God is something different from the Bible to which the Bible only bears witness but with which it is not to be identified. This is a modern form of un-belief. Some others declare that the Word of God is to be identified with a tradition which can exist in addition to the Bible and thus impart additional information about Mary, the mother of Jesus, purgatory, the authority of Peter, confession, and other doctrines. This adding to the Word of God is also heretical. The Christian view has been and is that the Word of God is now inscripturated so that the Bible can be called "The Word of God" and every doctrine must be tested by it.

The historical view of the Bible as the Word of God has three parts: first, God has spoken; second, the spoken word is inscripturated in the Bible by inspiration; third, the recorded word is authoritative for faith and life. All this is implied in what Paul wrote to the Thessalonians.

II. *The Word of Preaching*

In speaking of the Word of God, Paul adds, ". . . which ye heard of us . . ." (I Thess. 2:13). The message which he preached and which is to be preached today is the Word of God. This message is derived from the Bible. What Paul originally delivered to them is now inscripturated in this first Epistle to the Thessalonians and from it the same message can be derived as was declared by Paul personally. Preaching ought to be devoted to God's Word of salvation. This is nothing light, frivolous, or subsidiary. It is of prime impor-tance and nothing ought to be allowed to substitute for the Word of God. It has its message concerning sin and its conse-quences, concerning the atonement through the cross, con-cerning repentance and faith, and concerning forgiveness and life. It is our duty to preach it as dying men to dying men and to stand in the gap between the living and the dying. He who recognizes the gospel as the Word of God has a sense of burden, of responsibility, and of faithfulness.

The messengers who declare the Word of God are fallible men. Paul himself did not claim perfection (Phil. 3:13) or infallibility except as he was the vehicle of an authoritative and trustworthy message, which was given to him by God. He describes this as carrying the treasure in earthen vessels. An awful responsibility rests upon the preacher to impart this message. Thus he should speak effectively, achieving the finest presentation which is possible. This demands careful preparation and diligent performance. He is to redeem the time. The preacher has so few moments to get at the souls of men that not one of them should be lost. Perhaps it is the only time that these souls will ever hear the message, which only increases the preacher's responsibility. He is to witness to all, both small and great. Thus Paul himself did in his whole life and could bear witness to the fact before Agrippa. A true call consists of a desire to make known these unsearchable riches of Christ to the souls of men.

God's Word is mediated through preaching today. Sometimes people feel that preaching is nothing more than words, words, and more words. Yet in them is God's Word and God's plan through the foolishness of preaching to save those who believe. We have a right, therefore, to trust God's Word to work today. Not our words and thoughts, but His Word is able to save. The Word is quick and powerful and sharp as any two-edged sword. God speaks through it. Our faithfulness to the divine revelation will enable us to mediate the Word of God to those who need life.

III. *The Word of Faith*

Paul added, ". . . ye received it not as the word of men, but as it is in truth, the word of God . . ." (I Thess. 2:13).

In receiving the Word, it is possible to ascribe it to man. If the Bible is of man, then we are in a position to sit in judgment on it, to accept what we approve and to reject what we do not approve. This attitude is taken by the intelligencia who ascribe much of the Bible to man—as fallible, erroneous, and undependable. One intellectual leader declared that the Bible has been made a shambles by historical criticism. To ascribe it to man is to invalidate its authority and power, for then there must be some higher standard to determine what in the Bible is true or false. What is that standard? Is it my idea of what is true, or is it your idea of what is true?

On the other hand, it is possible to receive the Word by ascribing it to God. They took it as ". . . the word of God" (*Ibid.*). You can accept the message of repentance and faith to salvation as divine, as originating in God. Then you must acknowledge its authority and authenticity by obeying it. This action must be contrasted with the reaction an individual has if the Bible is ascribed to man. We either must give submission or we will revolt against it. The attitude of intellect which we take affects the action of our will. These intellectual problems concerning the Word of God are very important to our faith. We must retain our integrity. To be able honestly to ascribe the Bible to God is to validate Christianity. Paul made this definite affirmation and claimed to be speaking for God. If his message were not of God, the moral implications of pawning off his own words as God's Word is more reprehensible and has far-reaching consequences for our acceptance of anything which Paul says. At this point intellectual honesty will make one diverge from or follow through Paulinism.

Paul says, ". . . you that believe" (*Ibid.*), that is, when men received the gospel as the Word of God, they believed it. Faith is elemental to Christianity, yet faith is dependent upon knowledge. It is necessary for men to grasp the content of the gospel intellectually before assent can be given. How great a degree of enlightenment is necessary before such assent can be given is debatable. At least we know that the content of I Thessalonians declares the amount of knowledge Paul presented to the Thessalonians. Acceptance of God's Word on appropriate evidence of prophecy fulfilled, miracles performed, of the resurrection of Christ and the moral tone of the teaching constitute assent to it. Beyond this, however, the believing soul must make a committal, so that his destiny is determined by the attitude which he takes. Decisions come from the heart.

Entrance to the Kingdom of God is contingent upon this believing. Such believing persons become justified by faith, not by works. They receive the new birth which is wrought in their hearts by the Holy Spirit and they are constituted righteous in the sight of God through a faith righteousness.

This kind of believing manifests itself in obedience to the will of God. It is inevitably followed by action, adventure and achievement, illustrated by the roster of the heroes of the faith in Hebrews 11.

Those who respond by receiving the Word and believing the Word also experience the Word. Paul says, ". . . which effectually worketh also in you . . ." (*Ibid.*). When an individual believes the Word, he finds that it is a living power (Heb. 4:12; Psa. 119:130). Through the Word, God's power operates in the individual. It may be called a quickening Word because it convicts, it converts, it cleanses, and it transforms, bringing about the salvation of the individual. Thus Peter declared, "Being born again, not of corruptible seed, but of incorruptible, by the word of God, which liveth and abideth for ever" (I Pet. 1:23).

The choice of what we will do with the Word of God in the gospel must be faced by individuals and churches. The happy reaction of Thessalonica may be repeated. When it is, the Word of God will work effectively. Individually, one may receive the Word of God and its effective work in him will prove that it is the Word of God in power and in truth.

VIII

The Church and the Jew

*... the Jews ... both killed the Lord Jesus, and their
own prophets, and have persecuted us; and they please not
God, and are contrary to all men.*

—I THESSALONIANS 2:15

ANTI-SEMITISM IS THE FUNGUS WHICH GROWS ON A DECAYING
and corrupt society. The Jew too often has been the scapegoat
of irresponsible politicians and of self-exonerating but bun-
gling statesmen. The Jew has been blamed for war, for depres-
sion, for moral debacle, for communism, and for revolution.
No doubt some Jews, along with many Gentiles, have had
their part in these things, but to lay the responsibility upon
them as a people is to be guilty of anti-Semitism.

Anti-Semitism has appeared periodically throughout history
from the days of Egypt's Pharaohs, Babylon's Ahasuerus,
Greece's Antiochus Ephiphanes, Rome's Titus, Spain's Torquemada, Russia's Alexander V, Germany's Hitler, and
America's Father Coglan and Gerald Smith. Only a few
weeks ago a retired engineer handed me a copy of "The
Protocols of Zion," which attributes to the Jews the plan to
overthrow all morals, all law, and all government and to set
up on the ruins of society a Davidic Dynasty. These protocols

have been the source of anti-Semitism for decades. A score of other letters and magazines in America are devoted to heaping hatred upon the Jew. The objective of such persons engaged in anti-Semitism is to prosper upon the hate and prejudice, which to a limited extent is possible for them to do. In the political elections of 1936 and 1940, anti-Semitism played a very prominent part, and the members of the Roosevelt administration were openly accused of being Jewish-dominated.

Anti-Semitism has recently reared its ugly head in Russia. In that mysterious country, pogroms, persecutions, and ghettos thrived under the Czars. I shall never forget the exhibits in the anti-religious museums of Russia, which I saw in the year 1933. Many of them contained huge photographs of Jewish people lying in rows or in heaps after they had been massacred in pogroms. The purpose of these pictures was to show the people of Russia, including the Jewish population, that religion had inspired the Czaristic regime to the perpetration of these cruel deeds. The Soviet regime proclaimed its freedom from all race prejudice and from all anti-Semitism. The tragedy is that when the State of Israel was established and the Jews of Russia thronged the bureaus to obtain passports and visas to go to Israel, once again the reproaches of persecution and anti-Semitism were heaped upon them. Thousands of Jews sought to emigrate and tens of thousands of them were dispossessed and sent off into Siberia. The old names, epithets, and accusations of the Czaristic regime were revived, all because the leaders of the Soviet state thought that these Jews were not loyal. Thus the modern example of so-called freedom and equality of all races has reverted to anti-Semitism. This is paradoxical because the Communists are often said to be Jewish, and yet these so-called Jewish Communists are guilty of anti-Semitism or of the persecution of the Jews. This in itself is anomalous.

Anti-Semitism exists in America. The Federal Council survey, included in its information service published a few years ago, declared that there were anywhere from fifty to eight hundred organizations in America devoted to anti-Semitism. Its studied conclusion was that there were probably one hundred fifty such organizations as would be worthy of note. At almost the same time, *Fortune* Magazine made a survey of anti-Semitism in America and found that among eighty-six per cent of Americans there was absolutely no anti-Semitism and among the fourteen remaining per cent, it was insignificant. It was *Fortune's* conclusion that the Jews do not play a dominating part in industry, whether heavy or light, in communications, whether radio, movies, or newspapers, or even in retailing, so that there was no danger of Jewish influences taking over America. However, these surveys did point out that the aggressive, defensive measures and organizations taken and established by the Jews themselves were often provocative of an anti-Jewish feeling, and it was pointed out that though anti-Semitism was insignificant in America, as any disease, it could grow if it were not watched.

In reverting to our text, which contains one of the most explosive denunciations of Jewry, we are compelled to ask the question, "Was St. Paul anti-Semitic? Was he guilty of laying the foundations for such outbreaks of persecution and ostracism as have from time to time befallen the Jews? Was this statement of St. Paul an outburst of feeling due to the opposition staged against him by the Jews or was it his studied opinion?" Certainly nobody had a better right to indignation against the Jews as a people than did St. Paul. When he was first converted, they persecuted him at Damascus, so that he had to flee surreptitiously to save his life (Acts 9:22-25). When he gave his testimony at Jerusalem, they went about to slay him (Acts 9:29). When he did his missionary work in Galatia, they undermined the authority of his apostleship and they questioned his gospel (Acts 14:1-20). In Paul's second missionary journey as he entered Europe, they stirred up the populace at Thessalonica to riot against him (Acts 17:5), then they repeated the process at Berea (Acts 17:13), and they blasphemed and made insurrection against him and the gospel in Corinth (Acts 18:12). Since Paul was writing at this moment from Corinth and had all these experiences back of him, it was only human that he should have such a reaction against the Jews, his own countrymen. But was this a human reaction of a harassed man or was it the Word of God about a race? Listen again to the text, ". . . the Jews . . . both killed the Lord Jesus, and their own prophets, and have persecuted us; and they please not God, and are contrary to all men" (I Thess. 2:15). In no other place does St. Paul speak like this. Faithfulness to the Scripture necessitates our investigation of the broad biblical attitude toward the Jews, especially the teaching of St. Paul. At the outset, we must say that the Bible always condemns anti-Semitism, whether it was in the time of Abraham, or Ahasuerus and Haman, or of Paul, or of our day.

I. *The Indictment of the Jew*

Because of fear of anti-Semitism, one must not close his eyes to the historical position of the Jewish race nor to the individual sins of its people, condoning them because they are the chosen people. Wrong is wrong whether it is found in a Gentile or a Jew. Because Paul found considerable wrong among the Jews, he made a sevenfold indictment of them. We must give our attention to this passage of Scripture.

The sin of the Jews as a people—Paul affirmed that ". . . the Jews . . . killed the Lord Jesus . . ." (I Thess. 2:15). The responsibility for the death of the Lord Jesus must rest upon the Jews. This categoric statement declares that they are responsible. We are aware of the long debate over responsibility in this matter. Several years ago, I was invited to Town Hall in New York City to speak with John Hayne Holmes, Joseph Sizoo, and William Ward Ayer on the question, "Did the Jews Kill Jesus?" Dr. Holmes and Dr. Sizoo tried their best to prove that the Jews did not kill Jesus, but they had a very difficult case set out for them. The Bible makes it clear that the primary responsibility for the death of Jesus rested upon the Jews. One need only go back to the New Testament narratives to read of their plotting against the Lord Jesus, their intention to put Him to death, their judgment that He was guilty of death, their request of Pilate that He be put to death, their insistence upon His crucifixion, and their willingness to accept the responsibility for it. The plot, the purpose, and the perseverance in the accomplishing of it all prove that they were responsible. Those wild scenes in which they rent their garments and said, ". . . He hath spoken blasphemy . . ." (Matt. 26:65), or when they cried ". . . Crucify him, crucify him" (Luke 23:21), or when they cried ". . . His blood be on us, and on our children" (Matt. 27:25) all bespeak this fact.

The deed of the crucifixion was done by the Romans only because the legal authority was in their hands. That fact does not lessen their responsibility for injustice, for indifference to righteousness, and for inflicting cruel torture upon an innocent man, but the intention lay not with the Romans, but with the Jews. In the final analysis, both must share their guilt, but our text still stands.

It is utterly wrong, however, to pass such guilt of the contemporaries of Jesus on to the descendants of them in the Jews of this generation and thus use that guilt as the ground for anti-Semitic activity. That this has been done in different generations must be admitted, especially in so-called Christian countries. That the hierarchy of Israel who perpetrated Christ's death did not represent the people is explicitly stated. We read, ". . . they . . . feared the people . . ." (Mark 12:12), for the people were the friends of Jesus and these people were Jews. We also read, ". . . And the common people heard him gladly" (Mark 12:37), and those people also were Jews. It was the hierarchy who feared Him, hated Him, and sought His death. That the church itself in its initial stages was Jewish in its founder, its apostles, its first hundred and twenty adherents, and those converted on the day of Pentecost must also have a bearing upon this question. Not all of the Jews were opposed to Jesus Christ.

The rejection of Christ by any man, whether Jew or Gentile, brings upon him the responsibility of the blood of Christ today. There is no difference between Jew and Gentile, and the Jews are no more to be singled out as responsible for the death of Christ than the modern pagan Gentiles are. Their guilt is equal before God. Thus all ground for anti-Semitism in the charge that they killed Jesus is removed.

Paul declares, ". . . the Jews . . . killed the Lord Jesus, and their own prophets, and have persecuted us . . ." (I Thess. 2:15). The phrase "their own prophets" may be taken either with the previous part of the sentence, which describes the killing of the Lord Jesus, or with the succeeding part that describes the persecution of the Christians. Grammarians are divided in their interpretation of this. However, both are true for they most certainly did persecute and did kill their own prophets. The Lord Jesus denounced the scribes, Pharisees, and Sadducees of His day for hypocrisy, for guilt, and for responsibility of exactly such actions as are recorded in the twenty-third chapter of Matthew. He said, "Wherefore, behold, I send unto you prophets, and wise men, and scribes: and some of them ye shall kill and crucify; and some of them shall ye scourge in your synagogues, and persecute them from city to city: That upon you may come all the righteous blood shed upon the earth, from the blood of righteous Abel unto the blood of Zacharias son of Barachias, whom ye slew between the temple and the altar. Verily I say unto you, All these things shall come upon this generation" (Matt. 23:34-36). The description of Israel's treatment of its own prophets is given clearly in the eleventh chapter of the Book of Hebrews. Here the heroes of the faith were beheaded, slain with the sword, sawn asunder, crucified, and driven out to wander as wild animals on the earth. They were not accepted by their people.

Another terrible arraignment of the Jews for mistreatment of their own prophets is given in the address by Stephen before the Sanhedrin and contained in the seventh chapter of the Acts. He concludes it with the words, "Ye stiffnecked and uncircumcised in heart and ears, ye do always resist the Holy Ghost: as your fathers did, so do ye. Which of the prophets have not your fathers persecuted? and they have slain them which shewed before of the coming of the Just One; of whom ye have been now the betrayers and murderers" (Acts 7:51,52).

Thus also Paul himself condemns the Jews in the eleventh chapter of Romans which constitutes his greatest defense of Israel. Here he quotes several Old Testament passages of Scripture to show Israel's fall. "Israel hath not obtained that which he seeketh for; but the election hath obtained it, and the rest were blinded (According as it is written, God hath given them the spirit of slumber, eyes that they should not see, and ears that they should not hear;) unto this day. And David saith, Let their table be made a snare, and a trap, and a stumblingblock, and a recompense unto them: Let their eyes be darkened, that they may not see, and bow down their back alway. I say then, Have they stumbled that they should fall? God forbid . . ." (Rom. 11:7-11). Here an imprecation is brought upon the Jews during this present time because of their blindness to the truth brought by their own prophets.

The third count in the indictment of St. Paul is ". . . they . . . have persecuted us . . ." (I Thess. 2:15). We already mentioned Paul's experience of persecution at the hands of his fellow countrymen which illustrated their antipathy to the church. They hated the universalism of Christianity. They did not believe that God would accept men without making them become Jews first. The persecution of the Thessalonians was stimulated by their fellow countrymen who were also Jews. These Jews had not only stirred up a riot against St. Paul and then had slandered him in his absence when he left, but they also continued their persecution of those people who did believe in Thessalonica. St. Paul tells these Christians that in this they were also imitators of the churches which were in Judea who suffered under the persecution that raged against them by their fellow countrymen—also the Jews. It was Paul himself who led this persecution before he was converted, and it was as he went to Damascus to apprehend people to cast them in prison and to give his voice against them when they were put to death that he was finally converted to the Lord Jesus. What Paul had done, they continued to do.

The fourth count in the indictment is that ". . . they please not God . . ." (*Ibid.*). The end for which God chose the Jews, to be a holy people, an example unto the nations, a delight of the Lord, has not been fulfilled. No nation has been privileged as has this nation. It is the chosen people. It was singled out among all nations of the earth to become the means of the Divine revelation and of the giving of the Messiah. The privileges of this nation are listed by St. Paul in the Book of Romans. Yet at the time of the captivity, the prophet Ezekiel declared how that neither the Israelites nor their children nor their children's children had obeyed the divine statutes and commandments and laws and therefore had been driven into captivity (Ez. 20-22).

The evaluation of the Jews by the New Testament is a stiffnecked, rebellious and sinful people. Jesus' parable of the householder, who let out his vineyard unto husbandmen which took his servants and beat one and killed another and stoned another in refusing to bring forth the fruits thereof until finally they took his son who was the prince and heir and killed him, illustrates this truth. His punishment of the husbandmen was that he destroyed them and let his vineyard out to other husbandmen, which would render him the fruits in their season. Then comes the application which says, "The kingdom of God shall be taken from you, and given to a nation bringing forth the fruits thereof" (Matt. 21:33-43). The elective purpose of God for this people has been nullified by their obduracy.

The fifth item in the indictment is ". . . they . . . are contrary to all men" (I Thess. 2:15). The word contrary means hostile or at enmity or against. This almost sounds like a quotation from the heathen of Paul's own day. Tacitus, the historian, characterizes the race with "an attitude of hostility and hatred towards all others." Juvenal is said to make the same accusation, that they are like no other race, a nation of misanthropes. Did St. Paul lapse into the heathen estimate of his own people? The answer comes in the meaning of this word contrary. It is qualified by the modifying clause which says, "forbidding us to speak to the Gentiles that they might be saved . . ." (I Thess. 2:16). Their contrariety lay in their opposition to the gospel, not in that they were contrary to all men, as Benjamin Franklin accused them of being when he pled for their exclusion from America. In that they had hindered the eternal salvation of men by opposing the preaching of the gospel under Paul and others, they were contrary to all men. In this their sin was very great.

The next count against them by St. Paul was, ". . . they . . . fill up their sins alway . . ." (I Thess. 2:16). The figure is of a cup which is filled to overflowing and is taken from the Old Testament. At times it has been used to express blessing such as in the twenty-third Psalm— ". . . my cup runneth over . . ." (Psa. 23:5), at other times to express indignation, such as being forced to drink the cup of the wrath of God (Hab. 2:16). The cup of Israel's sin was not full until she rejected Christ and repudiated the gospel. Then judgment inevitably followed. The Bible tells us that the cup of the Amorites was not yet full. When Abraham lived in Palestine, he had to wait four hundred years before judgment would fall upon these people. Thus also the cup of the Russians and the cup of the Americans is not yet full, but Israel's was filled, according to Paul, in her rejection of Christ. The final dispersion came a few years later in the destruction of Jerusalem and the driving of the people into the four corners of the earth, but the evidences of this coming judgment were already present.

The last count in Paul's indictment was ". . . the wrath is come upon them to the uttermost" (I Thess. 2:16). This is the same wrath from which all believers are delivered by Jesus. It is the wrath to come. It has an eschatological meaning, but it is also wrath which is coming constantly upon them. This wrath was already operative upon the nation in the days of Paul. The word "to come upon" is in the perfect tense and means that it has already come. What we have seen in the history of the Jews throughout two thousand years is evidence of the fact that this wrath did come upon the Jews, but that does not hinder the fulfillment of Scripture that the history of Israel will culminate in the time of Jacob's trouble in the great tribulation for Israel, a time of the wrath of God.

This then is the terrible indictment drawn by St. Paul upon the Jews. It is not anti-Semitism, but it gives the Jewish relationship to God according to its position.

II. *The Interpretation of the Jew by Paul*

This outburst of feeling against his own fellow countrymen must be understood in Paul's studied philosophy of Israel's place in the divine purpose. This is contained in Romans, chapters nine to eleven. It is opened by a protestation of Paul's own love and burden for his kinsmen according to the flesh. "I have great heaviness and continual sorrow in my heart. For I could wish that myself were accursed from Christ for my brethren, my kinsmen according to the flesh" (Rom. 9:2,3). This came from one who was an Hebrew of the Hebrews. The truth concerning the Jews as presented in this great section of Paul's epistle is compared to the horticultural practice of breaking off branches from a fruit tree and grafting in other branches. Three truths are declared. First, that the branches which were natural, namely, Israel, were broken off. Second, that the branches which were unnatural, namely, the Gentiles, were grafted in. And third, that the Gentiles would ultimately be broken off and the Jews grafted in again.

In chapter nine we have the description of Israel as the chosen people of God, as the natural branches of the olive tree, which represents God's redeemed people. Theirs was the election. They were chosen of God. Through them the promised blessing to Abraham was to come to the world. Through them God's revelation and Saviour were to be given to the world. For them God did wonders. He delivered them from Egypt with an high hand, He guided and cared for them in the wilderness with a pillar of cloud by day and a pillar of fire by night, He enabled them to triumphantly enter and possess Canaan land, He gave them the judges, the symbolism of the tabernacle, the rulership of kings, and the guidance of the prophets—all of this evinced the fact that they were the apple of His eye, Jeshurun or God's darling.

They enjoyed the privileges of election and of divine favor. Paul describes them as ". . . the adoption, and the glory, and the covenants, and the giving of the law, and the service of God, and the promises; whose are the fathers, and of whom as concerning the flesh Christ came, who is over all, God blessed for ever" (Rom. 9:4,5). They are compared to the vineyard of the Lord which He pruned, purged, chastened in a series of blessings, calamities, and judgments in order that as a vineyard it might bear fruit.

However, they rejected their privilege and now are not the people of God. When the Messiah came, they rejected Him revealing their blindness and obduracy. When the righteousness which is of faith was revealed, they would have none of it but wanted righteousness which was by the law (Rom. 9: 30-32). When this choice was made, the natural branches were broken off and the wild branches were grafted in. Israel today is not the people of God.

The branches grafted in to take Israel's place were the Gentiles. It was another nation to which the divine vineyard was given for cultivation and care and for the bringing forth of fruit. Yet not all Israel was rejected nor were all the branches broken off. There was still a remnant of Israel. Thus the branches at present in the olive tree of God's redeemed people consist, not of any chosen nation, but of individuals of all nations who by repentance and faith become the Israel of God, the children of Abraham by faith (Gal. 3:6,14; I Pet. 2:9). There is now no difference between Jew and Gentile. Outside of Christ both Jew and Gentile are lost. In believing and confessing Christ, both Jew and Gentile are saved (Rom. 10:9,10; Eph. 2:11-17). The nation of Israel has no special place in God's redemptive scheme today. Those Israelites repenting and believing constitute the remnant of grace for God has not cast away His people. But those rejecting Christ are described in Romans 10:21: ". . . a disobedient and gainsaying people." To these the Lord had spread forth His hands all through the generations but they had rejected. Now the gospel goes to all men indiscriminately and whosoever will call upon the name of the Lord shall be saved. Jew and Gentile are on equal ground today. Paul and the Gentiles were on equal ground then. We and Israel are on equal ground today.

Yet God has a future purpose for Israel and it will as a nation be ingrafted into the olive tree. The purpose of God with Israel is not done. His Word declares that God has not cast away His people but that all Israel will be saved (Rom. 11:26), and that the veil of blindness will be removed. Hence the preservation of Israel through all the vicissitudes of persecution, pogrom, and anti-Semitism through the ages. This remarkable phenomenon in spite of its dispersion, its tribulation, and suffering testifies to its future place in God's plan. The present salvation of the Gentiles came about through the fall of Israel and the resultant crucifixion of Christ, and the future blessing which will come to the Gentiles through the conversion of Israel will be like a resurrection from the dead (Rom. 11:13-15). The whole race will be renewed. Hence, the believer, realizing how indebted he is to the Jews, must forever be a friend of the Jew.

III. *The Invitation to the Jew by St. Paul*

In Paul's last recorded experience in Rome, he is described as calling together the chief of the Jews for a conference (Acts 28:17). When the chief men of the Jews were gathered together, Paul preached unto them the gospel. It was his custom to take the gospel to the Jews first (Rom. 1:16,17). Thus at Rome he also summoned them to him to hear the gospel. There he spoke of the claims of Christ. ". . . he expounded and testified the kingdom of God, persuading them concerning Jesus, both out of the law of Moses, and out of the prophets, from morning till evening" (Acts 28:23). As a result, some believed the things which were spoken, and some believed not. Paul's sorrow in the rejection of his people of the Messiah was here repeated. Only a remnant believed.

Consequently, Paul prophesied that salvation thereafter was no longer confined to the Jews and his primary responsibility was no longer to the Jews, but he would go to the Gentiles. Said he, ". . . Well spake the Holy Ghost by Esaias the prophet unto our fathers, saying, Go unto this people, and say, Hearing ye shall hear, and shall not understand; and seeing ye shall see, and not perceive: for the heart of this people is waxed gross, and their ears are dull of hearing, and their eyes have they closed; lest they should see with their eyes, and hear with their ears, and understand with their heart, and should be converted, and I should heal them. Be it known therefore unto you, that the salvation of God is sent unto the Gentiles, and that they will hear it" (Acts 28:25-28). Following Pentecost, St. Peter had preached unto the nation as a whole in its authoritative Sanhedrin the gospel of Jesus Christ, but they had rejected that preaching (Acts 3-5). Later they had heard from St. Paul before the Sanhedrin (Acts 21) and had again rejected the gospel. Seriatim as he went from city to city, Paul presented the gospel to the Jews first and they rejected it. Therefore, they were no longer to be first in the order or reception of the gospel. The Jew lost his priority and now stands on an equality with the Gentile concerning salvation. He either is to be saved as a Gentile is to be saved through repentance and faith in Jesus Christ or he is to be lost as a Gentile is lost by rejecting Jesus Christ.

Paul's preaching today would call all men—Jew and Gentile—to repentance and faith in the Messiah, the Jesus of history, the Christ of God. This also is our message. There is no other name given under heaven whereby men must be saved, but the name of Jesus. The Christian must neither have an inordinate affection for the Jew, placing him first through sentimentalism, nor should he have an antipathy to the Jew, treating him with prejudice and hatred.

The dispensational purposes of God for the Jew still stand. They are yet to be converted as a nation. They are yet to be greatly blessed of God in an age which is yet to come. Touch not this people in hate, but preach to them Jesus Christ, pray for them, and thank God for the blessing received through them. This is the attitude of the church toward the Jew.

IX

Satan's Means of Hindering the Church

*Wherefore we would have come unto you, even I Paul, once
and again; but Satan hindered us.*

—I THESSALONIANS 2:18

PAUL WAS NOT THE ONLY ONE WHO STRUGGLED WITH SATAN.
Martin Luther's life was marked by contact with the devil.
His call from a secular to a religious life occurred during a
thunderstorm, while he was traveling from Mansfeld to Erfurt
in July, 1505. Just outside the city of Stotternheim, he was
knocked to the ground by a bolt of lightning and he cried
out in terror, "St. Anne help me! I will become a monk." [1] and
he did within two weeks, entering the Augustinian Monastery.
He always believed his vocation was from heaven.

When Luther's father learned of his transfer from the field
of law to the field of religion, he was highly enraged, for he
had educated his son in order to support himself and his wife
in their old age. But two years later when Luther became a
priest and celebrated his first mass, his father attended. At
the dinner table following the ceremony, Luther said, "Dear
Father, why were you so contrary to my becoming a monk?
And perhaps you are not quite satisfied even now. The life is
so quiet and godly." [2]

Old Hans flared up in the presence of the doctors, monks and guests, "You learned scholar, have you never read in the Bible that you should honor your father and your mother? And here you have left me and your dear mother to look after ourselves in our old age." [3]

Martin, according to the views of his day, answered, "But Father, I could do you more good by prayers than if I had stayed in the world." [4]

"God grant," said old Hans, "it was not an apparition of the Devil." [5]

Roland Bainton comments, "The medieval man entertained no doubt of the supernatural world, but that world itself was divided. There were saints, and there were demons. There was God, and there was the Devil. And the Devil could disguise himself as an angel of light. Had Luther, then, been right to follow a vision which might after all have been the arch fiend, in preference to the plain clear word of Scripture to honor father and mother?" [6]

This doubt sometimes troubled Luther, even as late as his voluntary incarceration in the Wartburg Castle after the tumultuous Diet of Worms, where he had faced the emperor, the princes, the cardinals, the doctors of theology, and had taken his stand on the Word of God alone. On his return, he was captured by four knights and placed in the Wartburg Castle, where the owls and bats wheeled about in the darkness of the untenanted castle. Then came the temptation of the prince of darkness, "Are you alone wise? Have so many centuries gone wrong? What if you are in error and are taking so many others with you to eternal damnation?" [7] The devil to Luther was a very real person indeed.

Luther was even bound by some of the superstitions of his day in reference to satanic activity. Bainton quotes Luther as saying, "Many regions are inhabited by devils. Prussia is full of them . . . In my native country on the top of a high mountain called the Pubelsberg is a lake into which if a stone be thrown a tempest will arise over the whole region because the waters are the abode of captive demons." [8]

Scripture sanctions no such superstitions, and we do not know whether Luther was emancipated from them or not. When I visited the Wartburg Castle, the guide showed me a spot on the wall of Luther's study, in which he had translated the Bible from the Vulgate to the German, where he had supposedly thrown an ink stand at the devil who appeared to him while at work. Luther gives the same conviction, though it may only have been a figure of speech, when he determined to go to Worms in spite of the adverse advice of his friends Sickingen and Hutten. They wished to dissuade him from this course because of the end of John Hus, but Luther would enter Worms "though there be as many devils as tiles on the roofs." [9]

Luther also expressed his belief in demons in his great hymn:

> A mighty fortress is our God,
> A bulwark never failing;
> Our helper He, amid the flood
> Of mortal ills prevailing.
> For still our ancient foe
> Doth seek to work us woe;
> His craft and pow'r are great,
> And, armed with cruel hate,
> On earth is not his equal.
>
> Did we in our own strength confide,
> Our striving would be losing;
> Were not the right Man on our side,
> The Man of God's own choosing.
> Dost ask who that may be?
> Christ Jesus, it is He;
> Lord Sabaoth is His name,
> From age to age the same,
> And He must win the battle.

And tho' this world, with devils filled,
Should threaten to undo us;
We will not fear, for God hath willed
His truth to triumph through us.
The prince of darkness grim—
We tremble not for him;
His rage we can endure,
For lo! his doom is sure,
One little word shall fell him.

Like Luther, Paul had controversies with Satan. It is very analogous to find that he had ". . . a thorn in the flesh, the messenger of Satan to buffet . . ." (II Cor. 12:7) him, and that he was hindered by Satan (I Thess. 2:18), and that he wrestled ". . . against the rulers of the darkness . . ." (Eph. 6:12), and that he believed "the god of this world hath blinded the minds of them which believe not . . ." (II Cor. 4:4), and that the unsaved ". . . walked according to the course of this world, according to the prince of the power of the air, the spirit that now worketh in the children of disobedience" (Eph. 2:2).

Paul was able to discern when he was hindered by God (Acts 16:7) and when he was hindered by Satan (I Thess. 2:18) and when he was hindered by his own spirit. The external hindrances, adversaries, illnesses, and accidents may be ascribed to Satan's activity, but Paul also had inward obstacles of feeling and conviction which were placed there by God's Spirit. He knew the difference between the two.

Some give an answer to this problem by saying that the same event may be ascribed to Satan and to God, for Satan works within the permissive will of God, but that is only a partial answer (James 1:12; Job 1:1-10). There is more in the ability to discern between the obstacles God places in our path and the obstacles Satan places in our path than this mere distinction.

We too may have controversies with Satan. He is described

as our adversary (Rev. 12:10; I Pet. 5:8), seeking to sift us as wheat (Luke 22:31) and to tempt us. (Matt. 4:3-11).

We may be called the children of the devil (John 8:44) or the children of God, and our deeds may be motivated by allegiance either to God or the devil. Thus it was that Jesus excoriated the Pharisees as being children of the devil. (Matt. 23:13-36).

The Christian takes his stand with Luther, with Paul, and with Jesus on the reality of Satan and of his power to hinder the church. The church and the devil are in conflict, but the gates of hell shall not prevail against the church. Moderns may refer to Christians as medievalists because they believe in Satan, but they do so on biblical ground.

I. *The Persecution of the Church by Satan*

In the twelfth chapter of Revelation, the picture is drawn of a woman waiting to give birth to a child and standing before the woman a dragon seeking to devour the child as soon as it was born. The child was rescued from the dragon, but he persecuted the woman and also made war with the remnant of her seed which kept the commandments of God and have the testimony of Jesus Christ. This is a picture of the persecution of the church by Satan.

We here adopt the broad view of the church. It is natural to identify this woman with Israel, but it includes her seed who have the testimony of Jesus. Thus not only the Old Testament form of the people of God, but also the New Testament form of the church is included in this figure of the persecuted woman. It includes the Israel of God (Rom. 11:15-24). We must insist that Abraham, David, and Paul were redeemed as are we through Christ and therefore that we are one in the church (Gal. 3:7,14,29).

Many have been Satan's attacks to overwhelm the church. We question as to the nature of the hindrance which obstructed St. Paul from going to Thessalonica. Was it the opposition of the Jews? Was it illness? Was it pressure from other work? That we do not know. The presumption is that it could be identified with the persecution and tribulations which raged in Thessalonica. Some have had a tendency to identify it with his temptation in the flesh (Gal. 4:14) to which he later referred. However Satan attacked St. Paul, it was to hinder his work with the church. The long history of such persecutions upon the Israel of God are a matter of record. There was Pharaoh's persecution of Israel, there was Ahasuerus' attempt to blot out Israel, there was Herod's attack upon Jesus with the slaughter of the innocents at Bethlehem, there was the Roman persecution which continued through the reign of ten Caesars, there was the Inquisition, and there have been modern persecutions in Russia, in Germany, and in China. All this may be ascribed to Satan.

The church is always given an opportunity to compromise in the form of a subtle temptation to amalgamate with the world. Thus after Christianity was legalized by Constantine, it made the great compromise. It took the glory, pomp, and power of the world into its hands as holding two swords instead of one. Thus the temptation which the devil placed before Jesus of the world, of power, and of leadership was effective when it was presented to the church. What would the church want more than to change and to lead the world, but this must be accomplished by the cross and not by worldly power.

There were tribulations in this Thessalonian Church. St. Paul said, ". . . no man should be moved by these afflictions: for yourselves know that we are appointed thereunto. For verily, when we were with you, we told you before that we should suffer tribulation; even as it came to pass, and ye know" (I Thess. 3:3,4). Paul had warned them when he was present with them that the gospel would entail tribulation. They very soon experienced it from their own countrymen as well as from the Jews. They suffered ostracism, physical attacks, and real suffering. This warning might well be repeated to all Christians. We are not to count it a strange thing when we are tried by a fiery trial. Peter in fact declares, "For if any man suffer as a Christian, let him not be ashamed; but let him glorify God on this behalf" (I Pet. 4:16). Thus Luther in writing to Frederick, the Elector of Saxony, rejoiced that he was counted worthy to suffer for Christ's sake. Thus did the early Christians such as Paul and Ignatius as illustrations of the teaching that ". . . we must through much tribulation enter into the kingdom of God" (Acts 14:22). The church cannot be at ease. It must be a marching church, a contending church, assaulting the gates of hell. If we are at ease, we betray our purpose, for when we are an aggressive church, there will be trouble through the hindrances and obstacles of Satan.

In our day there is a resurgence of this conflict. A new interest in demonism, in malignant forces which invade the souls of men with torments of mental disorder, with indescribable cruelty to one another, and with the planning of cataclysmic destructions is widespread. It is understood that electric lights alone will not banish the attacks of darkness. Before the end time all Christians must face severe trouble.

II. *The Preservation of the Church from Satan*

Paul said, ". . . I sent to know your faith, lest by some means the tempter have tempted you, and our labour be in vain" (I Thess. 3:5). Though Satan can tempt, obstruct, and hinder the church, he is a defeated person. The climax of conflict in the attack upon the woman came against Christ as He hung upon the cross, but by that very event, God was reconciled, sin was forgiven, and the dominion of Satan was broken. The entire evil machinations of the devil were turned to good when the cross became the means of glory. The conquest and the victory are declared in Scripture (John 12:31; Col. 2:14,15). As a result, Satan was vanquished and appointed unto a judgment of consignment to eternal fire (Matt. 25:41; Rev. 20:10). The execution of this judgment awaits the second coming of Christ, but the victory has been won and he is a defeated power.

The church then is composed of delivered people. Hence, St. Paul was instructed ". . . to turn them . . . from the power of Satan unto God . . ." (Acts 26:18). The devil has no power over God's people who have been delivered from his dominion and control. They belong to God. They are redeemed. Satan can touch them only with divine permission. Moreover, death, which is the instrument of Satan, has lost its sting and its fear (Heb. 2:14). This great deliverance is the fruit of the cross and of the resurrection. Hence, the dominion of Christ's kingdom is challenged, attacked, hindered by the devil who tempts, sifts, and tries every device and means to turn souls from Christ. The means of Satan's control over men is through their own sin. He is our accuser, and when we sin, he gains a ground for a claim against us to God. Not every saint is delivered from the lion's mouth. God may have a purpose in permitting us to suffer.

The believers are God's heritage in the saints and He will defend that heritage. Our security rests in Christ, the Man of God's own choosing, the redeemer—incarnate, perfect, glorious, and conquering. He is able to keep His own which He purchased by His own blood. He will not suffer us to be tempted above that we are able, but with the temptation will provide a way of escape. Through this divine inheritance, namely, the saints, God will show forth the riches of His grace in the ages which are to come. Our assurance rests in Christ's sovereignty, rule, and victory (I Cor. 15:24; Acts 2:26-33).

III. *The Prevailing of the Church over Satan*

Since the church has a defeated foe, it should be on the aggressive, marching in conquest for Christ. Jesus said, ". . .

the gates of hell shall not prevail against it" (Matt. 16:18). Campbell Morgan has shown that this is the picture of the church attacking the City of Destruction and the gates of hell cannot prevail against the aggression of the church. If the church is truly evangelistic in declaring the unsearchable riches of Christ with a passion for lost souls, if the church is truly a witness unto the resurrection life, if the church is teaching the content of the gospel, the gates of hell cannot stand such an attack. The church will be victorious over Satan and over his demons.

The church also is delivered from the wrath to come. When God's wrath and judgment is poured out upon the devil, his angels, and wicked men at His coming, the believers will be transformed into the image of Christ and will share His glory, for He will come to be glorified in them. When the Lord Jesus in that day divides between the sheep and the goats, when He says to those on His left hand, ". . . Depart . . . into everlasting fire, prepared for the devil and his angels" (Matt. 25:41), He will not speak to those who belong to the church.

The church is destined to share the sovereignty of Christ its Lord over all foes. The picture given in the twenty-fourth Psalm of the Lord of Hosts entering the gates of heaven which are lifted up for His presence is a picture which includes the glory of the church of Jesus Christ. This is the victory which Christ has won for us.

The Lord has not left us without help to counteract the hindrances of the devil. Christ is our conqueror, but Christ has given us another advocate who will help our infirmities and enable us to be more than conquerors. That advocate is the Holy Spirit. How paradoxical it seems that the Lord Jesus was driven of the Spirit into the wilderness to be tempted of the devil, for it is the Spirit who strengthens us and who compensates for our infirmities when we are in trial or temptation (Rom. 8:26).

The Lord Jesus vanquished the devil through His use of the Word of God. He said of Scripture, ". . . it is written . . ." (Matt. 4:10) and the devil left Him. Scripture is the greatest weapon in our armory, and when the Holy Spirit brings it to our minds in an hour of temptation, it is the sword of God with which we can overcome the enemy.

God is faithful. He will not suffer us to be tempted above what we are able. Our enemy is not too much for us, for when we are united with Christ through His Holy Spirit, we are more than conquerors. Thanks be unto God who always causes us to triumph in Christ Jesus!

X

The Crown Rewarding the Church's Labors

*For what is our hope, or joy, or crown of rejoicing? Are
not even ye in the presence of our Lord Jesus Christ at his
coming? For ye are our glory and joy.*

—I THESSALONIANS 2:19,20

PAUL HAD IN MIND WHAT IS TO TAKE PLACE AT THE COMING
of our Lord Jesus Christ. Before we are through with this
book, it will be necessary for us to analyze Paul's teaching
concerning the second coming of the Lord. When the Lord
comes again, He will judge the believers concerning rewards.
At that time the church shall receive her crown rewarding her
labors.

Compare this Scripture with I Corinthians 3:11-15 where
we are told that some build upon the one foundation with
wood, hay, and stubble while others build with gold, silver,
and precious stones, and that every man's work shall be
made manifest when it shall be tried by fire. If any man's
work survive the fire, he shall receive a reward, the others
shall suffer loss. Obviously this passage of Scripture is a sym-
bolic presentation of the reward for one's labors. It declares
that there is a time coming when our work will be tested,

when we shall stand before the judgment seat of Christ and answer for the deeds which we have accomplished, and when we shall receive a reward or shall suffer loss.

This does not mean that the believer will not be saved nor does it mean that he works in order to merit his salvation, nor does it mean that he shall be justified or condemned according to the works that he has done. That whole question was settled for the believer at the cross when he accepted the Lord Jesus Christ. At that time he was justified in the sight of God and possesses eternal life. Nevertheless, that same believer will be judged concerning his work as a result of which he will receive his status in the life to come called heaven. Our condition in that eternal state will depend upon the works which we have done here upon earth. That state will mean a great deal to us and to it we should give some consideration.

In the Book of Proverbs we read the statement, ". . . he that winneth souls is wise" (Prov. 11:30) or, as is translated in the Revised Version, ". . . he that is wise winneth souls." Daniel declared, "They that be wise shall shine as the brightness of the firmament; and they that turn many to righteousness as the stars for ever and ever" (Dan. 12:3). Hebrew parallelism is the practice of using two clauses to say the same thing and is quite common in the Psalms, the Proverbs, and the prophetic writings. Here Daniel says, "they that be wise shall shine as the brightness of the firmament" and the second clause says, "they that turn many to righteousness as the stars for ever and ever." The meaning is that they that be wise are those who turn many to righteousness and that these wise will receive glory in the life to come in accordance with their works in this world. The content is the same as that of our text. An analysis of Daniel twelve reveals that the wise are the righteous and the unwise are the wicked. (Dan. 12:10). Thus we conclude that the wise are the saved, the purified, and the righteous who are engaged in turning many to righteousness, i.e. in propagating the faith or in soul-winning. These soul-winners are declared to be assured of shining like the stars forever and ever.

The Bible makes it plain that there will be a differentiation of glory for the redeemed. Paul declares, "There is one glory of the sun, and another glory of the moon, and another glory of the stars: for one star differeth from another star in glory" (I Cor. 15:41). Then Paul declared, "So also is the resurrection of the dead . . ." (I Cor. 15:42). There is to be a great difference in the glory which believers receive in God's eternal kingdom and that difference will depend upon the work which they have done here upon earth.

Jesus declared the parable of the nobleman who went into a far country. (Luke 19:11-27). Before leaving he called his servants and delivered unto them ten pounds and said, ". . . Occupy till I come" (Luke 19:13). When after the passage of time he returned, he commanded the servants to be called unto him to give an accounting as to how much had been gained by trading. The first said, ". . . Lord, thy pound hath gained ten pounds. And he said unto him, Well, thou good servant: because thou hast been faithful in a very little, have thou authority over ten cities. And the second came, saying, Lord, thy pound hath gained five pounds. And he said likewise to him, Be thou also over five cities. And another came, saying, Lord, behold, here is thy pound, which I have kept laid up in a napkin: for I feared thee, because thou art an austere man: thou takest up that thou layedst not down, and reapest that thou didst not sow. And he saith unto him, Out of thine own mouth will I judge thee, thou wicked servant. Thou knewest that I was an austere man, taking up that I laid not down, and reaping that I did not sow: wherefore then gavest not thou my money into the bank, that at my coming I might have required mine own with usury? And he said unto them that stood by, Take from him the pound, and give it to him that hath ten pounds" (Luke 19:16-24). The obvious teaching is that God expects His servants to use that which He has committed unto them. Scripture buttresses this fact by declaring that there is a day coming when the Lord will take inventory of that which we have done with what He has committed unto us. What will be your experience in that day? Will it be glory, honor, and rejoicing? St. Paul declares in our text, "For what is our hope, or joy, or crown of rejoicing?" And then he answers, "Are not even ye in the presence of our Lord Jesus Christ at his coming? For ye are our glory and joy" (I Thess. 2:19,20). His crown was to consist of the converts whom he had led to a faith in Jesus Christ and who had received eternal life through his preaching and his ministry. They were to constitute his hope, his glory, his crown of rejoicing in the day of the Lord Jesus Christ. We have all sung the hymn "Will There Be Any Stars in My Crown?" It is true that glory will be granted to those who have engaged in soul-winning work upon earth.

The Bible makes it plain that God has endowed us to be soul-winners, He has equipped us with the instruments necessary for soul-winning, and He has pronounced an encomium on us for being engaged in soul-winning.

I. *The Endowment for Soul-Winning*

It is axiomatic that a soul-winner must already have received spiritual life from God, he must be a child of God. To impart life we must have life. We must already be quickened from being dead in trespasses and sins and be alive unto righteousness. That means that a soul-winner must have already experienced conversion, regeneration, and the beginning of sanctification. This is the life which God has given to us. It is not of ourselves but is of Jesus Christ. John the Apostle declared, "And this is the record, that God hath given to us eternal life, and this life is in his Son. He that hath the Son hath life; and he that hath not the Son of God hath not life" (I John 5:11,12). Spiritual life, abundant life, eternal life is God's gift to the repenting and believing man. This is the first requirement of being an effective soul-winner.

God has provided power to do this very work of witnessing (Acts 1:8; Matt. 28:18-20). The reception of such divine power is assured us through our consecration to the working of God's will, our cleansing from all defilements of the flesh, and our separation from sin. Joined with this is the experience of being filled with the Holy Spirit, who endues us with power from on high. This is the believer's heritage—to have power, pentecostal, divine, Holy Spirit power. Such power always comes through the Holy Spirit as Jesus promised in the fourteenth and sixteenth chapters of John's Gospel. It is when the Holy Spirit comes upon us that He will ". . . reprove the world of sin, and of righteousness, and of judgment" (John 16:8).

It is when the Spirit comes upon and fills us that we are enabled to love men. It is impossible simply to will to love unlovable persons. Such a love is given to us by the Holy Spirit. Missionaries do not go to repulsive, filthy, immoral areas of the world because they love those people. They go because they love the Lord Jesus Christ and the Holy Spirit has enabled them to transfer that love unto the unlovely ones of the world.

Christ has put into our hands the instruments of soul-winning. First is the truth. It is essential that the soul-winner have a knowledge of the Word, for this is the means of convicting and converting men. It is the sword of the Spirit which is quick and powerful and which on entering the mind brings light. (Hebrews 4:12; Psalm 119:130; II Timothy 3:16,17; Ephesians 6:17). He who knows the Word embraces the revealed doctrines of God's Word. The preaching of these doctrines and of the Word assures us of blessing in our outreach for the unconverted. Only Christ can save and the Word is the inscripturated Christ whom we are to present unto people in order to lead them to a knowledge of the person of Christ.

For this purpose the Lord has given us His Holy Spirit. It is a basic truth that the Spirit works only in conjunction with the Word of God and that the Word of God is only effective when it is attended by the quickening Spirit (John 16:8; 15:26; 16:13). The soul-winner must utterly depend upon the Holy Spirit to do his work of salvation.

Another instrument is prayer. We are told in the Word that it is the will of God that all men should come to the knowledge of the truth (I Tim. 2:4), and that if we pray anything according to His will, He heareth us and we know that we have the things that we ask (I John 5:15; John 15:7; 14:14). Thus we know that God will not withhold from us the conversion of people if we pray that the Lord of the harvest would thrust forth laborers for this very work (Matt. 9:37,38). Moreover, he who is engaged in soul-winning must depend utterly upon prayer. Paul prayed that Christ might be perfectly formed in his converts (Gal. 4:19), and we are told that the birth of souls into the kingdom is conditioned upon the prayers of the church (Isaiah 66:8). It is utterly foolish to attempt the work of soul-winning without prayer, preparation and practice.

Once we have put these instruments at our disposal, it is then necessary for us to bear testimony to the individual to be reached. The Lord has declared that we are His witnesses. It is ours not to argue, to persuade, to command, but to bear witness to the truth, to the Lord as revealed in His Word which He has exemplified in our experience. When the record of God's Word agrees with our testimony, the individual is convicted in the mouth of two witnesses (I John 5:11). Certainly the Lord has not left His church without the necessary equipment to be effective in soul-winning.

II. *The Employment in Soul-Winning*

Once we possess this equipment, if souls are to be saved, we must get busy and win them. There is no other way. All the theory in the world will not enable a man to play the piano, the violin, or the trumpet. He must put his knowledge into practice and make a beginning. The Lord said, "If any man will come after me, let him deny himself, and take up his cross daily, and follow me" (Luke 9:23). This means more than an initial acceptance of Christ as Saviour. The Lord Himself was constantly engaged in winning souls. A hasty reading of the gospels will reveal His dealing with the woman at the well, His interview with Zacchaeus, His call to Matthew, His summoning of the apostles, His reaching for the soul of the rich young ruler, and many other cases which reveal His readiness night or day to win a soul. He promised His disciples that He would make them fishers of men. Fishing is not only business but it is great fun and thousands of people follow it for sport and relaxation. They may not be great fishers or good fishers, but they enjoy fishing. The Lord Jesus wants us to make this our avocation, even if it is not the full-time vocation of our lives. There is nothing more entrancing than fishing for men. Anyone can be a soul-winner.

The seventh Earl of Shaftsbury, Anthony Ashley Cooper, was won by a faithful nurse who prayed with him, taught him, and led him to the Lord. All the work he accomplished in the House of Commons and the House of Lords for the reform of treatment of the insane, for the benefit of laborers in mills and factories, for the lifting of children from sweatshop labor, for the reform of housing, for the freedom of chimney-sweeps, all can be placed at the door of that faithful nurse who won him to the Lord Jesus Christ. Mr. Dwight L. Moody was won to the Lord Jesus Christ by his Sunday-school teacher, Mr. Kimball. The countless thousands of souls who were brought to God through the preaching of Dwight

L. Moody may be laid directly at the door of Mr. Kimball's faithful witnessing for Jesus Christ. We are also responsible for people who are brought under our care. Recently I received a letter from our missionary in Oicha, Africa. This young lady had formerly been the superintendent of a school of nursing in greater Boston and had laid it all aside to take up work in a hospital in Africa. Of her work she wrote, "All other things mean nothing if I am not a soul-winner . . . I must be a soul-winner. I must be winning these people to Jesus Christ." So must you, whether it is the man who reads your light meter, who delivers your groceries, who services your car, or the lady who dresses your hair, or sells you materials, you must be attempting to win him or her to Jesus Christ.

We as Christians have no right to send someone to a mission field to do what we are unwilling to do at home. Why should we expect a missionary to do a pioneer work by making contacts with a foreign people, inviting them into her home, preaching the gospel, leading them to Christ, building a church, unless we at home are willing to do the same thing. What about that person who has been working side by side with you for ten, twenty, or thirty years in the office? Maybe he knows that you are a Christian, that you have made a profession of faith, that you are an officer in the church, or a Sunday-school teacher, or a member of a Christian organization. Do you not think he wonders why you have not said anything to him about Christ? You say, Oh, he would laugh at me. Perhaps he would laugh at you. He might even now and then poke a little fun at you behind your back, but the day is coming when that same individual will condemn you because you have not spoken to him about the salvation of his soul. What will you do in the day of the revelation of Jesus Christ when a person with whom you have worked for years has never heard the gospel from your lips?

No one will be an effective soul-winner unless he is abiding in Jesus (John 15:1-16). As the branch abides in the vine, the believer must abide in Christ. He must permit the husbandman to cut away the unnecessary wood, that is, practices which would hinder the bearing of fruit. He must remember that his primary purpose is to pass the life from the vine into the fruit. Thus he bears the pruning knife and continues the selfless activity for the glory of this high purpose.

The believer is to be an ambassador for Jesus Christ (II Cor. 5:20), beseeching men to be reconciled to God. Every believer becomes the divine representative to those with whom he comes in contact for the purpose of winning them to Jesus Christ.

Let your emotions as a soul-winner be kept at a white heat. Be fervent in this business of the Lord (Acts 18:25; II Timothy 4:2; 1:6). Let the world be your parish, let the constraining love of Christ move you to enlist every man as a follower of the Lord.

III. *The Encomium of Soul-Winning*

When the grand totals of life are balanced, it is the soul-winner who will receive the crown of rejoicing. Have you lived for self-gratification or for Christ and His Kingdom? What will the balance of your life show? No deed in the realm of soul-winning shall lose its reward (Matt. 10:42; 25:45). The weight of a life spent in winning multitudes to Jesus Christ has been to save souls from death and to cover a multitude of sins.

The day will come when we are gathered at the throne with elders, angels, cherubim, and the redeemed to receive for the deeds done in the body. On that crystal pavement the crowns will be dispensed to those who have been faithful in soul-winning. There the praise of Christ will be heard by the redeemed and will echo with the songs of the angels, ". . . Well done, good and faithful servant . . ." (Matt. 25:23).

Then the glory will be comparable to the self-denial and

sacrifice which we have experienced here. Active soul-winners will inevitably experience ridicule, rejection, and even persecution in some cases. Yet these light afflictions which are but for a moment will work for us a far more eternal and exceeding weight of glory (Matt. 5:11,12; John 15:18-20; II Cor. 4:17). Our joy will be that those who have been saved through our witness will be there to share in the glory. They will constitute our crown of rejoicing. Our state of responsibility, of usefulness, and of service as well as honor in that eternal kingdom will depend upon our faithfulness here (Matt. 25:21). The different spheres of responsibility which we have in this world only call for faithfulness. If you are faithful where God has placed you, He will give you souls—the souls of your children, of your relatives, of your friends. It is not necessary that you should be a preacher and labor in public in order that you might have souls for your hire. As far as we know, Andrew, the brother of Peter, was not a great preacher nor did he gain great honor, but he won Peter, he shared in all of the triumphs that Peter attained.

Are you a soul-winner? Are you wise? Will you shine as the brightness of the firmament and the stars for ever and ever? Will you have a crown of rejoicing? Are there any stars in your crown? Paul expected that he would have them because he was a soul-winner. Let us give ourselves to the same activity.

XI

The Provision for the Church's Lack

Night and day praying exceedingly that we might see your face, and might perfect that which is lacking in your faith.
—I THESSALONIANS 3:10

ST. PAUL HAD A GREAT BURDEN FOR HIS CONVERTS. HE FELT the same affection and responsibility for them that a father would feel for his children, and, if they did not mature, if they did not come to a full knowledge of the faith, it greatly concerned him. It was his purpose, therefore, to visit the Thessalonian Church a second time in order that he might be able to perfect their faith, to bring them into the maturity of a Christian experience and not to leave them dangling with an imperfect knowledge of the things of God. So he had hoped to come, but according to chapter two, verse eighteen, he found that he was hindered, prevented by perhaps sickness, or perhaps the persecution that had befallen him of the Jews, his fellow countrymen. He said that it was Satan that hindered him. He ascribed it to the activities of his adversary, the evil one.

Being not able to go and minister to these people personally, he made a substitute plan. He dispatched his co-laborer and fellow minister in the gospel, his dearly beloved son in the faith, Timothy. And though he needed Timothy, probably because of sickness because he came to Corinth in much weakness and trembling, he dispatched him to Thessalonica. As the third chapter, verses one and two, tell us, he was left alone at Athens, Timothy going on to visit the Thessalonians and to establish them in the faith. Timothy was sent for that purpose. After all, it makes little difference whether it is Apollos, Paul, or Peter; for Paul may sow, and Apollos water, but God gives the increase. We must always remember that the gospel is not connected with any particular man, but that God can use and does use many men to preach His Word and communicate the truth.

When, therefore, Timothy returned to Paul while he was at Corinth, for he had moved on to preach the gospel there, he found Paul in affliction and discouragement. He reported about the way the Thessalonians had received his ministry: that there were new converts, that they had grown in grace, that they were matured in the faith, that in fact they were even preaching the gospel, and that through them the gospel was sounding forth in Macedonia and in Achaia to the glory of God. St. Paul was thrilled, filled with gladness, comforted in his affliction and his distress, and he penned his letter with an outburst of thanksgiving to God and of praise, stating, "For what thanks can we render to God again for you, for all the joy wherewith we joy for your sakes before our God" (I Thess. 3:9), because God had established a people in grace. This then was the way in which he came to write these words.

But at the same time he had a passion for these converts. He had a passion for them that they might enter into the completion of their faith. He said in verse eight, "For now we live, if ye stand fast in the Lord." He wasn't exaggerating. He meant that his life took on new color, new strength, and new vibrancy when he knew that his converts were established. After all we can't blame people who enter the Christian faith for vacillation, for foolish actions, and for even slipping into error from time to time if they are not thoroughly indoctrinated and trained in the truth. That leads us to say that there should not only be an evangelistic emphasis in which we thoroughly believe, but that there must be a teaching emphasis and that the indoctrination of converts is as necessary and as important as the first winning of these converts to the Lord Jesus Christ. That is why often in the kind of evangelistic campaigns in which I participate, we have great emphasis on teaching as well as exhortation and persuasion. That is why here in our church we have always emphasized the teaching ministry, believing that it is the teaching ministry that causes people to grow and to mature and to have a full experience of salvation such as that Paul desired them to have at this time. So his concern was manifested and he was going now to make this transition into teaching for the rest of the epistle. But before doing it he prayed for them and verses eleven through thirteen state his prayer. Let me read them to you.

Now God himself and our Father, and our Lord Jesus Christ, direct our way unto you. And the Lord make you to increase and abound in love one toward another, and toward all men, even as we do toward you: to the end he may stablish your hearts unblameable in holiness before God, even our Father, at the coming of our Lord Jesus Christ with all his saints.

Paul saw that though he could not get to Thessalonica, yet he could directly influence them by his prayers. Would God that that thought would clearly come home to us as believers. So many of us at one time or another are incapacitated by some illness or accident or trouble, so that we are limited in our activities and cannot go to church, cannot do what we would otherwise do. We chafe against it. It could become, if we would let it, one of the greatest means of influencing the church of Christ and the work of Christ in the world by the reaching out through the realm of intercession as St. Paul here did. Many a minister has found that when he had an intercessor behind him, his work is intensified with a geometrical increase, more so than if he had prayed alone. Moody found that, Finney found that, many others have found it. Usually, when you find a great work, you will find that there are people of prayer behind it. What an influence every one of us could exert in those periods of inactivity if only we would do it. But how few of us do it. St. Paul reached out then, limited by Satan in that he could not go personally, reached across the line and released by his prayer life that which otherwise could not have taken place.

Notice what he prayed about. He prayed for them that they should have an experience of being perfected in the faith. Here again he says, ". . . Praying exceedingly . . ." (I Thess. 3:10). What an intercessory life that was! ". . . that we might see your face, and might perfect that which is lacking in your faith" (*Ibid.*). He wanted in them a perfection of Christian spirit.

Then he wanted them to exhibit that Christian perfection of faith. Notice here in the twelfth verse, "And the Lord make you to increase and abound in love one toward another, and toward all men, even as we do toward you." That would exhibit their perfection in the faith. Then he wanted them to be established in holiness as a result of that perfection in the faith, "To the end he may stablish your hearts unblameable in holiness before God, even our Father, at the coming of our Lord Jesus Christ with all his saints" (I Thess. 3:13). Now let us look at it.

I. *The Experience of Perfection in Faith*

In the Book of Hebrews (whether written by Paul, or Apollos, or some other apostle of the New Testament time) we have the statement that we should leave the ". . . prin-

ciples of the doctrine of Christ" and "go on unto perfection
. . ." (Heb. 6:1).

What are those first principles? The writer names them.
He said, ". . . repentance from dead works, and of faith
toward God, of the doctrine of baptisms . . . resurrection
of the dead, and of eternal judgment" (Heb. 6:1,2). Think
of them a moment. They are very essential. You never can
eliminate them from the gospel. They are basic things to our
faith. They are principles which must be inculcated in men
if they are going to enter the Kingdom of God, but they are
not to be the final principles. I find that people, in part at
least, are trusting in their church membership, in their baptism, in the experiences which they have had, in the things
which they have done for entering into the Kingdom of God
instead of trusting in Jesus Christ.

Let me give you an illustration. During an evangelistic
campaign in Moncton, New Brunswick, the manager of an
insurance company knocked at my hotel door one morning,
came in, and in short order we found that he had been serious enough about his faith to go and join the church, serious
enough to be baptized, and to participate in works of the
church. But as he sat there, a bit nervously, he said, "I have
not achieved that which I have sought," and I said, "What
have you sought?" He said, "That I might really be forgiven
and that I might know that I am a child of God." And so we
had the privilege of pointing out to him how God makes
known to a man that he is His child through repentance,
through conversion by exposing himself to Christ and what
Christ has done, through his committal unto Jesus Christ as
Saviour and Lord, through recognition of his own sinfulness
and his confession of faith in Christ and what He has done.
He said he was willing to do it. He did. When he finished,
with tears in his eyes and with a smile upon his lips, and as
he went out, he said, "Well, now, I feel better. That is what I
wanted to do." He was amazed that this all happened instan-

taneously, suddenly, and that he was converted. He was just one of many.

What this writer of the Book of Hebrews says is this. He says we must leave these things of repentance from dead works, we must leave this matter of faith toward Christ, that initial step of salvation, we must leave this matter of being baptized into the body of Christ by the Holy Spirit so that we participate in His death, in His resurrection and in His present position, we must leave this matter of an ultimate resurrection, and we must leave the matter even of judgment. We are not going to tell you about those things all the time. Those are the things that should awaken a man and turn him away from his sins and bring him into a knowledge of salvation in Jesus Christ. If we are Christians, if we are believers, if we are children of God, then we must move on.

How true that is. Paul said here that he was burdened for these Thessalonian believers because they had not had the instruction that would lead them to the perfection of their faith. He knew that there would come a day when they would be thoroughly disillusioned by the vestigial remains of their unconverted life that still remained in their converted experience. He knew that there would be times when there would be things that would come out of their sinful nature; for they knew, and he knew, that they had this nature in spite of the seed of God's planting within them and that they were now God's children. He knew that there would be motions of concupiscence, and lasciviousness and evil that would come out of the old nature, and he wanted them to be instructed and established in the faith so that those things which disillusioned them might not drive them away, those things that would make them become a prey to sects which dwell upon the aberrations of Christians. He told them that he longed to come and, since he could not come, that Timothy would come in order that they might be established in the faith and that they might know what God had in addition to their conversion for them. He wanted them to know that the Lord had provided the ministry of the Holy Spirit who, being released in a converted crucified man by the crucified, resurrected, and glorified Christ, would begin to produce attributes and characteristics which would demonstrate that man to be the child of God, which would make him different from other people in the world, and would give him a measure of deliverance and of victory and power in his life. That is what Paul wanted them to have. He wanted them to enter that great experience of Christian perfection. So he longed that they should come to such an experience.

When he got through telling them about this experience of perfection, he went on to tell them how it would exhibit itself. If I had been St. Paul with the knowledge that he had at this time, this is what I would have written. I would have written to them about the things that had happened on my missionary journeys, about the things that are recalled in the Book of Acts. You remember when St. Paul came to Ephesus on his second missionary journey what happened? At the very beginning of this journey which is now described, he found there certain disciples who had believed in the Lord, who had the baptism of John, but who were deficient somewhere in their Christian experience. They simply were lacking, that is all.

Now St. Paul may have noted an ethical lack. Maybe they were doing things that they ought not to do as the children of God. Maybe they had a lack of knowledge and he noticed their ignorance in their testimony, or their prayers, or whatever they were doing, or maybe he noticed some other deficiency in the joy or the fruitfulness of their lives, but he saw that something was lacking. So he said to them, "Have ye received the Holy Ghost since ye believed? And they said unto him, We have not so much as heard whether there be any Holy Ghost" (Acts 19:2). Twenty-two years after Pentecost and they did not know anything about the Holy Spirit. And so St. Paul indoctrinated them, he taught them, and when they were taught, they came out into the experience of the perfection of the faith.

There is an illustration in the previous chapter given of Apollos, a man who was mighty in the Scriptures, eloquent, fervent in the spirit, who taught diligently the things of the Lord, but when two of Paul's believers had been with him at Corinth for a few months and had listened to him, they believed he was deficient in knowledge, experience, and blessing. They took him aside and expounded to him the way of God more perfectly. Now when Apollos received that in Ephesus and was disposed to go on over into Achaia to preach there, the brethren wrote a recommendation of him, and the Bible says that when he was come, he mightily helped them which believed through grace and he convinced the Jews that Jesus was the Christ.

Apollos had a more perfect instruction in the way. If that were necessary for Peter, for Stephen, for Philip, for Paul, for the twelve, for Apollos, for the Thessalonian Christians, and for so many others, do you suppose that it is unnecessary for us? Do you think for one moment that we too can get along without having our faith matured and perfected under the teaching of the New Testament?

Well, God undoubtedly has that experience for us for which Paul prayed for the Thessalonians.

II. *The Exhibition of Perfection of Faith*

Now I want you to see how Paul desired them to exhibit the perfection of their faith. He prayed for them in the twelfth verse, "And the Lord make you to increase and abound in love one toward another, and toward all men, even as we do toward you." Paul lifted up a standard of this kind of perfection of faith and he used one word. It is the word love. It is not only used in this, but when he came to the maturity of his writing in that greatest theological treatise that exists in the whole world, the Book of Romans, in the thirteenth chapter he declared that we are to "owe no man any thing, but to love one another: for he that loveth another hath fulfilled the law" (Rom. 13:8). And he went on to say, "Thou shalt not commit adultery, Thou shalt not kill, Thou shalt not steal, Thou shalt not bear false witness, Thou shalt not covet; and if there be any other commandment, it is briefly comprehended in this saying, namely, Thou shalt love thy neighbour as thyself. Love worketh no ill to his neighbour: therefore love is the fulfilling of the law" (Rom. 13:9, 10). Love! Love then is God's norm of righteousness, the plumb line to reveal our deficiencies and weaknesses and sinfulness in life. But we are not to be conforming constantly to a negative standard of Thou shalt nots. We ought to be under the power of love, and love goes far beyond any law. Love is the fulfillment of the law. The law stands as the standard of righteousness, but the love of God in Christ Jesus, transforming the human heart, brings charity, purity, integrity, loyalty, honesty, and all these things into an aggressive and dynamic movement that reaches out. When the lawyer said to Jesus, ". . . which is the great commandment in the law? Jesus said unto him, Thou shalt love the Lord thy God with all thy heart, and with all thy soul, and with all thy mind. This is the first and great commandment. And the second is like unto it, Thou shalt love thy neighbour as thyself" (Matt. 22:36-39).

The Lord knew that those first four commandments: "Thou shalt have none other gods before me," "Thou shalt not make thee any graven image, . . ." "Thou shalt not take the name of the Lord thy God in vain, . . ." "Keep the sabbath day to sanctify it . . ." (Deut. 5:7,8,11,12), dealt with man's relationship to God, but he summarized them in one simple word and said, ". . . love the Lord thy God with all thy heart, and with all thy soul, and with all thy mind" (Matt. 22:37). He knew that the second part of the Decalogue, the section dealing with honesty, purity, and all these things was on a horizontal level, and He summarized them by saying, ". . . love thy neighbour as thyself" (Matt. 22:39).

Then He went further. One of the lawyers said to him later, ". . . And who is my neighbour?" (Luke 10:29). He pointed out the beautiful, immortal parable of the Good Samaritan, how we are not only to love those who love us, how we are not only to love the brethren, but when the priests, the Levites, and all pass by the needy of earth, we, like the good Samaritan, are to step in and lift those burdens and do good unto all men.

St. Paul said here that we are to abound in love one toward another. Yes, but then he goes on to say, ". . . toward all men . . ." (I Thess. 3:12). Real love is the most radical philosophy in all the world and would make us act upon maxims that would deal with every problem in human relationships. Love delivers from all fear, heals the divided personality, makes a man once again able to stand forth as a child of God. Love! So this would exhibit, Paul says, their maturity and faith. They were children of love.

When we take inventory, how little we love. How much we probably need to be perfected in our faith. How little we really accomplish in the world after all. That is why the Marxists make their progress. That is why the radical philosophies rule and reign and prey upon people everywhere, because we forget what the Bible tells us about the exhibition of the perfection of our spirits.

III. *The End of the Perfection of Faith—Holiness*

Now he adds one more thing. The thirteenth verse reveals the purpose of this to be the establishment of these people in holiness and blamelessness before Christ at His coming. Beloved, I thank God that there is an imputed holiness that is given to us in the Lord Jesus Christ when we are accepted before Him and it is perfect when we receive it or we should never have a right to eternal life. It is given to us through our substitute, our Redeemer, Jesus Christ who perfectly obeyed the law.

But here is something more. Here Paul is praying for a holiness, a blamelessness before Christ at His coming through the exercise of love and through the perfection of their faith. It goes beyond that which every Christian receives when he becomes a convert of Jesus Christ. He is praying now for something that can be called I think rightly, not what the Methodists call "an imparted righteousness" such as is given to us in holiness all at once, but an "achieved righteousness," an attained righteousness that comes through the maturity of faith and obedience to the teaching of the gospel and the exercise of the conditions of righteousness in the sight of God. That kind of thing must come through a moment-by-moment cleansing, through consecration, and through undertaking the things of God, the kind of thing that takes us out of that state of vacillation where we as Christians are not doing as we ought to do and brings us into the state whereby God can release His Holy Spirit within us and we may live in the position of deliverance and power and victory. Paul says, "Let us therefore, as many as be perfect, be thus minded . . ." (Phil. 3:15), so that we may know some of these things in life. Paul longed for it for those believers.

Finally, there is just one illustration about a man who was a good and faithful member of my church for many years and has gone home to be with the Lord now. Any time when I called at his home he showed me some new things he had gathered from some secondhand place, covered with yellow or red or green paint, that someone with no aesthetic sense had ruined. He would gather those things because of their lines and use his sanding machine and his tools on them and when he would get through with them, they would be perfect little works of art. In fact, I possess one that he transformed. He used to take such pleasure in redeeming a thing that once had been made to grace somebody's home. Then with the wood all sanded and oiled, and with the inlay standing out and the other parts made perfect again, it would stand forth in glory, an object of art. Do you not think that our praying, interceding Lord is just as interested that we who were created in His image, that we whom He once redeemed and recalled from destruction and from misuse and from maybe even the ash heap of life, that we should exhibit His glory, and love, and holiness, and beauty, and His perfecting grace? He really is. And we with Paul should pray that according to the will of God and believe also that it is the will of God for us to be so transformed and made perfect.

XII

The Church's Standard of Moral Purity

God hath not called us unto uncleanness, but unto holiness.
—I THESSALONIANS 4:7

MUNDANE MATTERS BULK LARGE IN THE THOUGHT AND WRIT-
ing of Paul. He knew that Christians were living in a world of
pressures. There was no cellophane separation in that age and
I doubt that there can be any cellophane preservation from
impurities in this age. The questions of sex, of work, of death,
of sanctification, of authority all had to be met by the Thessalonian Christians, as they must be met by us. Timothy,
returning from his brief visit and ministry to the Thessalonians, expressed to Paul at Corinth the problems which were
facing them and now Paul addressed himself to them. That
Paul did not sidestep the issue of sex is clear from this passage
which deals with it. In the first verse he refers to his teachings, "as ye have received of us," and in the sixth verse, "as
we also have forewarned you and testified." In his ministry to
the Thessalonians and in his writings to them, he did not
hesitate to point out the dangers of impurity and the demands
for purity on the part of the Christian. Laxity in this realm
cannot be condoned.

Let us recognize that the fourth chapter marks a transition in this epistle, from the apologetic writing to the appeal of exhortation and instruction. Here is the point of division in his writing between the section dealing with his mutual relations with them and the section dealing with his encouragement to them in their walk of life.

Nobody could be more brusque or harsher than Paul when occasion demanded, but nobody could be more diplomatic and considerate when the occasion demanded. Here Paul undoubtedly intended to urge the Thessalonian Christians to walk in accordance with the ethical standards which he had imparted to them when he was present, but considering what they had faced and what they had achieved, he tempered his statement by adding, ". . . as ye have received of us how ye ought to walk and to please God, so ye would abound more and more" (I Thess. 4:1). He wanted them to do better, but he did not want to discourage them in what they had already done. A lesson for us all lies in this attitude toward fellow Christians.

The needs Timothy had related to St. Paul on behalf of the Thessalonian Christians and their walk of conduct pertained to the perennial pressures of sex in a pagan society, to the matter of creative work, independence and accumulation, to the question of what happens to believers who die, to the question of the second coming of our Lord, to recognition of authority in harmony with peace among the brethren, and to the high practices of a sanctified Christian life. The new life of these converted pagans must attain to these standards. If so, how much more should we. The gospel is never divorced from the law. The imperative of a righteous life always lies before us.

The division opens with the word "furthermore" (*Ibid.*). It literally should be translated "for the rest" or "finally." Here Paul was giving a summarized statement of the walk which pleases God. It was not particularly bringing the epistle to a conclusion. He declared, "how ye ought to walk and to please God" (*Ibid.*). The highest motive of all Christian conduct is to live pleasing God. In his Corinthian epistle (II Cor. 5:9), Paul declares that our honor aim is ". . . that, whether present or absent, we may be accepted of him." The great objective of a Christian should be to live acceptably in the sight of our God and Saviour. Happy is the believer whose conduct is oriented around God's will rather than what pleases men. Paul made a specific point in his Galatian epistle that he was trying to please God and not to please men. In this lies the freedom of a believer and the possibility of independent action. He who pleases men is in slavery; he who pleases God is free. Paul wanted the consciousness of God's "well done." Do you? I firmly believe that the teaching which he gave here in these eight verses is in harmony with the instructions which he had given to the Thessalonians during his campaign. It is obvious that Paul instructed them upon matters pertaining to sex, for he said, "as ye have received of us" (I Thess. 4:1). This implies a very strong emphasis upon the ethical content of the Christian message under the authority of the Lord Jesus. That ethical content is described in the Bible as a walk, a way, and here one's walk with God, or pleasing to God, is the life which he leads. From the Pauline authority then we approach this subject on the church's teaching on sex.

The early church had great trouble with this problem of sex. Converts of the apostles were called out of pagan communities and immorality was very closely associated with idolatry then as it is now in sections of the world, like India and Africa. Hence it was necessary for the Jerusalem Council described in the Book of Acts (Acts 15:29) to legislate that the early Christians ". . . abstain from meats offered to idols, and from blood, and from things strangled, and from fornication. . . ." It seems rather surprising to us, as also does Paul's teaching injected here in the Thessalonian Epistle, that those

Christians had to be taught how to live, and in a resurging paganism of our day, we need also to learn how to live.

In that new translation by J. B. Phillips called *Letters to Young Churches*, the text is translated, "The calling of God is not to impurity but to the most thorough purity." (P. 135.) Without question this passage deals with physical and moral purity. The indications are that the Thessalonian Christians had not fallen into sexual laxity, for had they, more stringent discipline would have been exercised by the Apostle and the laudatory tone of the epistle would have been impossible. However, the lascivious pressures of the day were being felt by the church and this teaching was given as a preventative to their falling into evil practices. In these eight verses we have instructions on how to please God in sex behavior and how to live the Christian way, which demanded a clean breach from the pagan standards of the day. Paul was writing from Corinth and the immoral excesses connected with religion in the temples of Corinth were enough to prompt him to give such advice and teaching.

We ought not to be too smug about this matter concerning our own age. Sex is now making its way into the homes, the schools, the churches, the life of the families of America. We must face these facts as they are and then determine the antidote to them. *The Woman's Home Companion* of November, 1951, had an article entitled "Smut Peddlers" describing a huge industry of peddling of obscene pictures, pornographic literature and stories which incite young people to moral looseness. The extent and reach of this traffic in America is astounding. Fortunately, the article revealed how the situation had been cleaned up in the city of Chicago and can be cleaned up in any other city. No teenage child is safe from the smut peddler.

Recently a lady in this congregation attempted to buy a novel and asked the saleswoman to give her one that didn't have any questionable sections in it. The saleslady conferred with the manager of the store about several novels and they concluded that there was no novel that did not have these questionable moral sections in them. The modern realistic novel has descended to a new depth of sex expression and the publishers seem to vie with one another in printing them and offering them to the American public.

My attention was recently called to the filthy literature which is being read in the name of literature in our schools. The parent of a child in Bryn Mawr College for girls handed me a book called *That Moll Flanders* by DeFoe and asked me to look it over to see what was being taught in that college. I did look it over and it was one of the vilest things that I had ever seen, bringing into the life of the supposed heroine of the story every possible kind of immorality and incest. Just a few days ago I was asked by the mother of a boy in a famous preparatory school to read a book of short stories which was required reading in that school. It likewise was dealing in smut. Young people are told that they must read this to appreciate that kind of literature.

We hardly need to mention the strip-tease that is called advertising, whether it is of oranges, automobile tires, Coca-Cola or what. It seems that people cannot sell an item without advertising it along with sex. Is there any wonder then that we have 900,000 abortions annually in the United States and 300,000 high-school girls who become mothers outside of wedlock?

Our newspapers are full of sex crimes which seem to be the most prevalent of all. In *Coronet Magazine* for September, 1950, we read that we have 8,000,000 homosexuals in the United States, a sin for which God judged Sodom and one which is the most revolting of all.

Our age is parallel to the age of Noah and the age of Lot which were given to such great immorality that God judged both of them, for the specific reason stated for the judgment on the antediluvians was their physical immorality, as was also the judgment on the day of Lot, which immorality carried over from Sodom into his own family, even after the judgment of Sodom and Gomorrah. Interesting it is that the Lord Jesus told us that our day, or the day of the coming of the Lord, will be parallel to Noah's day and to Lot's day as far as sexual immorality was concerned. A reference in the Kinsey Report which revealed the conduct of the American male is enough to tell us that the parallel is already perfect.

Such an investigation clearly tells us that our conditions are parallel to the conditions in which Paul found the Thessalonian Christians and that we have a great obligation to declare the standards of righteousness.

I. *The Standard of Christian Morals—Purity*

Our text declares that God has called us not "unto uncleanness, but unto holiness" (I Thess. 4:7). The section begins with an exhortation to walk in this way of purity before God. Says Paul, ". . . we beseech you, brethren, and exhort you by the Lord Jesus, that as ye have received of us how ye ought to walk and to please God, so ye would abound more and more" (I Thess. 4:1). The invitation and exhortation to purity suggests that man has a measure of freedom in this realm of his physical life. Not the victim of his past, or of his environment, or of his teaching, as we are told by certain interests, man has a measure of freedom in this realm. If the evolutionary theory is true and man is merely a product of his past, then he would be totally unable to conquer physical desires. If he is the product of the reactions to the stimulus of his environment, as the behaviorist tells us, then again his conduct would be determined by external forces, and if all conduct is relativistic and what was considered wrong in the Bible times may be right in our age, moral connotations are removed from such action. In this way the freedom, the responsibility, and the culpability for immoral actions are removed in much of modern society. But not only this text but the whole Bible declares that man has freedom, is responsible, and will be judged.

The standard of purity has already been imparted. Paul said, ". . . how ye ought to walk . . ." (*Ibid.*). Wherever the sense of ought exists, there is the presence of law or of a standard and ought implies a lawgiver. The standard of purity is changeless whether in the Greek, the Roman, or American age.

Sinfulness and culpability result from failure in such matters. Such individuals will be judged of God whether they are Christian or non-Christian. That this can happen in the Christian life is implied in this passage of Scripture. Hence, we are urged to abound more and more in the way that is pleasing to God. Christians must more and more die unto sin and more and more live unto righteousness, conquering the possibility of this evil in their lives.

The standard of Christian purity was exhibited in the life and teachings of the Lord Jesus. Paul said, "For ye know what commandments we gave you by the Lord Jesus" (I Thess. 4:2). These commandments were given under the authority of Christ, they were not Paul's own invention. I am convinced that they were the Ten Commandments for I do not believe that the moral standard has ever been abrogated. It is as permanent and as eternal as the nature of God. The seventh commandment authoritatively holds sway over our lives today. This commandment was revealed in the Mosaic Law, but it also is part of a work of God written on the human heart, convicting and condemning us when we break it.

The Lord Jesus also delivered the Sermon on the Mount in which He interpreted the law. Here He pressed the matter of fornication and adultery into the heart, declaring that not only our actions constitute us guilty, but our thoughts and feelings. He that looketh upon a woman to lust after her has committed adultery in his heart. The life of Jesus was one glorious standard and example of moral purity. He declared and exhibited that life which is pleasing unto God and which God expects of us.

The standard of Christian morals was explained as that of sanctification. Paul declared that it was ". . . even your sanctification . . ." (I Thess. 4:3). The word sanctification, *hagiosmos*, means consecration or the sanctification of heart and life, which is the effect of our consecration.[1] The emphasis is upon our surrender, our act of consecration, our yielding unto God. Sanctification means that we take our place with Jesus Christ as crucified on the cross and dead unto sin, especially the sins of the body. The same word is used in the fourth and in the seventh verses revealing that God holds the standard of our consecration to this absolute purity.

Christ Himself is the means of our sanctification (I Cor. 1:30). The means of our sanctification from physical lust is the same as our sanctification from any other sin of life. It comes by union with Christ through faith, thus releasing the Holy Spirit who sanctifies us by producing holy desires and virtues in our lives. The consequence of this sanctification is a state of holiness. It is a totally different word, namely, *hagiosune*, meaning the state of moral purity. It is in this state of holiness that we desire to be found when Jesus comes again.

II. *Separation from Heathen Immorality*

Phillips translates verses three and four as follows: "God's plan is to make you holy, and that entails first of all a clean cut with sexual immorality."[2] The Revised Version adds, "That ye should abstain from fornication." Neil declares, "From this basic attitude it follows that you abstain from sexual vice."[3]

The believer is to flee the fornication of the pagan world because of his obligation to consecrate himself and achieve holiness of character. That was true in Paul's day and it is true now. We are not to regard our bodies as "an instrument of self-gratification as do pagans with no knowledge of God." [4] One does not have to look far to find that self-gratification today. The repeated marriages in many lives, notably of the screen stars, or some public family, or popular singer vividly illustrate the increasing divorce rate, the popular practice of exchanging mates with the season. Jesus' teaching is that all such practices are adultery and in them the Christian can have no part.

We need only note that promiscuity about which comedy is made over the radio and in literature. Easy women are plentiful, looseness of life before marriage is common. The wise man will remember the warning of Solomon that there shall be ". . . a dart strike through his liver . . ." (Prov. 7:23).

Kept women in America are also multiplying. One does not have to search far to find such conditions. Those who engage in them are fools.

The motive in all the pagan sex of Paul's day was self-gratification. The same ideal is held forth today in the theory that everyone has the right to be happy. If one is not happy in his physical relations, then change mates like cats do, not as the sons of God.

Over against this our Scripture declares the Christian must form the Christian view of the body. Paul said, "every one of you should know how to possess his vessel in sanctification and honour; not in the lust of concupiscence, even as the Gentiles which know not God" (I Thess. 4:4,5). This word vessel may be understood in one of two ways. Some commentators think it means wife, others think it means body. We believe that the latter is the most consistent, most ethical, and most elevated interpretation and so we adopt it. The *skeuos* or vessel then is one's body. Thus Paul uses the word when he says, ". . . we have this treasure in earthen vessels . . ." (II Cor. 4:7), referring to his body. The Christian then must learn to control his body, to discipline it, whether in marriage or out of marriage. We are not pleading for asceticism that perverts the views of the Bible in reference to marriage and the physical relationships of this world, which perversion divides the spirits of men and women, but only for a sanctification of the marriage relation in purity and in love and the sanctification of the bodies of the people out of the marriage relation unto the glory of God. This is the Bible view.

Our bodies are the temples of the Holy Spirit (I Cor. 3:16; 6:19). Thus the body must be sanctified or consecrated to God as well as the mind and the spirit of man. Such consecration is demonstrated by the mastery of the body.

Paul then adds, "that no man go beyond and defraud his brother in any matter . . ." (I Thess. 4:6). The literal translation speaks of "the matter" and is a delicate way of referring back to the subject under discussion. All sin of a physical nature cannot be indulged without defrauding some neighbor of that which is rightly his. It is an over-reaching, a defrauding, a going beyond of what is within the bounds of justice and propriety. He who rejects Christ who is the way, the truth, and the life will ultimately be led into this sin. Let a man beware of thinking he can stand in his own strength for the Scripture clearly declares unto us in Romans 1:20 and following that he who rejected the knowledge of God went down, down, down until he ended up in moral uncleanness. As idolaters the Thessalonians were engaged in this practice and their conversion meant a tremendous change in their lives.

Immoral relations based on gratification or selfishness always defraud, hurt, and wound another. One thinks of the millions of wounded women whose lives have been blighted because they have gone contrary to the sanctions of society through the desire for self-gratification on the part of others or of themselves. Even those who have not been hurt in such a way have been hurt in their souls. Christian love of one another would certainly rectify this cruelty of selfishness. Recognition of men and women in their dignity as the children of God, as created in His image, would deter us from treating them as chattel. They would be elevated to the dignity of personality and this in itself would be a great deterrent to this sin.

III. *The Source of Christian Purity*

Purity is according to God's will. Paul said, "this is the will of God, even your sanctification . . ." (I Thess. 4:3). In this passage Paul does not leave us with mere condemnation of this sin, but he tells us about God's plan, God's punishment, and God's provision. The word "will" is *thelema* and refers to the desire or the plan of God for a life. This plan is purity. God's eternal plan for the relation of men and women is the sanctified standard of monogamous marriage with procreation, love, responsibility, and character development involved. In the hardness of his heart man may have changed that standard from time to time, but God's standard never changes and God's plan is that our bodies, whether in or out of marriage, shall be totally consecrated unto Him and to the purposes which He has revealed in His Word. For this He has provided a means of our purification that when He comes we may be holy in body, soul, and spirit. We will be like unto Christ for we shall see Him as He is.

Paul also mentions that God will punish the violation of this standard of purity. He said, ". . . the Lord is the avenger of all such . . ." (I Thess. 4:6). The phrase "all such" is in the plural, revealing the whole range of impure, unclean, and immoral acts of man. Judgment is the function of God and it is committed to Jesus Christ as His representative. The day will come when He will judge the world in righteousness by that man whom He has appointed, namely, Jesus Christ. The judgment in which God will avenge such sins will be executed upon the wicked in the day of Christ's coming, or the day of His wrath, and the result will be eternal death, separation from God, and condemnation to the lake of fire.

Justice is executed in this world by the subjective effects of such sin, but it is not final. Such justice hardens the soul rather than remedies it. Oftentimes an individual who experiences such subjective hardening will go on in his selfish indulgent ways, gratifying his desires and actually enjoying the process. Karl Heim declares that an immoral man first will be severely convicted of his sin and as he performs his act the second time and the third time and the fourth time, he gradually loses all compunctions of conscience on the matter and enjoys it. For such there is only one way of justice and that is a future judgment. All those who plunge into an unclean and immoral life stand in jeopardy of their eternal souls. Such actions soil and spoil everything in their lives.

Our passage of Scripture, however, tells us that God has made a provision for man to be cleansed from such sin and to have victory over it. He declared, "He therefore that despiseth, despiseth not man, but God, who hath also given unto us his holy Spirit" (I Thess. 4:8). The Holy Spirit is the gift of God, the third person of the Trinity, who comes to take up His abode in the life of the believer at his adoption as a child of God. The Spirit regenerates us, indwells us, and empowers us to be holy. He is a partaker of the holiness of God and He cannot brook uncleanness or lack of consecration in the life of a believer in whom He dwells. Therefore he who has the Spirit in him must sanctify himself. He must cleanse himself from all filthiness of the flesh and spirit, perfecting holiness in the fear of God. The work of the Spirit in the believer is entirely opposed to the work of the flesh.

Paul urges us to grieve not the Spirit by which we are sealed against the day of redemption. Nothing will more quickly grieve the Spirit of God than the physical sins by which an individual is joined unto another person in immoral relations. He will terminate all of his ministry until there is total repentance, confession, and obedience in that soul. No man or woman is to believe, however, that there can be no forgiveness for such sin. The Lord forgave the woman taken in adultery and in itself sin of that nature is no different from even the more refined sins of the spirit which do great damage. All sin can be forgiven except sin against the Holy Ghost. He who will in godly sorrow over his sin turn to Jesus Christ confessing that sin and desiring to be cleansed of it with a high purpose to live in obedience to Jesus Christ will find that the Lord is gracious and merciful, that He will abundantly pardon. It was for the purpose of forgiving sin that Jesus Christ came into this world and died upon the cross. The depth of His love led Him to go lower in His suffering than any human being will ever have to go for his sin, for His suffering was sufficient for the sins of the race including that sin. Take that sin then and lay it upon Jesus. Let God cleanse you and constitute you a new creature in Him so that you can be holy. The promise is, "Come now, and let us reason together, saith the Lord: though your sins be as scarlet, they shall be as white as snow; though they be red like crimson, they shall be as wool" (Isaiah 1:18).

God makes this offer, God gives this commandment, God warns of this punishment and he who sets aside all this is not despising man, but he is setting aside or despising God, rejecting God's will, His plan, and His provision for our cleansing. To disregard God is to be established for the inevitable judgment. "But . . . whoremongers . . . shall have their part in the lake which burneth with fire and brimstone: which is the second death" (Rev. 21:8).

No more than Paul could condone this sin in the church of his day can the church of our day condone the sin of immorality. We must not accommodate ourselves unto the lax moral standards of our day but unto the revealed standards given to us by God. The expectation concerning purity is absolute, ". . . holiness, without which no man shall see the Lord" (Heb. 12:14). For the believer there must be a clean breach with all physical uncleanness and moral impurity. "For God hath not called us unto uncleanness, but unto holiness" (I Thess. 4:7).

XIII

The Church's Attitude toward Work

. . . study to be quiet, and to do your own business, and to work with your own hands. . . .

—I THESSALONIANS 4:11

THE PRACTICAL SECTION OF THE THESSALONIAN EPISTLE IS continued by the discussion of work. Paul introduces it by referring to brotherly love. This brotherly love is the touchstone of Christian conduct and action. It is an intuitive experience for a Christian. Said Paul, ". . . ye need not that I write unto you: for ye yourselves are taught of God to love one another" (I Thess. 4:9). There is what may be called an evangelical intuition of both truth and practice. The evangelical intuition of truth is described in I John 2:20 and 27, "But ye have an unction from the Holy One, and ye know all things . . . the anointing which ye have received of him abideth in you, and ye need not that any man teach you: but as the same anointing teacheth you of all things, and is truth, and is no lie, and even as it hath taught you, ye shall abide in him." This is the experience of a born-again Christian. He is predisposed to biblical teaching and senses that something is wrong with the isms which are parading themselves in the name of Christianity today. Similarly a true evangelical Christian has the urge to love, which experience is described in I Corinthians 13. The love which beareth all things, believeth all things, endureth all things is the characteristic of an evangelical Christian. This love comes intuitively to those who are born of the Spirit and united with Christ. The Spirit of God teaches sincere Christians how to love.

Evangelical Christians who are harsh, strident, quarrelsome, contentious, and unlovely have something wrong with their Christian experience. Such people have not grasped the Christian teaching and the Christian standard of living as revealed in the Word and in Christ, or else they have not been renewed in their life and are having a false trust concerning their experience.

This truth was illustrated by these infant Christians in a new church. Paul said, "And indeed ye do it toward all the brethren which are in all Macedonia . . ." (I Thess. 4:10). Apparently this was a spontaneous outreach of loving fellowship with other Christians in Macedonia. These newly converted Thessalonian Christians found the outreach of love. The most natural thing is for believers to join hands with other believers in loving work, witness, and worship. They experience the sense of oneness in the body of Christ.

The very antithesis of this exists in Christian churches today because of so many departures from the truth. A truly converted evangelical church often has hesitancy and reluctance to join hands with other churches where the most precious truths, like the deity of Christ, the atonement for sin, and the second coming of our Lord are denied. From 1780 to 1805, the great Unitarian apostasy in the Congregationalist churches swept Boston and New England. Instead of unity, evangelical believers found that they were separated from other so-called churches. That separation has continued even unto this day, and it has intensified in the modernistic Unitarian emphasis that exists in some so-called Christian churches.

An appreciation of Christian teaching and living wherever it is found was manifested in the early church and should be manifested today by loving fellowship. True believers must allow nothing to curb or to destroy that outreach of love, for it is the core of our divine experience. We Christians need each other and must join hands with each other in truth and in love.

Granting all this, St. Paul enjoins the Thessalonian Church to grow in love. He said, ". . . but we beseech you, brethren, that ye increase more and more." (*Ibid.*) Exercise in love will increase one's capacity to love, whereas idleness of this affection will make love atrophy. New England prides itself upon being unsentimental, on being sharp, on being keen, and yet that is not true with Christian people. They are openhearted, kind, hospitable, and thoughtful. They have learned to love.

Notable is it that the exhortations of the New Testament writers are not to exercise judgment or to evaluate the actions of one another or to fight in society, but they are to love. Would that we had ears to hear and hearts to understand, for we might well experience much of heaven on earth were we truly to love.

This elemental teaching of Christianity on the quality of life with its implications is opposed to the pagan concepts which existed in Paul's day and which are pressing in upon us again today. What we gather from this Scripture is contrary to the life which most of us are leading. We need, therefore, to take it as God's message to us as of today. I would like, therefore, to point out to you the composure of spirit, the creative activity, and the community testimony of the true Christian.

I. *The Composure of Spirit*

Paul says, ". . . study to be quiet . . ." (I Thess. 4:11). This literally should be translated, "Make it your ambition to lead a quiet life." Thayer, the lexicographer, says of this quiet that it is "said of those who are not running hither and thither, but stay at home and mind their own business." [1] Some of us need to blush as we read this interpretation of Paul's words. The Greek speaks of making it our honor aim to keep quiet. Phillips' *Letters to Young Churches* translates it, "make it your ambition to have no ambition!" [2] Now let us say at the outset that we must not misunderstand this so as to seek in this world to amount to nothing. Rather we must join it with the practice of willing the will of God, for God has a will for each of us, and we should be in the proper place.

The teaching is that we must be content. It suggests peace, contentedness, calmness, and happiness even in the throbbing, bustling, changing, challenging day. Be assured that such an existence must be sought, pursued, and studied or it can never be experienced. It does not just happen. What a refreshing experience it is to witness a Christian family with a love for a piece of land, a love for a house, a love for the members of the family which continues through the years. Each one of us can visualize such a tidy, attractive, peaceful home where love reigns and where the members of the family have a mutual regard one for another.

This contentedness is consistent with other teaching of the Scripture. The prophet Isaiah declares, ". . . in quietness and in confidence shall be your strength . . ." (Isaiah 30:15). That quietness consists of resting in the will of God. God has a will for each of us and this purpose or plan may involve the most strenuous work, but while engaged in it, we will find strength and rest. Jesus said, ". . . my yoke is easy, and my burden is light" (Matt. 11:30). He who is conformed to the will of God will find this experience to be true.

When we contrast such an experience with the modern view and activity of life, we Christians are convicted. Our day makes an appeal of glamour, of fame, of power, of travel, of excitement, of success, and of romance. In many ways this is very wonderful and it has its lure for the minds of every one of us, but it does not make for the quietness of spirit spoken of in our text here in the Bible. Activity at home has taken on a rush, a selfish movement if not even conflict, quarrels, and divisions which drive out peace and contentment. The modern day has totally lost the appreciation of ancestral homes, of family farms, of historic cottages with their associations and their memories. One real estate man in trying to sell a home to me made the statement, "People change their homes to suit their needs as they do their cars." God help America when our dwelling places and homes are traded in every four or five years as are our cars. The ambition to keep up with our neighbors places such tension and strain upon many breadwinners that any degree of contentment or peace is impossible.

Composure of spirit can better be known by a Christian than anyone else. It is the effect of righteousness. Isaiah said, "the work of righteousness shall be peace; and the effect of righteousness quietness and assurance for ever." (Isaiah 32: 17). The right relationship to God determines the source of true confidence in Him. The conviction that God is sovereign over the universe, that He is controlling and superintending the affairs of life, and that He has a plan for each one of us instills a sense of quietness. If, on the other hand, God has no such control, no plan, and no direction of our lives, we must do this for ourselves. Such independence of a benign providence makes for restlessness, anxiety, and pressure. Such a characteristic of restlessness is found with the unrighteous. Isaiah also said, "the wicked are like the troubled sea, when it cannot rest, whose waters cast up mire and dirt. There is no peace, saith my God, to the wicked" (Isaiah 57:20,21). The entrance to the Kingdom of God by the new birth is the prerequisite of this composure of spirit. It will not be found as a characteristic of those who are non-Christians. Nevertheless, many Christians do not possess it because they do not make it their ambition to be quiet.

II. *The Creative Activity*

Paul then adds, ". . . we beseech you, brethren . . . to do your own business, and to work with your own hands . . ." (I Thess. 4:10,11). In modern life, work has assumed a certain degree of a curse. Throughout the ages men have found creative work to be the means of the release of their energy, their interest, their ability, and their peace, but for countless millions, such release is today impossible. Work has now been disassociated from the means of production. Whereas once men had the implements of production in their own possession, they today must work on assembly-line production. They have little connection with the process and no identity with the finished product. All sense of creativity and craftsmanship is removed. The workmen become mere robots in a continuous production. As a result, if one works too fast, he steps up the necessary work of his fellows and a premium is put on mediocrity of production and also of quality. The workman has little interest in what he is doing and, consequently, he keeps his eye upon the clock. His only reason for continuing in such activity is that he might earn the money to buy bread and butter and the good things of this life.

Much of modern work puts a disparagement upon personality, on the meaning of life, and on the purpose of existence. It leaves no satisfaction for achievement and no possibility of the individual losing himself in a work which is greater than he. William James once said, "The great use of a life is to spend it for something that will outlast it." How one can feel he is making a great use of his life by working on Christmas tree lights, or on tinsel, or on balloons, or on cigarettes, or on liquor, or any other such thing is beyond our conception.

Modern work also determines social conditions of housing, of the location of where one lives, of the type of pleasure in which he indulges, and of the cultural interests which he enjoys. Men are tied to their factories just as migrant laborers are tied to the crops which they harvest, both being disassociated from the means of production and from the possession of the product.

A certain drudgery accompanies the engagement in the frivolous or useless toil so common to our modern civilization but so necessary for individuals to make a living. Such workmen have no reward, no pride, no compensation in their labor. There are thousands of them who would never go back to their benches or their machines were it not necessary for them to do it in order to live. Consequently, they seek to escape from their work when they are not at work—by drink, by gambling, by immorality, and by other sins. The flourishing condition of the night clubs, the taverns, the race tracks, and such amusements witness to the fact that the average worker does not receive the thrill at his work which he should receive. Elton Trueblood has said, "The man who is not enthralled with his work, labors only for the money and then he must use a considerable portion of his money to secure the thrill which the work does not give." [3]

He who exercises his freedom by getting out of such types of labor and changing into something which is productive and worthwhile in this world is a happy man. It takes courage to pull out of a useless engagement and seek a more worthy employment, but the man who does it is going to get great satisfactions out of this life. Ask yourself whether if you could retire today, you would continue to do the thing you now do from sheer enjoyment and from productively desirable occupation. If not, then you had better give some thought to beginning that activity in your odd time so that when you are through work, your life will still have meaning.

There is no greater experience of happiness than to be engaged in work which draws forth all the capacities which a man possesses. Such a man lives to work instead of works to live. It was Edison who, at the close of his life, declared that he had never worked a day but that it was all fun, and yet sometimes he only had three or four hours of sleep a night because of the devotion to his task.

Granting all that I have said above, there still must be a recognition and a discernment of the creative possibility within the routines of necessary assembly-line labor. Men who have taken advantage of their time to think and to converse in such routine jobs have sometimes been able to set loose the genius of creative capitalism by invention and discovery of new methods of production which have lifted our standards of living to their present heights. No one wants to go back to the good old days of the Dark Ages or to the days of the pre-industrial revolution, but he does need a compensation in his present life.

A measure of this compensation comes in the shorter hours of the work week, which has been brought about through the industrial and power revolution. Today a man works, at most, eight hours a day and, for the most part, five days a week. This grants him what is called "the long weekend," and it grants him a considerable period of time every day to pursue objectives which he desires. Some men use this in an avocation or subsidiary employment or in some hobby. Many young men work a full eight-hour shift every day, and yet go through college and get a degree so that they can better their condition and improve their cultural understanding. Others take up gardening and work harder at their gardening than they do at anything else in life. This is because they enjoy it and feel the creative impulse and gain the satisfactions which accompany it. Others do similar things with woodworking, photography, music, writing, painting, raising pets, and in countless activities. The same emotion which an artist, musician, singer, or actor gets in his achievement, men may have in their work where they exercise craftsmanship and creativity.

Let us remember that the industrial society makes this possible. Since we cannot turn back the hands of the clock, we must accept our present situation and turn our attention toward getting the best out of it. Such rewards will not be reaped by a constant round of social life or indulgence in pleasure but by attention to creative activity.

Such activity joined with the pride of possession or ownership make a happy combination. Great amounts of work can be done on a piece of property, a house, a car, or some other possession in accordance with our abilities. The individual who seeks a little piece of land which he can improve and use in his spare time is usually a happy individual. Pride of ownership and community respect are joined with creative labor to bring about the rewards of achievement in one's life.

It takes courage to do something about this kind of employment. One may apprehend these truths but do nothing about them, but to exercise craftsmanship, to create, to make something, to exercise one's powers as a first cause is to sense the fact that one has been created in the image of God and that he is happiest when he is working as God would have him work. This work may be physical, it may be intellectual, or it may be spiritual, but it must be creative so that the satisfactions of beholding the product are present. In such activity men forget themselves, they get lost in their interest, and when they finish an object, they are thrilled. To such craftsmen time is no element. Most creative workers wish that they could have two or three extra days in every week instead of finding boring time on their hands.

It is possible to substitute for the lack of creative initiative at our daily work by the balance of interest which comes in the long weekends, in vacation periods, and in unused parts of the day for valuable employment in things that we love. Thus the day may be divided into chapters or life itself may be divided into chapters, when at one period we do one thing and at another period we do another thing. This avoids the frustration of trying to do everything at the same time. Women who have devoted their lives to raising families know that there comes a day when the families are gone, and then they can have a new chapter of real creative responsibility which is just as valuable and just as productive as the creative chapter in the raising of children. Again referring to Mr. Trueblood, we quote: "Every man who works for the sake of work instead of reward is an aristocrat at heart." [4]

Compensation may be also found in service to the community, to mankind, and to others, which lies at the doorstep of us all. This brings a true thrill. Happy then is the man who has a sense of vocation in both his labor and in his avocation. Do the things which pertain to you and to your interest and do not fail to work with your own hands.

III. *The Community Testimony*

Paul added, "That ye may walk honestly toward them that are without, and that ye may have lack of nothing" (I Thess. 4:12). The Christian ought to live a life which is commendable to the non-Christian community. He should walk seemingly. Unbelievers are alert to the Christian testimony. Does Christianity work? Does it bring peace and contentment to the individual? Does it make a difference in work habits, in ethics, and in human relations? "Those without" are always watching those who are within. The life that we lead means much to our community.

Consistency of testimony is essential. Paul's word translated "honestly" is really seemingly or appropriately, but it has the meaning of honestly as well. It seems that we who are Christians working in an office of non-Christians must give a full labor value for the time for which we are paid. We cannot be chiselers, or clock-watchers, we cannot give fifty minutes for our sixty minutes pay, or seven hours work for our eight hours pay. To do so is to steal from those for whom we work. Some of the practices of our unions in America approximate that. When bricklayers are required to lay only two hundred bricks when they could lay twice that many in one day or when the machine that could lay several times that many is kept off the market, it is a dishonest practice. This can be multiplied in many instances. On the other hand, when companies deliberately keep down the basic wages of employees, they encourage unions in such practices, or when companies refuse to share the profits which have been made by these employees, there is a certain degree of dishonesty involved, and Christians should give heed to these things. The Christian should be able to produce a better day's work, a better service, a better product than the man who is a non-Christian. This is the highest commendation of the Christian way of life. It is a seeming walk.

With this will come a commensurate prosperity. Paul said, ". . . that ye may have lack of nothing." (*Ibid.*) The Bible puts no premium on poverty. A careful study of the life of Job will find that the Lord attached prosperity to righteousness and obedience. The same was true with Abraham who became a very wealthy man. Likewise, Jacob was prospered of the Lord when he obeyed the Lord and fulfilled his covenant. There is no reason to believe that the Lord intends that a righteous, industrious, thrifty individual shall not be prospered. The promise is that we will lack nothing, but we will have a state of independence, a state of stability, and a measure of wealth. Modern disparagement of wealth and success is not Christian. The whole emphasis upon paternalism in the state, upon the welfare society, and upon left-wing socialism generates incompetence, indolence, and irresponsibility. It destroys the true Christian virtues, which are social virtues.

The blessings of work which result in prosperity are that we have to give to others. The biblical standard of such giving is tithing in recognition of God's goodness and the prosperity which He bestows upon us. He who has, as a result of his labors, is able to help the poor. He can give to those who have not. But if he does not have, he cannot give. The practice of social legislation to confiscate that which one has earned and saved in order to give to those who have not is just as wrong as if we in turn should take it by dishonest means. Moreover, the man who earns and saves and has will never be a burden upon others in society, and this is no little satisfaction in personal self-respect. Thus he who works with his hands and attends to his own business will "have lack of nothing."

This is the one great antidote to the dissipation of our glorious heritage of wealth and freedom as we have known it in this nation.

In this brief passage of Paul's letter to the Thessalonians, we have the clue to a social theory which will solve many of societies most pressing problems and will bring peace and blessing to individuals without number. Quiteness of spirit, creative activity, and community testimony of honesty is the Christian theory of work. May each one of us follow it to the best of his ability.

XIV

What the Church Teaches about the Dead and Their Resurrection

But I would not have you to be ignorant, brethren, concerning them which are asleep, that ye sorrow not, even as others which have no hope.

—I THESSALONIANS 4:13

IGNORANCE CONCERNING THE STATE OF THE DEAD IS GENERAL. This teaching of St. Paul to the Thessalonian Church was intended to banish that ignorance. The expression "I would not have you to be ignorant" is used by St. Paul when dealing with practical problems, difficult questions and personal matters of perplexity.[1]

Misconceptions concerning the dead arise from ignorance of biblical teaching. The Lord Jesus Christ corrected the Sadducees in their materialistic conception of the resurrection by saying, "Ye do err, not knowing the scriptures, nor the power of God. For in the resurrection they neither marry, nor are given in marriage, but are as the angels of God in heaven" (Matt. 22:29,30). Sleep of the soul in the unconscious state in death is a modern misconception very widely taught. It is completely contrary to the Scriptures and arises from the figurative use of sleep in reference to death. Sorrow born of doubt concerning the future of lost loved ones is common to those who have no biblical hope and faith. The misconception that they cease to exist at death is enough to distract the average individual who is bereaved. Skepticism about immortality is also a widespread result of misconception.

There is a manifest ignorance of God's teaching in His Word. As an authority for His teaching, St. Paul here declared, "this we say unto you by the word of the Lord . . ." (I Thess. 4:15). There is no other source of knowledge concerning the dead except God's revelation. All else is speculation and has no certainty. Paul claimed that God's revelation had been made to him. He was not here referring to some teaching of Jesus which was handed down by tradition but to the revelation which had been made to him and which is now inscripturated for us in the Bible. The neglect of this source of information is universal. Once we could presume that people knew the stories and characters of the Bible, but that is utterly impossible today. A reference to a biblical parable or a biblical story must now be told in detail or people will not understand. It is amazing how people will turn to writings of the philosophers, the historians, and biographers and then neglect the Word of God. The great need is to expound this body of teaching contained in God's Word. There we find no doubt about the state of the dead.

The message of St. Paul was calculated to bring comfort to the Thessalonians. He said, "Wherefore comfort one another with these words" (I Thess. 4:18). As a result of Paul's preaching, the Thessalonians had faith that the Lord would come to take them into His eternal kingdom of glory by His second coming. They based their faith upon what Paul had taught them when he was present at Thessalonica. They actually expected that He would come during their lifetime, as is shown by II Thessalonians 2:2. They were not alone in this, however, for there are other instances of the disturbing effects of such an unchastened anticipation in later ages of the church. "In the tenth century for instance, the expectation of the approaching end of the world in or about the year 1000 A.D. was almost universal. This event was to usher in the seventh sabbatical period of a thousand years, the preceding six millennia being calculated as five between Adam and Christ, and one after the nativity. Again, amidst the plagues and famines of the fourteenth century, the Flagallantes were prominent in their announcements of the speedy approach of the end." [2] These Thessalonians had lost members of their families since Paul had evangelized them. Their questions and perplexities about these dead and their sharing in the *parousia* or coming of Christ caused St. Paul to propound new doctrine at this point in order to meet the difficulty.[3] This was no imaginary difficulty but a very real problem that agitated the church and which had been reported to St. Paul by Timothy on his return. As the loved ones of the Thessalonians died, they wondered if they would participate in the kingdom of glory. They asked Timothy, What is the state of our dead? Timothy propounded the question to Paul and, as a result, there came this teaching which has been of inestimable blessing to the church ever since.

In brief, Paul told them that their loved ones were in the hands of the Lord and that they will participate with them or with whoever is living at the time of the coming of the Lord in the resurrection and in the *parousia*. They will be resurrected first, they will be caught up together with the living believers to meet the Lord in the air, and so they will together ever be with the Lord. This passage along with chapter five, verses one to eleven, gives the dominant note to the epistle. The suggestions in each of the three previous chapters are now given full amplification in this practical section of the epistle.

I. *The Experience of Death*

Paul refers in verse thirteen to "them which are asleep" and in verse fourteen to "them which sleep in Jesus." This is the New Testament designation of those who have died in Christ. Only believers are in question here. This is quite in contrast with I Corinthians 15:29 where the unbelievers are in consideration. There the question was, What happens to those unsaved dead? Paul uses the Hebrew method of parallelism, which makes clear the meaning. He declared that Jesus died but believers sleep in Jesus. He declared that Jesus rose again but believers who sleep in Jesus will God bring with Christ. The phrase "in Jesus" actually is through Jesus and it is the means of limiting all who sleep, so that not all the dead are meant, but only those who are dead in Christ. It is rather startling to read of death through Christ. Usually we read of life through Christ, and the explanation is to be sought in the fact that it is a resting in Christ from which there will be an awakening but that it is not the kind of death which is the effect of sin.

This figure of sleeping was not something new. It was commonly used by the heathen to describe their dead. It was used in the Old Testament to describe those who had demitted this world—they ". . . slept with (their) fathers" (II Kings 24:6)—and it referred to the outward appearance of death in a sleep of the body. It is used more than a dozen times in the New Testament as a beautiful figure of the way in which we die when the sting of death is gone, but we affirm unqualifiedly that it does not teach psychopannychism or the sleep of the soul in death. The union of the believer with Christ is such that he is in Jesus in death as he is in life. Thus we will come to ". . . the spirits of just men made perfect, and to Jesus the mediator of the new covenant. . . ." (Heb. 12:23, 24). Thus for us it is better to go and to be with Christ (Phil. 1:23). Thus to be "absent from the body" is to be "present with the Lord" (II Cor. 5:8). Thus the thief was with Christ in Paradise on the day of his death. Now we are united to Christ in His death and new life by faith. When we depart this world, we shall sleep in Jesus, and when Jesus comes, we will have resurrection life in Him.

The description of the sorrow of ". . . others which have no hope" (I Thess. 4:13) is in great contrast to the Christian viewpoint of death. Death for the pagan was the end. There was no resurrection, no immortality, no knowledge beyond the grave. A simple consulting of any good classical commentary will give you quotations from the pagan world concerning their dead which expressed such sentiments. Even Solomon viewing man from under the sun or with a materialistic outlook declared, ". . . for there is no work, nor device, nor knowledge, nor wisdom, in the grave, whither thou goest" (Ecc. 9:10). Wherever people are without God, they are without hope (Eph. 2:12). In ancient Israel, there was a true hope of resurrection and immortality as expressed in the words of Job, "For I know that my redeemer liveth, and that he shall stand at the latter day upon the earth: and though after my skin worms destroy this body, yet in my flesh shall I see God" (Job 19:25,26).

The dirge and despair of those who say a final farewell to their dead in excessive grief is contrasted with the comfort, hope, and expectancy of those who have the Christian assurance. This excessive sorrow is differentiated from Christian sorrow, which is moderated by the hope of the resurrection and is only instigated by the loss of the presence of such loved ones.

The doctrine of Scripture concerning the state of the dead in Christ is that they are naked, disembodied, unclothed souls in the interim between death and resurrection but that they are in the presence of Christ. "For in this we groan, earnestly desiring to be clothed upon with our house which is from heaven: if so be that being clothed we shall not be found naked. For we that are in this tabernacle do groan, being burdened: not for that we would be unclothed, but clothed upon, that mortality might be swallowed up of life" (II Cor. 5:2-4). Such souls are described in the Book of Revelation with the words, ". . . I saw under the altar the souls of them that were slain for the word of God, and for the testimony which they held: and they cried with a loud voice, saying, How long, O Lord. . . ." (Rev. 6:9,10). These souls in the presence of God and Christ were awaiting the resurrection. In this interim period, the believer goes to be with Christ, awaiting the day of His coming and the manifestation of glory. The story of Dives and Lazarus describes their state in the interim of waiting.

II. *The Example of Christ*

It is informative that as Paul introduces the subject of those who are asleep in Jesus, he does it with a declaration of the historical facts of the death and resurrection of Jesus Himself. He said, "For if we believe that Jesus died and rose again . . ." (I Thess. 4:14). The fact that Jesus of Nazareth died is indisputable. He died by crucifixion in a shameful, ignominious, painful way. He died indeed that we might be able to sleep in Him because the sting of death has been pulled. The Bible uses the word death as the fruit of sin. It is the God-forsaken experience of a condemned soul. This is the death which Jesus died upon the cross and the death of which Scripture warns. The Bible may say that we sleep, but it never says that Jesus slept. Jesus died a terrible death which is the result of sin. That death was confirmed by the authorities and it was concluded in burial with a sense of finality connected with it, so that He fully identified Himself with the human race.

Similarly, a fact is involved in the resurrection. This occurred in history and has had a tremendous influence upon the church and the world. The great apologetic doctrine of the apostolic preaching contained in the Book of Acts is the resurrection of Christ. Wherever they went, they preached the resurrection. It was the resurrection which galvanized them into activity, which stirred them out of their despair, which enabled them to turn the world upside down, and when they preached this doctrine, they argued that it has already been foretold in the Scripture and that Christ arose from the dead as the Scriptures had foretold. The famous speech of Peter on the day of Pentecost used the sixteenth Psalm as the justification for this biblical expectation.

The resurrection has become the intellectual ground of our faith in the supernatural. Only those who refuse to accept historical evidence, such as the records of the appearances of the Lord Jesus Christ, or logical evidence, such as the argument of the open tomb and of the transformation in the enemies of Jesus, or psychological evidence, such as the complete change in the attitude and outlook of the disciples themselves, can refuse to accept the resurrection as a fact. If it is a fact, then it substantiates the entrance of first cause into this world in the supernatural which justifies the complete Christian system.

This fact that Jesus died and rose again is of tremendous importance to our own future state. It is on this fact that Paul bases his full argument in the fifteenth chapter of I Corinthians when he is attempting to prove to these Corinthians the resurrection of the dead. He appeals to the commonly accepted faith of the church concerning the resurrection of Christ and on it he builds the truth of the resurrection of the believer. Thus also in this first writing concerning this subject Paul declares the great historic facts of the death of Christ and the resurrection of Christ as the ground for the hope and the comfort of the believer concerning his own dead.

All this is conditioned on the fact of faith. Paul introduced it with the words, "if we believe." (*Ibid.*) It is by faith that we are joined to Christ in His death and resurrection now so that we have died to the old nature and are living a resurrected life. It is by faith also that the sting of death is gone, for we know that in physical death we are joined to Christ and it has no power over us. By faith one may face the hour of death with perfect confidence, assurance, and peace believing that he goes into the presence of Christ. By faith also one knows that when Jesus comes, his body shall be transformed into the likeness of Jesus Christ and he shall be as Jesus is in his resurrection state.

III. *The Expectation of the Resurrection*

Then Paul declares, ". . . the dead in Christ shall rise first" (I Thess. 4:16). Let us note the order of the resurrection. He says first. The contrast here is between the resurrection of dead believers and the translation and transformation of the living believers. He says, "first . . . then." Unbelievers are not under consideration in this passage at all. There can thus be no comparison of this resurrection with a second resurrection of the unbeliever. This passage deals only with one resurrection. It is the resurrection of the believer at the coming of the Lord Jesus Christ. The others are not even in view. If the interpretation called premillenarianism is true, there is a division of a thousand years between the resurrection of the believer and the resurrection of the unbeliever. This interpretation is grounded upon Revelation 20:3-6. However, we must admit that in Daniel 12:2 there is no reference to two resurrections nor in John 5:29 is there a reference to two resurrections. Two resurrections must be read into these passages from the suggestion in Revelation 20. Since two resurrections are not mentioned here, we will not give our attention to the question of the state and resurrection of unbelieving dead.

Referring to I Corinthians 15:20-25, we find these events described. There a distinction is made between the resurrection of Christ as the firstfruits and the resurrection of believers as the full fruits. Following this Paul says, "Then cometh the end . . ." (I Cor. 15:24). The question arises as to whether the end is to come at Christ's coming or at a later time when we will be accompanied by a general resurrection. There is no implication in this passage that there is any interval of time between the resurrection of the believers and the end. The end here is implied as following immediately after the resurrection of believers. That end would certainly be attended by the resurrection of unbelievers as well. The only answer this passage can give is that the end cometh when He has ". . . delivered up the kingdom to God, even the Father; when he shall have put down all rule and all authority and power." (*Ibid.*) Either Christ is putting down His enemies now preceding the resurrection of believers and the end, or He must put down those enemies after He comes and the believers are resurrected. A millennial period cannot be substantiated from this passage of Scripture, but it may be read into it from other passages of Scripture if it is a true interpretation thereof. Suffice it to say that bodies of believers will rise from the dead when Jesus comes at the end of the age.

Let us note the time of the resurrection. Paul said, ". . . them . . . will God bring with him" (I Thess. 4:14) and "we which are alive and remain shall be caught up together with them in the clouds . . ." (I Thess. 4:17). This time is at the coming of Christ with glory, with angels, with clouds, with a shout, and with the sound of a trumpet. The word used for shout in this case is one that applies to a shout of encouragement given to rowers in a race, or to horses, or to dogs.[4] It leads us to say that from this passage there is no reference to a secret coming of Christ. The description is anything but an invisible and secret coming, in fact, it is just the opposite. The shout which will gather these believers is a shout of encouragement, and the sound of a trumpet is a great noise and the glory is visible. What a meeting of our dead and of the living believers that will be as we gather in the atmosphere of earth to meet the Lord as He descends from heaven!

This resurrection will be attended by the rapture of living believers. They will ". . . be caught up together with them . . ." (I Thess. 4:17). There will be some believers living in that day. What a wonderful expectation for one generation of believers who will go to be with Christ without death. They will be translated as Enoch was translated without death. They will be made like unto Christ in a moment, in the twinkling of an eye. They will be with Him for eternity. Corruptibility for them will put on incorruptibility and mortality will put on immortality. However, they will not precede those which are asleep, for both will have a part in the *parousia*. Here was the comfort which was given to these Thessalonians who had been bereaved.

This event will come at the close of this dispensation when the time of grace is over, when the acceptable year of the Lord has closed, when the number of the elect has been filled, when the times of the Gentiles are ended. Of that day and hour Paul and the apostles were ignorant. The Scripture says that not even the angels know it. It lay beyond the limit of inspiration given to God's people.

The nature of this resurrection is declared in Scripture. There is an absence of definition or description in this passage, and we must infer it from other passages of Scripture. We have a wide analogy from which to learn. In Philippians 3:20 and 21 we read, "For our conversation is in heaven; from whence also we look for the Saviour, the Lord Jesus Christ: who shall change our vile body, that it may be fashioned like unto his glorious body, according to the working whereby he is able even to subdue all things unto himself." In John's first epistle, the third chapter, the second verse, we read, "Now are we the sons of God, and it doth not yet appear what we shall be: but we know that, when he shall appear, we shall be like him; for we shall see him as he is." In II Corinthians 5:1 we read, "For we know that if our earthly house of this tabernacle were dissolved, we have a building of God, an house not made with hands, eternal in the heavens." And in Romans 8:23 we read, "And not only they, but ourselves also, which have the firstfruits of the Spirit, even we ourselves groan within ourselves, waiting for the adoption, to wit, the redemption of our body."

A full analysis of the fifteenth chapter of I Corinthians gives answer to the question, How are the dead raised up? We are told that each has his own body. In the resurrection, men shall have the same kind of body but transformed. There is an identity and yet a difference, just as there is an identity in the seed which is planted and the flower which grows from it. We are told that each kind of flesh is different and that there are various glories to even the same kinds of flesh. Thus in the resurrection, the believers will differ one from another in glory. We are also told that the resurrection aspect is in contrast with the earthly. As we have borne the image of the earthly, we will bear the image of the heavenly. We are to be sown in corruption and raised in incorruption, sown in dishonor and raised in glory, sown in weakness and raised in power, sown in a natural body and raised in a spiritual body, sown mortal and raised immortal, for flesh and blood cannot inherit the Kingdom of God, and if Jesus comes while we are yet living, we must be transformed without death into His likeness if we are to inherit that Kingdom.

Through the resurrection and the rapture believers will ever be with the Lord. They will never be separated from Him again. Wherever He is, we shall be. If He is to be on earth during a millenial kingdom, we shall be with Him. If He is to rule eternally in a spiritual, incorporeal, glorious kingdom represented by the depictions of the Scriptures, we shall be with Him. This is the comfort of Christian truth.

When Jesus comes we will go to the marriage supper of the Lamb. All who are members of the church of Jesus Christ are His bride and will enter eternal bliss and fellowship with their Lord. All such believers who have entered the kingdom by the new birth will now enter the kingdom of glory and will participate in the joys of a redeemed universe. In this will come the consummation of our physical and spiritual existence. Those who are in Christ will be with Christ forever. Wherefore comfort one another with these words.

XV

What the Church Teaches about the Coming of Christ

For yourselves know perfectly that the day of the Lord so cometh as a thief in the night.

—I THESSALONIANS 5:2

PAUL BEGINS HIS DISSERTATION ON THE SECOND COMING OF THE Lord by saying, "But of the times and the seasons, brethren, ye have no need that I write unto you" (I Thess. 5:1). The time to emphasize the advent of Christ is the season of His birth, namely, Christmas. We have the Lord's precept that we are to remember Him, and in conjunction with this, we are to look for His coming. Said He, ". . . this do ye . . . in remembrance of me" (I Cor. 11:25). There was a backward look and a forward look to the Lord's Supper. It will continue until Christ comes again. The Scripture which Christ used to initiate His ministry joins these two great events. The prophet Isaiah said, "The Spirit of the Lord God is upon me; because the Lord hath anointed me to preach good tidings unto the meek; he hath sent me to bind up the brokenhearted, to proclaim liberty to the captives, and the opening of the prison to them that are bound; to proclaim the acceptable year of the Lord, and the day of vengeance of our God . . ."

(Isa. 61:1,2). When Jesus used this text in His sermon at Nazareth, He stopped at the statement "to proclaim the acceptable year of the Lord," and He omitted the statement "the day of vengeance of our God." The reason was that He came to inaugurate the acceptable year of the Lord and the day of vengeance will be inaugurated when He comes again.

The prophecies pertaining to His first coming were all fulfilled. Isaiah's Messianic prophecies were quite detailed. He declared, "the Lord himself shall give you a sign; Behold, a virgin shall conceive, and bear a son, and shall call his name Immanuel" (Isa. 7:14), and "unto us a child is born, unto us a son is given: and the government shall be upon his shoulder: and his name shall be called Wonderful, Counsellor, The mighty God, The everlasting Father, The Prince of Peace" (Isa. 9:6). Micah declared, "But thou, Bethlehem Ephratah, though thou be little among the thousands of Judah, yet out of thee shall he come forth unto me that is to be ruler in Israel; whose goings forth have been from of old, from everlasting" (Mic. 5:2). Zechariah declared, ". . . shout, O daughter of Jerusalem: behold, thy King cometh unto thee: he is just, and having salvation; lowly, and riding upon an ass, and upon a colt the foal of an ass" (Zech. 9:9). Psalm twenty-two gives the very words which Christ used upon the cross in describing His suffering, "My God, my God, why hast thou forsaken me? . . . my tongue cleaveth to my jaws . . . they part my garments among them, and cast lots upon my vesture" (Psa. 22:1,15,18). Psalm sixty-nine also is very definite in application to Christ describing His sufferings on the cross in which He said, "They gave me also gall for my meat; and in my thirst they gave me vinegar to drink" (Psa. 69:21). Daniel is definite concerning the work of Christ in His first coming by saying, ". . . to finish the transgression, and to make an end of sins, and to make reconciliation for iniquity, and to bring in everlasting righteousness, and to seal up the vision and prophecy, and to anoint the most Holy" (Dan.

9:24). This is what Christ did when He came the first time.

The promises of the second advent will also be fulfilled. In the Old Testament, these promises are made by the same prophets who promised the first coming, which promises were fulfilled. Daniel declares, "I saw in the night visions, and, behold, one like the Son of man came with the clouds of heaven, and came to the Ancient of days, and they brought him near before him. And there was given him dominion, and glory, and a kingdom, that all people, nations, and languages, should serve him: his dominion is an everlasting dominion, which shall not pass away, and his kingdom that which shall not be destroyed" (Dan. 7:13). Zechariah declares, "And the Lord shall be king over all the earth: in that day shall there be one Lord, and his name one" (Zech. 14:9). In the New Testament, we have many references to the coming of Christ in glory, some of which I have quoted to you on previous occasions. As Christ ascended up into heaven, the angels said unto His disciples, "Ye men of Galilee, why stand ye gazing up into heaven? this same Jesus, which is taken up from you into heaven, shall so come in like manner as ye have seen him go into heaven" (Acts 1:11). "Behold, he cometh with clouds; and every eye shall see him, and they also which pierced him: and all kindreds of the earth shall wail because of him" (Rev. 1:7). The return of Christ is as certain as is the fact that His first coming took place. As there was a remnant looking for Him then, there will be a remnant who look for Him when He comes a second time without sin unto salvation.

Thought about the advent of Christ in glory turns one's attention to the times and seasons involved. People ask, When? How? What? in reference to His coming. His own disciples said unto Him, ". . . Tell us, when shall these things be? and what shall be the sign of thy coming, and of the end of the world?" (Matt. 24:3). When He was about to leave them, they said, ". . . Lord, wilt thou at this time restore again the kingdom to Israel? And he said unto them, It is not for you to know the times or the seasons, which the Father hath put in his own power" (Acts 1:6,7). The word translated time is *xronos* and "denotes a period of time whether long or short, and hence in reference to any particular event 'the date.' "[1] The word season or *kairos* not only applies to time but to place and signifies "the fit measure."[2] Hence "it is 'the right moment' . . . involving the idea of *adaptation*."[3] It means "the opportunity for doing, or avoiding to do, anything."[4] It denotes quality rather than quantity.[5] The implication of the word time is of duration until the event and the implication of season is of crisis or of signs which will designate the occasion. The two underlying questions might well be distinguished as: "How long will it be before the Lord comes? and What will happen before His coming?"[6]

The teaching of Christ and the apostles is that the time of the coming cannot be foreknown (Acts 1:7; Matt. 24:36), but that the signs may be watched and recognized. Those who are believers or, as Daniel calls them, wise will know the time of the end because they will give heed to the signs. They will not be caught unawares, or surprised, or confounded. Those who are unbelievers or, as Daniel calls them, wicked will not know or care because they are spiritually asleep and the day shall descend suddenly upon them.

The references given in this passage of Scripture are harmonious with those given in the Gospels, which Gospels were not yet written at this time, and show how the church had a common doctrinal position even before the Gospels were inscripturated. Paul had taught them and they knew about the signs of the coming. He said, "For yourselves know perfectly that the day of the Lord so cometh as a thief in the night" (I Thess. 5:2). Thus he felt that there was no necessity for him to write to them about the signs again.

In dealing with this event, there are certain questions which we want answered about the coming of the Lord.

I. *Is the Day of the Lord Any Different From the Day of Christ?*

Many expositors declare that there is a difference between the day of Christ and the day of the Lord. The Scofield Bible in its note on I Corinthians 1:8 declares, "The expression, 'day of Christ,' occurs in the following passages: I Cor. 1:8; 5:5; II Cor. 1:14; Phil. 1:6,10; 2:16. A.V. has 'day of Christ,' II Thess. 2:2, incorrectly, for 'day of the Lord' (Isa. 2:12; Rev. 19:11-21). The 'day of Christ' relates wholly to the reward and blessing of saints at His coming, as 'day of the Lord' is connected with judgment." [7]

Dr. Harry Ironside in *Addresses on the First and Second Epistles of Thessalonians* said, "This expression 'the day of the Lord' refers then, not as some have supposed to the descent of the Lord in the air to call His Church away, but to the manifestation of the Lord in visible glory to set up His kingdom." [8] Dr. Ironside believes in and declares a secret rapture followed by world evangelization, the appearance of the anti-Christ, the tribulation, and then the coming of the day of the Lord with judgment upon those on earth.

Dr. DeHaan, Dr. Gaebelein, Dr. Kelly, Dr. Darby and others all make a distinction here declaring that a week of years, namely, the seventieth week of Daniel's prophecy intervenes between "the day of Christ" and the "day of the Lord." They say that the *parousia* or rapture occurs first, that an interval of seven years elapses and then the *epiphaneia* or revelation occurs.

Let us analyze the biblical teaching on this subject. The Old Testament uses the "day of the Lord" to refer to a time of judgment, of wrath, and of tribulation. Isaiah 2:12,19 declares, "For the day of the Lord of hosts shall be upon every one that is proud and lofty, and upon every one that is lifted up; and he shall be brought low . . . and they shall go into the holes of the rocks, and into the caves of the earth, for fear of the Lord, and for the glory of his majesty, when he ariseth to shake terribly the earth."

Amos 5:18-20 says, "Woe unto you that desire the day of the Lord! to what end is it for you? the day of the Lord is darkness, and not light. As if a man did flee from a lion, and a bear met him; or went into the house, and leaned his hand on the wall, and a serpent bit him. Shall not the day of the Lord be darkness, and not light? even very dark and no brightness in it?"

Zephaniah 1:14,15 says, "The great day of the Lord is near, it is near, and hasteth greatly, even the voice of the day of the Lord: the mighty man shall cry there bitterly. That day is a day of wrath, a day of trouble and distress, a day of wasteness and desolation, a day of darkness and gloominess, a day of clouds and thick darkness."

Joel 2:1,2 says, "Blow ye the trumpet in Zion, and sound an alarm in my holy mountain: let all the inhabitants of the land tremble: for the day of the Lord cometh, for it is nigh at hand; a day of darkness and of gloominess, a day of clouds and of thick darkness. . . ."

Jeremiah 30:7 says, "Alas! for that day is great, so that none is like it: it is even the time of Jacob's trouble, but he shall be saved out of it."

In the New Testament there are many references to the "day of the Lord." I shall not quote these in detail but refer to them. In Matthew 24:29-31; Acts 2:19,20; II Thessalonians 2:1-3; II Peter 3:10; Jude 6: Revelation 6:12-17 those days are described as days of tribulation, as great and terrible, as the conclusion to the present form of the earth in which the heavens shall pass away with a great noise and the elements shall melt with fervent heat, as a time of judgment, and as the day of God's great wrath.

The New Testament referred to the "day of Christ" as a time of reward and blessing. I Corinthians 1:8 says, ". . . that ye may be blameless in the day of our Lord Jesus Christ." II Corinthians 1:14 says, "we are your rejoicing, even as ye also are ours in the day of the Lord Jesus." Philippians 1:6 says, ". . . he which hath begun a good work in you will perform it until the day of Jesus Christ." Philippians 1:10 says, ". . . that ye may be sincere and without offence till the day of Christ." Philippians 2:16 says, "Holding forth the word of life; that I may rejoice in the day of Christ. . . ." Similar testimony is given in I Thessalonians 2:19, 5:23, II Timothy 4:8.

If we were to summarize or give an account of the biblical teaching, we would have to say that the "day of Christ" or the "day of the Lord," for Christ is the Lord, refers to Christ's glorious coming to settle accounts in this world. It necessarily refers to a period of time longer than a twenty-four-hour day, as the original meaning of the word implies, so that numerous concomitants may occur during the day of the Lord. There will unquestionably be the resurrection (I Thess. 4:14), the rapture (I Thess. 4:17), the wrath of God (I Thess. 5:9), the tribulation and judgment (II Thess. 1:9).

The day of the Lord may be considered from two viewpoints, first, that of the believers who will be taken to be with Christ for reward and who will escape His outpoured wrath and, second, that of the wicked who remain to endure the terrible judgment described as taking place on the day of the Lord (II Thess. 1:7-9).

The day of the Lord is the catastrophic judgment ushered in by Christ's coming in glory toward which all signs are now pointing.

II. *Is the Day of the Lord Foreknown as to Time?*

The answer to this is, by unbelievers, that it is not foreknown. Such are in darkness. For them the coming of the

Lord will be unexpected—". . . the day of the Lord so cometh as a thief in the night" (I Thess. 5:2). This statement is repeated in II Peter 3:10 and Revelation 16:15. It was first taught by Christ who declared, "But know this, that if the good man of the house had known in what watch the thief would come, he would have watched, and would not have suffered his house to be broken up. Therefore be ye also ready: for in such an hour as ye think not the Son of man cometh" (Matt. 24:43,44). Such a thief came not to appropriate something and to depart stealthily, but he came as Christ said in John 10:10, "to steal, and to kill, and to destroy." Unbelievers shall be caught off guard and unprepared, just as the wicked steward was unprepared for his master's coming and as the foolish virgins were unprepared for the coming of the bridegroom.

The day of the Lord will come upon unbelievers suddenly. Paul said, "For when they shall say, Peace and safety; then sudden destruction cometh upon them . . ." (I Thess. 5:3). No doubt this is a reference by the Apostle to the preachments of Jeremiah and Ezekiel about the false prophets who cried, ". . . Peace, peace; when there is no peace" (Jer. 6:14; Ez. 13:10). It refers to his sense of security which is utterly false. Such a sense of security may be drawn by ungodly men from the world organization, or from defense preparations, or from power, or from international covenants, but they cannot produce peace. The individuals who put their trust in them are described as the children of darkness. They are those who seek pleasure, indulgence, wealth, power, fame, and satisfaction from the things which come in an earthly security. They are those to whom Peter referred as mockers who claim that since the days of the fathers, ". . . all things continue as they were . . ." (II Pet. 3:4). They are those whom Jesus described as ". . . eating and drinking, marrying and giving in marriage . . ." (Matt. 24:38). They are those who were like the people of Sodom in the days of Lot. In the time of their seeming security, a change will occur which will be as radical as that which occurred on the good ship Titanic when in one moment the people thought it was unsinkable and in the next moment it was sinking, having been sheared by an iceberg.

This day of the Lord shall come catastrophically and finally. Said Paul, ". . . then sudden destruction cometh upon them, as travail upon a woman with child . . ." (I Thess. 5:3). Neil declares that "the whole clearly refers, not to the Ecclesia, but to the unredeemed world." [9] If one wants a picture of it, Isaiah gives it in the thirteenth chapter, the sixth to the ninth verses, "Howl ye; for the day of the Lord is at hand; it shall come as a destruction from the Almighty. Therefore shall all hands be faint, and every man's heart shall melt: and they shall be afraid: pangs and sorrows shall take hold of them; they shall be in pain as a woman that travaileth: they shall be amazed one at another; their faces shall be as flames. Behold, the day of the Lord cometh, cruel both with wrath and fierce anger, to lay the land desolate: and he shall destroy the sinners thereof out of it."

The whole church shall either have been caught up with Christ or will at the moment of the beginning of this day of the Lord be caught up with Christ away from these tribulations, but the wicked will continue in their suffering. Thus the wicked must be warned of this impending doom. Paul says, ". . . they shall not escape" (I Thess. 5:3). Oh, sinner, repentance must be performed now. This is the acceptable year of the Lord. Next will come the day of vengeance and then it will be too late. That day of vengeance begins by the coming of our Lord Jesus Christ.

The time of the day of the Lord is known by believers in a general sense. Paul said, "But ye, brethren, are not in darkness, that that day should overtake you as a thief" (I Thess. 5:4). It is the illustration of the day dawning and startling thieves engaged in their activities. In the original, a variant reading

is to put the plural for thieves instead of the singular, so that
it is as if the day of the Lord discovered people as thieves. It
shall not be so for believers. They are the children of the
light, children of the day. They have understanding, wisdom
which is given to the righteous (Dan. 12:10). Hence they
know the seasons or the times of crises which constitute the
signs which the Lord originally defined for His church to
watch. They are not in darkness. On the contrary, they are
looking for His coming. This is the mark of a true believer.
He takes seriously the biblical teaching and the promise of his
Lord, since we are told that "the grace of God that bringeth
salvation hath appeared to all men, teaching us that, denying
ungodliness and worldly lusts, we should live soberly, righteously, and godly, in this present world; looking for that
blessed hope, and the glorious appearing of the great God and
our Saviour Jesus Christ; who gave himself for us . . ."
(Titus 2:11-14). The writer of Hebrews says, ". . . unto
them that look for him shall he appear the second time without sin unto salvation" (Heb. 9:28). As the signs are fulfilled
round about us, believers are to lift up their eyes for their
redemption draweth nigh. What do we see? Do we see world
evangelization? Do we see the return of Israel? Do we see the
building up of the Russian Confederacy including Islam? Do
we see the apostasy from biblical Christianity? Do we see
indulgence in sex immorality? Do we see increase in travel
and knowledge? Do we see the conquering of the universe
by atomic power? If we do, then let us note that these things
point to the near coming of the Lord.

But who are these sleeping Christians of whom Paul speaks
in this passage? They are those who are believers, but they
are not fulfilling their obligation. There are no distinctions
among Christians in that day. Paul said, "Ye are all children
of light . . . of the day . . ." (I Thess. 5:5). These words
are a reminder of the teaching of Christ that the children of
God are the children of light, and that they who follow Him

will not walk in darkness but will have the light of life, but the reference here is to the day of the Lord which, to the believer, will be a day of light and of glory, and he is a child of that day. When it dawns, the rapture will include all believers, all born-again ones, all children of God. There may be a difference among these believers and that difference will be marked by a difference in reward, but all of them will be taken to be with Christ.

Nevertheless, Paul encourages and exhorts us to be alert. Phillips translates it, "we men of the daylight should be alert, with faith and love as our breastplate and the hope of our salvation as our helmet." [10] It is an anomaly for Christians who are looking for the coming of Christ and to be made like Him to be walking in carnality as the world walks, in darkness and in sin, and to follow the course of this world. Such ought not to be. Ask yourself if you have a false confidence, if you are in error about your salvation, if you have been deceiving yourself when you find no difference between you, as a son of light, and others who are children of darkness. There must be a great difference between the children of God and the children of this world. The attribute of a believer is that he is awake, that he is watching, that he is living soberly (not in gloom but with radiant joy) by means of the gospel armor which has been provided for him. He has the breastplate of faith and love and he has the helmet of salvation so that he might live in holiness which is expected from the believer.

Such believers will not be condemned at the coming of Christ but will be saved from wrath. "For God hath not appointed (destined) us to wrath, but to obtain salvation by our Lord Jesus Christ" (I Thess. 5:9). The confidence of the believers is to escape the judgment of the day of the Lord. Christ did not save us to pour out God's wrath upon us. The believer will certainly escape the trials of that day. To the believer He gives the promise, "Because thou hast kept the word of my patience, I also will keep thee from the hour of temptation, which shall come upon all the world, to try them that dwell upon the earth" (Rev. 3:10). The salvation wrought by Christ is complete. It delivers from the penalty of sin which Christ took upon the cross. It delivers from the power of sin by the gift of the Holy Spirit in the believer's life, and it will deliver from the presence of sin by taking the believer to be with Christ. Let us preach and believe full deliverance from all phases of sin in Christ both now and to come. The cross hath wrought a finished work for us. Paul said, "who died for us . . ." (I Thess. 5:10). This is the ground of our hope of salvation in any phase of our deliverance. We must glory in the cross. Through the cross we have the right to participate in the glorious coming of our Lord on that great day.

III. *Is There Any Distinction Between the Dead and the Living Believers at the Day of the Lord?*

Paul says, "Who died for us, that, whether we wake or sleep, we should live together with him" (*Ibid.*). The death of Christ guaranteed the salvation of all believers whether they are sleeping or living. Let us remember Paul's teaching concerning the dead. He tells us that the believers at death go immediately to be with Christ, that they are there with Him in heaven in a disembodied state until the time of the resurrection. That state is a conscious, personal, continued existence with the Lord. At the resurrection we shall receive a new body which will be joined unto our redeemed souls so that those who are dead in Christ will arise with Him when He comes in glory. Then they will be joined with the translated believers who are living at the time of the coming, and together in resurrected bodies and redeemed souls they will enter into the eternal kingdom of our Lord which is both spiritual and material.

This then was a reply to the question of the Thessalonians concerning their dead saints. Paul said that they are now saved, that they are delivered from wrath and that they will participate in the coming of our Lord. How interesting that he returned in his thinking to Calvary, where Christ suffered the wrath of judgment for all who believe. He took the God-forsaken experience into Himself. He was judged as sin, and He died in our place. Because of what Christ did for us, we are delivered from the wrath to come.

The deliverance of the believer is complete. He is not a child of darkness but of light. He is not under the power of sin but walks in liberty. He does not face wrath but full deliverance.

Moreover, the destiny of the believer is to forever be with Christ. ". . . we should live together with him" (*Ibid.*). This mystical union begins now when we are joined to Christ by faith and receive the gift of the Holy Spirit, and it will never terminate. We shall be with Christ in death, and we shall be with Him in the resurrection, and we shall be with Him forever.

Is it any wonder then that Paul says, "Wherefore comfort yourselves together, and edify one another, even as also ye do" (I Thess. 5:11). The mutual comfort of knowing that we are bound together with Christ and each other in eternal fellowship, both now and in the ages to come, is most strengthening. By means of this apprehension of the truth concerning the day of the Lord, we are able to edify each other in the faith and in the Christian life. With such a faith, the believer can say, Even so come, Lord Jesus. The coming of the day of the Lord has no terror for the believer.

XVI

What the Church Expects of Her Sons

Ye are all the children of light, and the children of the day. . . . But let us, who are of the day, be sober, putting on the breastplate of faith and love; and for an helmet, the hope of salvation.

—I THESSALONIANS 5:5,8

THE LORD HIMSELF FIRST USED THE CONTRAST BETWEEN THE children of light and the children of darkness when He said, ". . . the children of this world are in their generation wiser than the children of light" (Luke 16:8). Paul here uses the contrast in reference to the second coming of the Lord. At no time does the distinction between the children of light and the children of darkness come into the open as much as it does in the way they celebrate the coming of a new year. I walked across the Common the other day with a businessman of Boston who is not a member of Park Street Church. We were commenting upon the celebration of New Year's Eve. He volunteered the information that for years he and fifteen of his friends have gone on New Year's Eve to the Toll House for a happy, enjoyable, and sober dinner party. Only two of the whole group smoke and no one drinks liquor. Laughingly he said, "Some day I will have to go on a rollicking drunk to see how the other half does it." It would be most appropriate for us to investigate the difference between the children of light and the children of darkness.

We remember that this passage was a little dissertation upon the moral and religious uses of the doctrine of our Lord's second coming. The topic of writing was the day of the Lord and His return for His church and the judgment of the ungodly. It was the teaching of St. Paul that the Lord Jesus Christ is coming back to earth personally, visibly, gloriously, and judiciously on a certain day. This event will be appended by the resurrection of the saints, by the rapture of these resurrected believers, along with the transformed living believers, and by the advent of the wrath of God in judgment upon the ungodly and wicked. According to Paul and all Scripture, the time of that coming is unknown, but the signs are given to warn believers in advance so that they may be prepared and ready.

Immediately Paul recognizes the application of this truth to both the church and the world. For the church, the children of light, the brethren as he calls them, whether asleep in Jesus or living, it will mean fulfillment in the redemption of their bodies and in the being taken away from this earthly scene of tribulation to the presence of the Lord. For the ungodly or the children of darkness, this will mean the wrath of God in cosmological upheavals, catastrophes, natural phenomena, and destruction in flaming fire. The terrible prophetic descriptions of the day of the Lord contained in the Bible are overwhelming. For some then, it is the blessed hope for which they have been longing and waiting, whereas for others it is a time of fear and torment. It was with this in mind that the demons cried unto the Lord, ". . . art thou come hither to torment us before the time?" (Matt. 8:29). It is for this day that the fallen angels and the wicked are kept reserved unto judgment.

The children of light must realize that certain moral standards go with their position as sons of the church. Being included in the ecclesia or the church gives the church a right to expect that we will walk as the sons of light and not darkness (from which we have been rescued). Because we are the sons of the church, a different criterion of judgment, a different quality of life, and a different mode of conduct is expected from us. This is just and proper. The very strength of the Christian cause lies in this differentiation from the children of darkness. There is a mistaken notion of the liturgical branch of Christendom, of the Oxford groups, and of some Christians in the movie colony that their religion enables them to do the same things in a different spirit or attitude from what they did them before they were Christians. Over against this, our present passage of Scripture and many others, such as Romans 13:11-14, declare that a totally different kind of life is necessary for the children of light. Before one can share the great hope of the coming of the Lord, he must believe the truth and exhibit the life of a Christian. From the emphasis upon Christian truth, Paul invariably turns to the emphasis upon Christian life. Every epistle has two sections, the theoretical and the practical. So it is here. At this point he strongly emphasizes the practical.

I. *The Character of the Children of the Church*

"But ye, brethren, are not in darkness. . . . Ye are all the children of light . . ." (I Thess. 5:4,5). The nature of man is the ground of the character of man. Fruit grows on a tree. Words come from the mind and heart. Actions arise from disposition. The Lord Jesus said, "But those things which proceed out of the mouth come forth from the heart; and they defile the man. For out of the heart proceed evil thoughts, murders, adulteries, fornications, thefts, false witness, blasphemies: these are the things which defile a man . . ." (Matt. 15:18-20). He also said, "A good man out of the good treasure of the heart bringeth forth good things: and an evil man out of the evil treasure bringeth forth evil things" (Matt. 12:35), and ". . . by their fruits ye shall know them" (Matt. 7:20). James said, "Doth a fountain send forth at the same place sweet water and bitter?" (James 3:11).

Fallen human beings are not children of light but of darkness. Jesus said, "Ye are of your father, the devil, and the lusts of your father ye will do . . ." (John 8:44). Paul said, "There is none righteous, no, not one: there is none that understandeth, there is none that seeketh after God. They are all gone out of the way, they are together become unprofitable; there is none that doeth good, no, not one" (Rom. 3:10-12). Jeremiah declared, "The heart is deceitful above all things, and desperately wicked: who can know it?" (Jer. 17:9). By common grace, such persons may simulate a character which resembles the Christian, but they do not possess that character. While simulating the position of children of the light, they are capable of the depths of evil, which is amazing. Elton Trueblood said, "We have had a revelation of the depths of wickedness in the human heart that makes naturalistic optimism seem particularly nonsensical. The war has revealed aspects of human life that we had supposed, in our innocence, had been outgrown by the human race." [1] Ivor Thomas, a former member of the Socialist Cabinet of Britain, declared, "For a confirmation of the argument of this chapter, that socialism is bound to be wrecked on human nature, we may profitably turn to the theologians. A sound political philosophy, like a sound theology, must start from the fall of man." [2] Thus fallen men wander in the maze of their own inventions and doings, having an appropriate character.

Fulfillment of human nature is bound in human character. If the nature is renewed by grace, it will be righteous. If it is unrenewed, it will be unrighteous, ungodly, and wicked. We must acknowledge that there is a state of conflict between the renewed and unrenewed nature in the believer so that his character at times may be inconsistent, but the objective to be reached through grace is the dominion and rule of the renewed nature over the unrenewed and unregenerate nature.

The new birth produces the nature and character of the children of light. This is defined in the Westminster Catechism as effectual calling. "Effectual calling is the work of God's Spirit, whereby, convincing us of our sin and misery, enlightening our minds in the knowledge of Christ, and renewing our wills, he doth persuade and enable us to embrace Jesus Christ, freely offered to us in the gospel." [3] The necessity of that new birth or regeneration is one of the most oft-repeated truths in the New Testament.

Jesus uses the figure of following Him to describe the character of one who has been born again. ". . . If any man will come after me, let him deny himself, and take up his cross, and follow me" (Matt. 16:24), ". . . I am the light of the world: he that followeth me shall not walk in darkness, but shall have the light of life" (John 8:12). To follow is to commit, to trust, to adopt, to pattern after. It is an expression which is synonymous with the new life in which the new nature or character of the individual is shown.

This new nature must have a point of beginning. It is called a new birth, which is instantaneous, complete, and permanent. There is wonderful hope in the fact that Christianity declares there is a land of beginning again. The kingdom of God is among us. It is at hand. It is right about us, and when we are born into that kingdom, an entirely new beginning occurs. That birth is described as a baptism by the Holy Spirit into the divine nature uniting us to Christ's death and resurrection so that we live together with Him.

Knowledge called "spiritual enlightenment" ensues from a change of one's nature by the new birth. "But ye . . . are not in darkness, that that day should overtake you as a thief" (I Thess. 5:4). The same Spirit who regenerates enlightens the new creature. This work is done in the mind. The mind is renewed (Titus 3:5; Rom. 12:2). The Spirit ". . . shall teach you all things, and bring all things to your remembrance . . ." (John 14:26), and ". . . will guide you into all truth . . . for he shall receive of mine, and shall shew it unto you" (John 16:13,14). ". . . the things of God knoweth no man, but the Spirit of God. Now we have received, not the spirit of the world, but the spirit which is of God; that we might know the things that are freely given to us of God" (I Cor. 2:11,12). Through such regeneration, the light of God breaks in the human mind.

A new convert gains understanding of God's revelation contained in the Bible which he could not grasp before. An unregenerate mind is in darkness, it mutilates the Scripture, it misses its meaning, while the regenerate mind delights in discovering new things in God's Word. Such discovery never ends. The doctrinal system of the Bible is a source of constant thought and new understanding to a child of the light, for new light constantly breaks from it over his mind.

Thus the signs of the advent of the day of the Lord will ever recall the son of the light to his profession and his conduct as a believer. The second coming is the great incentive to this moral consistency.

II. *The Conduct of the Children of the Church*

Paul said, ". . . let us not sleep, as do others; but let us watch and be sober" (I Thess. 5:6). Phillips translates it, "Let us then never fall into the sleep that stupefies the rest of the world: let us keep awake, with our wits about us." [4] The antithesis is drawn between the condition of the believer and that of the world. The world is said to be asleep. Here is a change of figure from the meaning of sleep as physical death to that of moral insensibility or spiritual death. On the other hand, to be alive is to be alert, to be watchful. The world is insensible to the invitation to life and grace given in the Scripture, to the admonishing wrath and judgments announced in Scripture, and to the exhortation to participate in spiritual things. This passage is particularly full of begging, beseeching, and exhortation, all of which falls on the deaf ears of unbelievers.

The world seeks indulgence in sinful things. The un-Christian world is preoccupied with pleasure, with material security and with power. The reference here to "others" brings us back to the fourth chapter and the fifth verse where he is describing the Gentiles who know not God and who walk in "the lust of concupiscence." Sin reigns over them and the inward habit of obeying sin is the course of their conduct" (Rom. 6:12; Eph. 2:1-3). The conscience of such persons is deadened and their moral nature is asleep (Isa. 6:10; Acts 28:26,27; Rom. 11:8).

When a believer is carnal, indulgent and worldly, he is belying his position. Paul said, ". . . ye . . . are not in darkness. . . . Ye are all the children of light . . ." (I Thess. 5:4,5). Consistency is to be expected in the Christian life. From the day of the Lord which is a day of light, Paul makes a transition to day proper as opposed to the darkness of the night. Children of darkness love darkness because their deeds are evil. The children of the light love the light because their deeds are righteous. The life of the child of light is pure, clean, and holy through God's Word, through the blood of Christ, and through the work of the Holy Spirit. Nevertheless, the Scripture recognizes two classes of Christians—one as living in the power of the flesh called carnal, immature, and worldly, the other as living in the power of the Spirit and called spiritual. Carnal Christians can hardly be distinguished from the "others," that is, non-Christians, and this ought not to be. Hence, condemnation is implied in the exhortation to be of the day and of the light. The great motive for such consistency is the approaching day of the Lord.

Alertness will mark the son of the church. He will watch and be sober. Sober does not mean lugubrious, as opposed to buoyancy and cheerfulness, but it means a self-restraint or discipline. The word sober has grown to refer to temperance over against drunkenness, and this is implied in this passage of Scripture wherein the drunken are declared to practice their indulgence in the night. The full implication of sobriety, however, is temperance in the use of all of life's possessions and pleasures. This temperance may be experienced in conjunction with joy, radiancy, and enthusiasm as described in verses sixteen to nineteen, where we are urged to rejoice evermore and to quench not the Spirit. The true believer is an enthusiastic, cheerful person.

MacLaren declares that the motive in such sobriety is that we belong to the day which is a realm of light, of purity, of righteousness, and of joy. Therefore, such cheerfulness and illumination will shine from the believer as a child of the light.[5]

The means of such a disciplined and directed life is the panoply of God as suggested here in Paul's first epistle and expounded after much further thought in Ephesians 6:13-17. No doubt, as Paul considered the subject of watchfulness concerning the coming of the Lord, there was suggested to him the means by which a man defends himself from the enemy. He who is in constant danger from the enemy will practice alertness for his life depends upon it. So it is with the believer.

III. *Characteristics of the Children of the Church*

Said Paul, ". . . putting on the breastplate of faith and love; and for an helmet, the hope of salvation" (I Thess. 5:8). Here he returns to the statement with which he began the epistle in chapter one, "Remembering without ceasing your work of faith, and labour of love, and patience of hope in our Lord Jesus Christ . . ." (I Thess. 1:3). This trilogy of faith, love, and hope is both a provision by God for the believer and a product of the character of the believer.

A son of the church is a child of faith. He has the faith

which justifies. This faith is the instrument through which salvation is received and through which the light is followed. "But without faith it is impossible to please him . . ." (Heb. 11:6). Such faith is the mark or characteristic of one who has become a child of the light. He lives by this faith. ". . . the just shall live by faith . . ." (Heb. 10:38). And he will go on ". . . from faith to faith . . ." (Rom 1:17). Thus it was with the heroes such as Abraham, Joseph, Moses, and David. They lived by believing God. Faith always works. He is a man of faith who prays, labors, sacrifices, perseveres, and who receives the blessings thereof. Thus the child of the light is a child of faith.

A son of the church is a child of love, and he puts on love. He has the first commandment, ". . . Thou shalt love the Lord thy God with all thy heart. . . . Thou shalt love thy neighbor as thyself" (Matt. 22:37,39). Such love fulfills the whole law contained in the Ten Commandments and embraces the requirements of God. It is the standard of Christian life. The philosophy of love is the most revolutionary philosophy in the world and it is not sentimental. We do not let wickedness and error take over because we believe in a philosophy of love, but we find that love puts sternness into our souls so that we will contend for the faith, we will conquer wickedness and we will face error unequivocally. The details of the practice of love may not always be clear, but the principle of love must always motivate us.

The third characteristic is that of the hope of salvation. This hope looks to that day of the revelation of Jesus Christ when we shall be saved from all that contaminates. Salvation is by hope, which hope is a very present reality. Christianity is a true optimism even in the midst of the most dread conditions in the world, for it looks toward the day of the triumph of our Lord Jesus Christ and of His cause.

Paul concludes by saying, "For God hath not appointed us to wrath, but to obtain salvation by our Lord Jesus Christ"

(I Thess. 5:9). God appoints those in Christ to be saved, to acquire salvation, to possess eternal life, to become a fellow heir with Jesus Christ. Two aspects of this experience are our alertness and God's appointment which are joined together in one sentence, just as they are joined together throughout Scripture. There are two aspects of salvation. One is the divine preservation and the other is our perseverance. Through this, we are apprehended of God so as to be saved from wrath, and we will have no part in the coming judgment. All this is through the divine atonement as the means of redemption, for Christ died for us. What a wonderful truth! Our redemption has been wrought by Christ and because He hath redeemed us and owns us, we are to live for Him as the children of the light.

XVII

The Ground of the Church's Confidence

*Who died for us, that, whether we wake or sleep, we should
live together with him.*

—I THESSALONIANS 5:10

THE GROUND OF THE CHURCH'S CONFIDENCE IS THE DOCTRINE
of redemption. Paul found it impossible to speak about our
future salvation without making an allusion to the ground of
that confidence. He did so in this text which says, "who died
for us." He makes an allusion to it but gives no exposition of
the great doctrine. It is only mentioned in the Thessalonian
Epistles, first in 1:9 and then in this reference; but in his next
series of epistles, namely, Romans, Galatians, and Corinthians,
the doctrine assumes a very great place. As we study the
Corinthian Epistles, we find that the doctrine of the cross
and of the atonement assumes a large place in both his preaching and teaching. Let us remember that Paul was at Corinth
when he wrote these Thessalonian Epistles so that if his
reference back to the items which were prominent in his
thinking and in his teaching during his visit to Corinth are
correct, this doctrine receives quite an emphasis. We may be
sure that it also received such an emphasis at Thessalonica.

The fact that Paul could make a passing reference to it reveals that he had said much about it when he was present with them and they understood the reference. But this time he was preoccupied with other matters which had been reported to him by Timothy on his return from the visit to Thessalonica. They were troubled about their dead, about members who would not work but were waiting for the second coming of Christ, about the rumors concerning Paul's own apostleship and manner of life, about sex and about items of sanctification. Paul dealt with all of these in his epistle to them.

Having completed his teaching about the day of the Lord with the declaration that God had not appointed us unto wrath but to obtain salvation through our Lord Jesus Christ, he went on to emphasize this with the brief statement of our text. The sense of the word "appointed" is that of election. Olshausen says that it is in the sense of predestination of the saints and not as of individuals that Paul was speaking.[1] We must interpret it in the light of the reference in I Thessalonians 1:4 and also in the light of Paul's teaching in his other epistles. The doctrine of election was very common in Pauline teaching. The elect are to escape the wrath of God in the day of the Lord. According to this epistle, they have been delivered from the wrath to come (I Thess. 1:9), and when that great and terrible day of the Lord comes, as a thief in the night, it will not overtake the believers as thieves, for they will be prepared for it. On the other hand, the believers have been appointed or elected unto salvation. The word describing salvation and translated "to obtain" means to possess, to purchase and it refers to the church of Christ, which He purchased with His own blood (Acts 20:28) and to our already purchased redemption, the earnest of which we receive in the gift of the Holy Spirit. (Eph. 1:13,14). This salvation is held by some to be the equivalent of election and to be the description of those who are purchased and set aside by God's own act.[2] Certainly this salvation represents both

198 THE CHURCH IN GOD

the present and the future aspects of our great deliverance through the Lord Jesus Christ.

The accomplishment of this redemption is through the Lord Jesus Christ. He finished salvation and there is nothing we can add to it. How common is the error of the necessity of our earning salvation is illustrated by an experience I had when getting a semi-annual checkup on health. As they strapped on the electrical apparatus for a cardiogram, I observed to the nurse that it made me wonder what a man would think about when he was having them strapped on in the electric chair. She replied, "I think he would probably think on what was coming after death." Said I, "What do you think comes after death?" "Oh," said she, "I believe in heaven and in the hot place." So, by the Socratic method I thought I would ascertain her own confidence. I asked, "And what makes the difference as to whether you go to one place or the other?" Quickly she responded, "Your life." "But what standard," said I, "do you have for a righteous life which will enable you to go to heaven?" She replied, "I suppose the Ten Commandments." Then I asked, "Have you obeyed the Ten Commandments?" She responded, "Oh, yes." So we began to examine them, starting with the tenth commandment and working backward. After a few minutes she admitted that she hadn't kept the commandments and thus according to that standard would not have a right to heaven. In the complete conversation which lasted considerably longer than this, I tried to elicit from her that her ground of hope rested in what Jesus Christ had done for her on the cross, namely, in the doctrine of redemption, but she did not have the faintest idea that that was her basis of salvation, if she had any. Multitudes of people are in exactly the same state of mind. Our salvation depends upon the historical work of Christ. Paul said, ". . . by our Lord Jesus Christ" (I Thess. 5:9). Jesus was born and died in history. Christ was the Son of God. The historical Jesus and the eternal Christ were united in the person of Jesus Christ and He through His death and resurrection has become our Lord. The mention of this future salvation launched Paul into this brief but important reference to the two aspects of salvation, which can come only through the atoning work of Christ.

I. *The Undertaking of Our Salvation by Christ*

Paul says, "Who died for us . . ." (I Thess. 5:10). The meaning of this statement may be but is not necessarily the vicarious atonement of our Saviour. We must be very careful never to claim more for a Scripture text than is taught in it. The practice of reading into the Bible things which are not there is not acceptable procedure. The preposition used before "us" in this text is the little Greek word *peri* which means "on behalf of" rather than "instead of." If the latter had been meant, the preposition *anti* would have been used. This would mark substitution. The most that can be claimed for this text is that Christ died on our behalf because He would rescue us from the wrath to come and save us. We think of an analogy in a soldier dying on our behalf because the administration made wrong decisions in reference to Russia. Such is not a vicarious death, but it is a death on our behalf.

Different points of view are built on this differentiation in Scripture. One is that Christ died as our example and thus on our behalf. By denying Himself, by following His teachings through to Calvary, by demonstrating sacrificial love, He gave us an example of how we too could come to God through such a means. This is not vicarious, but this would be on our behalf.

Others tell us that He died as an example or a demonstration of the penalty of law. God who is omnipotent can arbitrarily suspend the operation of law if He so desires and all He needed was the demonstration to men that this is a moral universe and that He is a holy God and that He does punish sin. He did this in the death of Christ on the cross. Again this would not be a vicarious or substitutionary death but would only be on our behalf.

Yet others tell us that He died to influence us and that because we are moved by His sufferings, therefore we repent of our sins and live a life which is pleasing to God. This is called a "moral influence" view of the atonement. Each of these in part is true, but none of them will redeem the world.

The meaning of the death of Christ as drawn from many other passages of Scripture is necessarily a vicarious atonement. The Old Testament doctrine of atonement is very clear. On the Day of Atonement, the high priest laid his hands upon the sacrifice, confessing the sins of the people over that scapegoat which was released into the wilderness. A second scapegoat was then killed in its place (Lev. 16). The blood was established as the means of atonement. The law said, "For the life of the flesh is in the blood: and I have given it to you upon the altar to make an atonement for your souls: for it is the blood that maketh an atonement for the soul" (Lev. 17:11). Blood is the life, and when the blood was poured out, the life or the soul is poured out. Blood which was shed in the land polluted the land unless expiation was made for that through capital punishment (Deut. 19:11-13). The principle of expiation is found in the law from the fourth chapter of Genesis onward.

The prophets are just as explicit. Isaiah 53 is universally accepted as referring to Christ and it is so interpreted by Philip in the eighth chapter of Acts and by Peter in his first epistle, the second chapter, so that there is no clearer presentation of a sacrificial substitutionary atonement than that given in the fifty-third chapter of Isaiah. In Daniel 9:24 there is the description of the sacrifice of the Messiah, ". . . to make an end of sins, and to make reconciliation for iniquity, and to bring in everlasting righteousness. . . ." This is exceedingly clear. No mistake can be made when one reads the Psalms, such as Psalm 22, which was quoted by Christ when He was on the cross, and Psalm 69, which describes the misery of His sorrow in His atoning sufferings.

The Gospels are equally explicit. Christ declares that He came to give His life a ransom for many (Matt. 20:28), that His blood was ". . . shed for many for the remission of sins" (Matt. 26:28), that He died that ". . . whosoever believeth in him should not perish, but have everlasting life (John 3:16), that ". . . it behoved the Christ to suffer, and to rise from the dead the third day: and that repentance and remission of sins should be preached in his name among all nations . . ." (Luke 24:46,47).

Paul is equally explicit in declaring that ". . . he hath made him to be sin for us, who knew no sin . . ." (II Cor. 5:21) and that "Christ . . . being made a curse for us . . ." (Gal. 3:13), that Christ is our Passover, ". . . that Christ died for our sins . . ." (I Cor. 15:3), and that Christ was a propitiation for our sins (Rom. 3:25).

The other writers of Scripture declare that "Christ was once offered to bear the sins of many . . ." (Heb. 9:28), that ". . . his own self bare our sins in his own body . . ." (I Pet. 2:24), that ". . . Christ also hath once suffered for sins, the just for the unjust . . ." (I Pet. 3:18), and "Unto him that loved us, and washed us from our sins in his own blood . . . be glory and dominion . . ." (Rev. 1:5), thus teaching the same doctrine of a vicarious atonement for sin. Alexander MacLaren says, "In what conceivable sense, except in the sense of bearing the world's sins, and, therefore, mine, is the death of Jesus Christ of advantage to me?" [3]

The message of Paul did not change from the earliest of his epistles to the last epistles which he wrote on such a vital subject. Some accuse Paul of preaching in this epistle a gospel of the coming of the Christ and not of His cross. How mistaken they are is shown from this brief insertion of the ground of our redemption and confidence. The gospel of the coming Saviour and the gospel of the cross are one and the same.

Christ came to die and He will come again to reign. The accomplishment of our salvation from wrath and to life is by the cross of Christ and by the death of the Son of God on it. This constituted Paul's Christology from I Thessalonians unto II Timothy. He never changed. He believed that the atonement was made by the historical death of Christ upon the cross and in it the power of redemption inheres (I Cor. 15: 1-3).

II. *The Union with Christ through Salvation*

Paul declares that through this death ". . . we should live together with him" (I Thess. 5:10). This is a description of mystical life. It is life which is identified with the eternal life belonging to the redeemed and derived from Christ by the grace of God given to us. This life is initiated in the individual by his being joined to Christ who has eternal life (I John 5:12). Christ was pre-existent and eternal. He became incarnate. He died. He rose again. He lives eternally. It is by being joined to Him that we who have a temporal beginning have the possession of eternal life, to become identified with Christ by faith so that we share in His death and resurrection, thus having imputed to us the righteousness which is His in a new standing, or resurrection standing, before our God. There is no end to that life. If one has that life, it is a contradiction in terms to say that he will die spiritually. We have reckoned ourselves to be dead with Him and thus we live with Him in mystical life.

Likewise we have a mystical union with Christ. The Bible gives numerous figures of this. Jesus Himself described it in the terminology of eating and drinking. Jesus said, "Except ye eat the flesh of the Son of man, and drink his blood, ye have no life in you. Whoso eateth my flesh, and drinketh my blood, hath eternal life; and I will raise him up at the last day. For my flesh is meat indeed, and my blood is drink indeed"

(John 6:53:55). The disciples thought that this was a hard saying and they turned away. Christ who was present in their midst spoke of His being the manna come down from heaven on which they were to feed spiritually and to be one with Him, for He said, "He that eateth my flesh, and drinketh my blood, dwelleth in me, and I in him" (John 6:56).

Another figure used was that of the head and the body. This was common to Paul's writings and is especially manifested in the fourth chapter of Ephesians. "Speaking the truth in love, may grow up into him in all things, which is the head . . . From whom the whole body fitly joined together and compacted by that which every joint supplieth, according to the effectual working in the measure of every part, maketh increase of the body unto the edifying of itself in love" (Eph. 4:15,16). We believers are members of His body receiving our direction, guidance, and mastery from the head which is Christ. This is a mystery.

Another figure used by St. Paul is that of the bride and the bridegroom. Christ is the bridegroom and the church is the bride. No man hateth his own flesh, but nourisheth and cherisheth it, so Christ loved the church and gave Himself for it. The wonderful love which is manifested between man and wife is an emblem of the mystery of the love and community of life between Christ and the church.

It was for this that Christ prayed in His high-priestly prayer, "Neither pray I for these alone, but for them also which shall believe on me through their word; that they all may be one; as thou, Father, art in me, and I in thee, that they also may be one in us: that the world may believe that thou hast sent me" (John 17:20,21). This is the description of that mystical union with Christ.

In this we share His suffering and ". . . fill up that which is behind of the afflictions of Christ . . ." (Col. 1:24), we share His position for ". . . if so be that we suffer with him, that we may be also glorified together" (Rom. 8:17), we share His life and we share His love. Thus we may realize His presence with us today in this mystical relationship.

A third truth of our union with Christ is emphasized in the word "together" which bespeaks also the union of believers one with another in the body. The suggestion is of social life. There are certain things that God hath joined together and that cannot be separated. One of them is the mutual life of believers who are members of His body. There is a sense in which the members are all one when they belong in one body, even though they are different members, for they all do the bidding of the head. So it is in the church. Because we are joined to Him, we are also joined one to another. Salvation is not only individual, it is social, it is for the church. We shall be saved together, we shall live together, we shall be caught up into heaven together, we shall ever be together with the Lord and with one another. We had better get used to it now.

III. *The Unbroken Life with Jesus Christ*

This text suggests yet another thing and that is our unbroken fellowship. Paul said, ". . . whether we wake or sleep . . ." (I Thess. 5:10). This is the metaphorical use of waking and sleeping to represent living and dying, as it does in the fourth chapter.

It is inconsequential whether one is living or dead as far as his union with Christ and salvation are concerned. In either case we shall live together with Him. This does not put it off to an indefinite future for it is a subjunctive which implies that it should begin whether we are living or dying. We do not believe that it refers only to the resurrection. This should be the deathblow to all theories of the sleep of the dead, but they certainly do persist. How those who advocate this can misinterpret Paul's teaching of being immediately with Christ when one dies is beyond my comprehension. The spiritual life, i.e. eternal life, is ours even in physical death. Those who fall asleep forfeit nothing of the blessedness. One doesn't miss anything by the sleep of death, for he is in the presence of Christ. The lordship of Christ extends both to the dead and to the living (Rom. 14:9).

It is important to note that the beginning of life with Christ marks the entrance upon life over which death has no power. From this the sting of death has been removed (Heb. 2:14). The present and the future are always with Christ (Phil. 1:23; II Cor. 5:7; I Thess. 5:10). The people of God have passed from death unto life, from condemnation to justification, from darkness to light, and this is an eternal state.

It was no longer important from this point of view whether the *parousia* was near or far, for the attitude of mind was more important. From this truth came the high consolation to those either who faced death or who were bereaved by the loss of their loved ones. They knew that their departed ones lived with Christ and Christ is alive. By the redemption of the body which is the full effect of the atonement, an additional blessing ultimately will be received even by those who are at present living with the Lord Jesus Christ. With this comfort he concludes the treatise on death. And this we say in the words of Frederick Knowles:

> This body is my house— It is not I;
> Herein I sojourn till, in some far sky,
> I lease a fairer dwelling, built to last
> Till all the carpentry of time is past . . .
>
> This body is my house— It is not I.
> Triumphant in this faith I live, and die.[4]

His concluding words are, "Wherefore comfort yourselves together, and edify one another, even as also ye do" (I Thess. 5:11). Such edification belongs to the church. Edification is a word that summarizes all the benefits a believer receives from fellowship in the church. It describes what he gets from worship, from teaching, from prayer, from contact with

God's people and from every phase of church life. God's people are to seek to build up each other in virtue, in knowledge, in service and in grace. This is the purpose of their meeting together regularly in worship, prayer and preaching. Paul has described the church as a building. He also described the individual as a building indwelt by the Holy Spirit (Eph. 2:21; I Cor. 6:19). Just as we are to study to build up ourselves in our holy faith, so we are also to exercise our Christian duty to build up the church, i.e. others in the holy faith. Sainthood comes from edification under God's tutelage. God Himself will build us into what He plans by His Spirit, Word, and Providence and then He will fill His temple with His glory.

XVIII

Some Rules for the Church

And we beseech you, brethren, to know them which labour among you, and are over you in the Lord, and admonish you.
—I THESSALONIANS 5:12

AFTER TURNING AWAY FROM THE PRACTICAL PROBLEMS WHICH had been suggested to him by Timothy, St. Paul summarized the general rules for church observance. He addressed his remarks to the brethren who represent the entire church, not some specific class. It is sometimes thought that verses twelve and thirteen are addressed to the congregation and refer to its relationship with the officers of the church, and that verses fourteen to twenty-two are addressed to the officers in relation to the congregation of the church. According to Paul, the church is one and there can be no distinction between the meaning of brethren in verse twelve and the meaning of brethren in verse fourteen. The individuals who are over the church in the Lord exercise their functions as representatives under the Lord. This is in contrast to the hierarchical view that the church consists of its clergy. By introduction, let us examine the threefold exhortation which pertains to the attitude of the congregation toward these officers.

Paul says, ". . . know them which labour among you, and

are over you in the Lord, and admonish you" (I Thess. 5:12). Their activity is described by the word *kopiao* which means to labor exhaustively or to toil.[1] Phillips translates it "work so hard." [2] These individuals represented by Jason and others made themselves responsible for the welfare of the new society. They consumed energy, time, and effort in their Christian leadership. There must always be some who take it on themselves to do the work of the congregation. There are multitudes of tasks in the operation of a Christian church. Some are spiritual, some are material, some are social. This very word describes Paul's own evangelistic labors among the Thessalonians (I Thess. 3:5), and his labors among the Christians (II Cor. 10:15). Such evangelistic labors take great energy from an individual.

Such persons were recognized as having authority, as being "over you in the Lord" (I Thess. 5:12). The word means to be a superintendent. If Paul followed the usual form of his activity, he ordained elders to carry on the work in the church before he left that church (cf. Titus 1:5). The early organization of the churches was simple, consisting of elders and deacons to whom were committed the spiritual and physical responsibilities of the congregation. Such officers were men who had displayed gifts and devotion in the work of the church and thus were selected for leadership and were subsequently ordained. Some commentators think it was too early at this time to find officers of the church. But we ask, Why? If Paul's doctrine was fully developed at this time, why should not also his organizational plan have been developed?

The assignment of these officers was to admonish. To the elders was assigned the great task of teaching, of warning, and of disciplining the congregation. Without these aspects of preaching the Word, of administering the sacraments, and of exercising discipline, there is no true church. Thus to know these officers means to be acquainted with them, to be affectionately disposed toward them, and to be obedient to their authority.

This is most fully expressed in the following verse which says, ". . . esteem them very highly in love for their work's sake . . ." (I Thess. 5:13). There certainly is honor among the brethren. The position of leadership must be recognized as honorable and must be respected as such. We ought never to treat the positions of leadership in the church in a light manner, nor should we elevate a novice to the position of leadership. But the highest recognition given to such persons is to be greatly loved by God's people. We are to "esteem them . . . in love" (*Ibid.*). This esteem, love, and honor constitutes the compensation or hire for their labors. These individuals work with no remuneration in their strenuous service for Christ, but they receive the satisfaction of doing God's will plus the love and esteem of God's people.

To the congregation Paul added, ". . . be at peace among yourselves" (*Ibid.*). Among them there were some, no doubt, who refused to submit to the authority and leadership of these officers and thus made for insubordination and for party spirit (cf. I Cor. 3:3,4). There certainly is a suggestion in this admonition that tensions may have already arisen which could have been between the workers and the idlers.[3] The result of such discords is to weaken the church, to leave it without power and without progress. The resentment of assumption of authority by some who also were from among the church is natural among many men. Often our church recruits men from among a class that is in the habit of being ordered around in business. When opportunity thus comes to express themselves, they will no longer let themselves be under authority but insist on having authority. However, Christian love and consideration for the good of the church should be sufficient to overcome this. Along with this attitude of the brethren toward those who are over them in the Lord is a body of instruction of the attitude of the brethren toward the general church members and toward the life of the church. In the following admonitions we find the rules about the problem children among the members, rules about the personal attributes of church members, and rules about public worship of the church members.

I. *The Problem Children Among the Members*

There always has been and there always will be some who must be warned and corrected and disciplined in a church membership. They are the disaffected, the offended, the jealous, the envious. Surely not all the remnants of the unconverted life are gone from church people. Sometimes these elements become more prominent after individuals are converted and express themselves in church life.

First, Paul says, ". . . warn them that are unruly . . ." (I Thess. 5:14). The word "unruly," *ataktos*, describes disorderly conduct among the Thessalonians. There were some who gave up positions and work in order to wait for the *parousia*. Hence, they became idlers, drones, burdens on the workers of the community. The word has been shown to describe those who have been truants from their work, who are guilty of absenteeism.[4] Such disorderly conduct destroyed the dignified, commendable, ethical life of the congregation by aberrations of character on the part of its members, resulting in discord and tension. Discipline must necessarily be exercised over such individuals. Today discipline is a lost practice in most churches. But in the same percentage that churches have abandoned the practice of discipline, they have also lost their witness to the purity of Christian life. The word "warn" may well be translated "reprimand" and those responsible for the life of a church were to reprimand such disorderly conduct.

Next Paul advises them to ". . . comfort the feebleminded . . ." (I Thess. 5:14). The word translated "feebleminded" actually means fainthearted or little-souled, not actually feebleminded. It describes the wavering, the halting, the hesitant, the wounded, the discouraged ones. Many were the things to discourage, to oppose, and to persecute the believers in those days, and some will always find themselves cast down. These fainthearted exist in every age of the church because of bereavement, of temptation, of obstacles, and of persecution. Perhaps we ought to say as an aside here that had the word actually meant feebleminded, we would still comfort them, for the feebleminded do seem to gather wherever the gospel is preached. Perhaps that is because they can understand it and the church has a duty to minister unto them. However, no premium is placed on feeblemindedness nor on feeble folk. At least their presence is a commentary that the preaching of the minister can be understood by those of low intelligence and, in a sense, that is a compliment. The great antidote for the faintheartedness of people is the fellowship of the believers. In unity there is strength. Today you may be stronghearted, but the day may come when your soul will be cast down and you will have little faith. Then you will stand in great need of the church.

Next Paul suggests that they ". . . support the weak . . ." (*Ibid.*). Thayer translates it, "hold to him firmly," [5] and Neil suggests, "put your arm round about them." [6] We must recognize that all of us are weak at some time or another. No one has ever reached the perfect ethic of Christ. Beware lest you find yourself weak when you think you are strong. Scripture has much to say about the weak brother being the touchstone of both our thought and our conduct (I Cor. 8:9-13; Rom. 14:1-23). One of the three primary rules of Christian conduct is *offend not*. Take heed lest you cause your brother to stumble. If that brother is weak, your conduct must never be such as to lead him into sin. On the other hand, we are required to bear one another's burdens and so fulfill the law of Christ. (Rom. 15:1-6). Finally, summarizing the attitude which the church member should have toward the problem children, he said, ". . . be patient toward all men" (I Thess. 5:14). The word "patience" is really great-heartedness and is the attitude to be manifested toward the foregoing classes, however provocative they may be in their actions. It is very easy to lose one's patience with the idlers, the fainthearted, the stubborn, the discouraged, the weak, but one of the manifestations of the spiritual life is patience (Gal. 5:22), and wherever love dominates the character, longsuffering, or patience toward others will be in evidence (I Cor. 13:4). God Himself is longsuffering to all of us who are believers, and even to the unbelievers, for He is not willing that any should perish (II Pet. 3:9; Rom. 2:4), and in so being patient and longsuffering, we are only like our Father which is in heaven. Had this advice been taken by all Christians, we would have had fewer divisions in the Christian church, which today is so tragically fragmentized in denominationalism.

II. *Personal Attributes of Church Members*

It is notable that these rules given by St. Paul are divided into three groups of four. The second four describe the high state of life approximating that required by the Sermon on the Mount. First, there is general benevolence. St. Paul said, "See that none render evil for evil unto any man; but ever follow that which is good, both among yourselves, and to all men" (I Thess. 5:15). This is a brief statement of the universal code of the Christian life as it is expressed in the Sermon on the Mount and in the practical section of St. Paul's Epistle to the Romans (Rom. 12:16 ff.). Retaliation and vengeance are prohibited in the Christian life. All vengeance is to be turned over to the Lord in whose superintending control, both by providence and by miracle, we have implicit trust. In this kind of action we follow the example and the teaching of the Lord Jesus, who when He was reviled, reviled not again. The uncooperative action and attitude of problem children of the church sometimes stimulate a reaction of retaliation. When it occurs, it is but a sad betrayal of the Christian life. Nevertheless, neither churches nor Christians are exempt from such retaliation. The rule is that we are to undertake to conquer our enemies, the world, and even hostile persons who may be in the Christian camp by pursuing the good which, according to St. Paul, is love. Ask ourselves, What does love dictate in this matter? Thus by following the absolute good, we overcome evil with good.

This high state includes good cheer. Paul declares, "Rejoice evermore" (I Thess. 5:16). The basis of such good cheer in the presence of tragedy, loss, disappointment, and trouble, which must be the lot of most people, is a faith in God who orders all things for good through His sovereign control over the world. It is only one who believes in God who can be of good cheer in the face of these difficulties. The Christian will often face suffering with joy because of his hope of future glory.

The rejoicing spoken of here is a blessedness, not a happiness which is so sought after by the world. Blessedness is the underlying current of a Christian disposition. Thus Peter could say, "Yet if any man suffer as a Christian, let him not be ashamed; but let him glorify God on this behalf" (I Pet. 4:16). Such a life is a benediction to all. Few even approximate such a standard. Each of us knows how woefully he has failed and to even project such a life on anything but a Christian standard would be utterly ridiculous.

Another manifestation of this high standard is glorious fellowship. Paul said, "Pray without ceasing" (I Thess. 5:17). This is an impossible standard if it means the vocal expression of petitions, praise, and intercession all through the day and all through the night. Paul himself didn't do this as his life work reveals. He was engaged in many activities, and yet he told others to pray without ceasing. One branch of Christendom has externalized this to enjoin certain priests to quote

"Pater Nosters" or "Hail Marys" without end. This cannot
be the meaning of the passage. The real sense is to practice
the presence of God in one's work, travel, conversation,
relaxation, and even sleep. He who knows the value of ejacu-
latory prayer in every exigency which arises knows what it
means to live in the presence of God, and it is also possible to
do everything as a sacrament, as being sanctified unto God.
Such a life is utterly impossible without seasons of real waiting, petitioning, praising, and worshiping God in order to
manifest and maintain this attitude.

The last characteristic of the high state is gratulation in
everything which happens. Paul said, "In every thing give
thanks . . ." (I Thess. 5:18). Thanksgiving is made parallel
to rejoicing in everything. One is to thank God even in bereavement, in persecution, in loss, and in trial. This reveals a
dependence upon God, a faith in His goodness, and a trust in
His wisdom. Such an individual does not believe that things
merely happen. He believes that a personal power is directing
the events that befall us. Such an attitude is far from fatalism,
which merely resigns itself to the blindness of inexorable fate.
Paul adds, ". . . this is the will of God in Christ Jesus concerning you" (*Ibid.*). God has a plan for every one of us who
is in Christ, and as that plan is being fulfilled, we are to be
thankful and to rejoice. Some day we will be like the plan
and will see the plan. Now it should be our most sincere
desire to be made conformable unto God's will.

III. *Public Worship of the Members of the Church*

Paul attacks the problem of public worship in the third
division of his rule. He introduces it by dealing with the subject of enthusiasm saying, "Quench not the Spirit" (I Thess.
5:19). The informal nature of the early Christian worship was
described in I Corinthians 14:23 ff. The Spirit played a very
important part in directing such meetings of worship. St.
Paul quite commended the fact that some of them came with

a Psalm, with a doctrine, with a tongue, with a revelation and with an interpretation, but he enjoined them that all should be done unto edifying. A real restraint should be placed upon speaking with tongues unless an authentic interpreter was present. Even the prophets who declared God's truth were to take their turn in speaking so that order might be observed.

The informality of this early Christian worship has had a heavy influence upon some groups who have reacted against formalism and have gone to extremes in their attempt to follow the leadership of the Spirit. As a result, enthusiasms and fanaticisms have developed which repel sincere or cultured persons. Hence, the impetus to quench all such individual expressions has manifested itself in the following of a set form of service. It should be said, however, that the Spirit must find it very difficult to break through some of these worship services which are so established.

The intention of St. Paul was to maintain a nice balance between order and the opportunity for the Spirit to work. The manifestation of the Spirit's workings is not to be despised nor is it to be courted. Let us not seek strange fire and let us take care not to dampen enthusiasm.

I think of my friend Dr. Martyn Lloyd-Jones, who has now preached for fourteen years in Westminster Chapel, London. He refuses to have any quartet or any prepared music and he has a very informal service, although it is attended by anywhere from one to two thousand people, because he wants to make room for the activity of the Spirit in the worship service. It would be well if more of us followed such an attitude in our greater churches.

In worship we must not despise prophesying. The essence of prophesying is not foretelling but forthtelling, namely, preaching. Some of it we admit is done very poorly, and all of us at times grow impatient with it. We say, Why all this preaching? Is it nothing but talk, talk, talk? God says it is the means by which His Word is made known and by which He is pleased to save souls. It is actually one of the highest gifts of the Spirit to the church (Eph. 4:11; I Cor. 14:3). Expository ministry today may be of a much higher order now that we have the completed revelation of God. In that day there was no written New Testament. It was just being developed and this was one of the first Books of the New Testament. Now one may be critical in a constructive sense because the Word is open to all. We should not put up with poor preaching. A word should be said, however, about the development and exercise of the ability of hearing well so as to discern God's truth and to grow in it. Those who criticize should do it with the analogy of Scripture which is now available. Thank God for a trained congregation such as this one which knows the art of hearing.

The standard to be applied in all worship services is "prove all things . . ." (I Thess. 5:21). In Corinthians St. Paul says that there is a gift of discerning of spirits. It is necessary to subject the claims of individuals to the collective conscience and judgment of the church. Psychotic individuals may thrust themselves upon us and infringe upon our liberty and our sanity. We must give them no place. The word "prove" is *dokimadzo*. It means to learn by experience and by trial. One soon recognizes the fakers and the dissemblers so as to be able to protect the church from them. When they are discovered, they must very speedily be disciplined. Never let the church lose her critical faculty when it comes to the matter of worship.

Finally, Paul declared, ". . . hold fast the good" (*Ibid.*). This is not the moral good but the genuine or the true. There is an old adage, "Do not throw away the baby with the bath." There is a tendency in social theory today to react against the welfare state and thus also to do away with many very beneficial social projects. The same tendency exists in the church. Because some have been fanatic and overenthusiastic, we quench and repudiate all such activities and thus lose some blessings of the Spirit.

Age-long practice or tradition has a great leveling experience. Men tend to cling to what has been approved. Sometimes they lean over backwards this way so that it is very hard for a man like John Wesley and his like to break through the traditions of the church. Those traditions are very good.

If we will accept the biblical standard as the means of testing the genuine and the counterfeit in every aspect of worship, we will be on safe ground. Then we may steer a middle course between the danger of quenching the Spirit and the danger of embracing that which is fanatic.

In conclusion, Paul presented an overall rule for the church by declaring, "Abstain from all appearance of evil" (I Thess. 5:22). This applies primarily to any charismatic practice which proves productive of evil in church worship. It must be interpreted in the light of the discussion in which Paul has been engaged. But we may really amplify it to embrace all that is really evil. It is a correct thing to say, Abstain from every form of evil or wrong. The appearance is not the emphasis here but the actual existence of evil, and from everything of such sort the church is to abstain. This is the ground for the true doctrine of the separation of the church from the world.

XIX

The Church's Doctrine of Sanctification

And the very God of peace sanctify you wholly; and I pray
God your whole spirit and soul and body be preserved
blameless unto the coming of our Lord Jesus Christ.

—I THESSALONIANS 5:23

ONE WOULD EXPECT THAT SOME SUCH DOCTRINE AS SANCTIFICA-
tion would immediately follow upon the general rules for the
church. Sanctification is the high state implied in the general
rules. Only an experience of intimate fellowship with God
would enable anyone to fulfill these rules. Who except the
sanctified can rejoice evermore, pray without ceasing, in
everything give thanks, quench not the Spirit, and abstain
from all appearance of evil?

The possibility of enjoying this quality of life depends
upon the experience of what the church has called sanctification. The very picture of this Christian character throws us
into a condition of conviction and realization of need. If the
previous teaching of St. Paul does not humble us, it is due to
our insensibility or else to a sense of achievement in the realm
of sanctification.

Holiness is the aim sought and desired as the result of redemption. The summary of the general rules for the church

is "Abstain from all appearance of evil" (I Thess. 5:22). This is the description of sanctification in the negative form of separation from evil. Such separation must have its place in the Christian life, but it must not be overemphasized. Our gospel is not a series of "Thou shalt nots." Holiness does not result from prohibitions. It comes from the sanctification of the entire nature of man resulting in holy desires, intentions, and affections, which is a positive doctrine. Holiness results from the subjection of the individual to the Holy Spirit who sanctifies rather than the subjection of the individual to the rules of conduct.

But how is the believer to enter this high state of holiness? It is not enough to hold the standard and aspiration of holiness before one. It is necessary to define the methodology of receiving the blessed experience of sanctification. Some people aspire and yearn for holiness all their lives and never attain to it. They live in a state of dissatisfaction. It befalls us, therefore, to examine this great teaching in the closing of this epistle which is directed to the infant church.

I. *The Meaning of Sanctification*

Paul said, "the very God of peace sanctify you wholly" (I Thess. 5:23). The term "sanctify" or *hagiadzo* is an action attributed to God. Just as the priest separated, consecrated, and hallowed an offering, so God sanctifies the believer. He sets him apart for Himself. The Psalmist declared, "But know that the Lord hath set apart him that is godly for himself . . ." (Psa. 4:3). Only God by His special grace could enable any man to fulfill these rules of church life. The preposition translated "very" actually is God Himself. He alone can do this work. The reference to peace may suggest the tensions which were developing in this infant church with the implication that if we worship God, we worship a God of peace and must live in peace.

Sanctification may be defined as "to purify internally by

reformation of the soul."[1] The noun *hagiasmos* means the sanctification of heart and life which is the effect of consecration. Thus when the individual is consecrated, he becomes sanctified. Paul adds to this the word "complete" translated "wholly." It means entire or complete sanctification which is perfect in all respects.

This state was desired by St. Paul for his new Christians. Lightfoot says that it "not only implies entirety, but involves the further idea of completion."[2] There can be no question but that this teaching deals with the most controverted subject of Christian sanctification unto perfection. Is such perfection possible? Am I to seek it? How shall I interpret my failures and my sins? What are the answers to these questions?

The church teaching on sanctification usually takes one of two forms, either the Wesleyan view or the Reformed view. The Wesleyan view treats sanctification as a term expressing full salvation or completeness of the Christian life. It is a synonym for entire sanctification. "Holiness in man is a moral or religious state; sanctification is a gracious work of God whereby that state is produced."[3] Sanctification begins in regeneration, which removes the corruption of our nature by an interior purification. This regeneration is sanctification begun, but it is incomplete in regeneration.[4] The actual Christian life is not immediately purified at regeneration.

Complete sanctification comes by a second blessing and may or may not be attainable in this present life. Most Wesleyans hold that it is attainable. Since the inner state is observed by the tempers, words, and acts of the believer, these must be effected by entire sanctification. Therefore, the completion of regeneration or the purification of nature occurs through the second blessing. This second blessing involves an eradication and destruction of the disordered affections in the regenerate individual, although some Wesleyans declare that it occurs by repression of the remnants of depravity, so that the disorderly affections yield to the dominance of the higher spiritual life. There is some division among the Wesleyans in reference to the means by which this entire sanctification occurs.[5]

The Reformed view defines sanctification as "Sanctification is the work of God's free grace, whereby we are renewed, in the whole man after the image of God, and are enabled more and more to die unto sin, and live unto righteousness." [6] Sanctification is the same work which is commenced in regeneration and it is wrought by the Holy Spirit. It is a work of God in which the believer cooperates by use of the means of grace placed at his disposal. It occurs over the believer's whole life and is never complete in this life but only at death. It consists of mortifying the old sinful nature and deeds by crucifixion and the quickening of the new nature unto good works affecting the whole man. The Reformed view may be differentiated from the Wesleyan in that there is no second work of grace but a constant process and it is never complete until death.

As we hear the exposition of these two views, the question arises, What is the biblical view? We derive these points of emphasis from the Scripture. It is essential that the believer be holy (I Pet. 1:16; Heb. 12:14). Holiness in the believer's position is obtained by him through justification. He is thereby declared righteous in sight of God and has a holy standing before God. In practice, holiness is begun by regeneration, which is the initial stage of sanctification. However, we must not overlook the fact that the Bible emphasizes an experience subsequent to regeneration in the Christian's life. One might declare that the apostles lived in a transition period and that when they believed on the Lord Jesus Christ, the Holy Spirit dispensation had not begun, all of which is true. The Holy Spirit came on the day of Pentecost to abide in the church, and no man can become a Christian without being baptized by the Spirit into the church of Jesus Christ. Nevertheless, experientially, the disciples had something occur in their lives subsequent to their personal committal to the Lord Jesus Christ which made a tremendous difference in their experience. It was their Pentecostal experience and it transformed the tenor of their lives. What was true in the case of these apostles and the larger group called "the one hundred twenty" was also true in the narration of subsequent characters in the Book of Acts. Stephen is designated as a man full of the Holy Ghost. Paul was acknowledged as a chosen vessel of Christ and he called Jesus Lord on the Damascus Road, but he was not filled with the Holy Ghost until Ananias came to lay hands on him. Simon, the Samaritan, and his fellow countrymen needed the coming of Peter and John that they in turn might lay hands on them so as to receive the Holy Ghost, for, in the ministry of Philip, He had fallen upon none of them. Cornelius, though a God-fearer and a believer in the truth with a very high ethical character, had a great experience when the Holy Spirit fell upon him and his household. Apollos, who believed on the Lord and who was ministering in Ephesus more than twenty years after Pentecost, had the way of God explained more perfectly to him by Aquilla and Priscilla. When Paul came to Ephesus, he found twelve disciples who had believed but who did not even so much as know whether there was any Holy Ghost, and these also received a subsequent experience. Examining the greatest theological treatise in the world, the Book of Romans, one finds that St. Paul similarly draws a clear distinction between justification from one's sins through the propitiation in Christ Jesus, which is described in chapters 1-5:12 of the Book of Romans, and the experience of sanctification which he describes from chapters 5:13-8:39. Unquestionably, St. Paul knew all the principles of the sanctified life as he declared them in the sixth chapter, but he autobiographically testified in the seventh chapter that he himself had not so entered that victorious and delivered life until Christ through His Holy

Spirit delivered him, as is described in chapter eight. Similarly, to these Thessalonians Paul wrote that he was ". . . praying exceedingly that we might see your face, and might perfect that which is lacking in your faith" (I Thess. 3:10). The implication of the Scripture is that the new Christian, having received the gift of salvation through faith in Jesus Christ, is not sufficiently instructed nor has he had sufficient personal experience to know what is entailed in a thorough consecration and complete surrender unto the will of God which will result in his sanctification. Therefore, this experience must be faced critically at a later time in his life.

The emphasis of Scripture is upon the inhabitation of the Holy Spirit, who does the purifying work in the individual. He comes to inhabit the believer at regeneration constituting him a new creature. It is possible for him to fill the believer immediately so that the new nature is in complete dominion over the old, but generally it does not so occur, and a believer must face a crisis in which he takes his position as crucified with Christ and subjects his old nature to Christ. He continues in this state only by a constant walk of fellowship. It is the Spirit who does the work. The work cannot be called eradication or suppression but inhabitation (Eph. 2:22). There is a state of Christian experience called spiritual which brings victory, fellowship, and satisfaction. God does not mock us with these yearnings (I Cor. 2:10-3:3; Matt. 5:7).

The time of sanctification should be pointed out. This great experience is initiated at regeneration by the Holy Spirit, who is given unto us (Acts 2:38; Eph. 4:22). Sanctification is enjoyed by consecration, yieldedness, and obedience to the Holy Spirit while we walk in this life. Sanctification is perfected so as to be immutable at our going to be with Christ. The mass of Christians may live in a higher spiritual state than they do now. As Paul said, "For ye are yet carnal . . ." (I Cor. 3:3).

II. *The Means of Sanctification*

Paul declared, ". . . I pray God . . ." and ". . . the very God of peace sanctify you . . ." (I Thess. 5:23). The means of sanctification according to Paul are threefold: first, prayer; second, God; and third, the self.

Prayer is essential for sanctification. St. Paul prayed for the sanctification of these Thessalonians. They were regenerated, but he wanted them completely sanctified in their experience and life. He held before them a much higher standard than they had attained. This was true also in his writing to the Ephesians (Eph. 1:15-19; 3:14-21). Similarly, Jesus prayed for the sanctification of His disciples and of those who should believe through their word. He said, "Sanctify them through thy truth. . . . Neither pray I for these alone, but for them also which shall believe on me through their word" (John 17:17,20). The burden of our prayers for our converts should be for their sanctification, meaning for their purification, preservation, and holiness. Moreover, we should pray for our own sanctification. Just as the disciples were taught to pray for the Holy Spirit who is the agent in sanctification, so we ought to do. Tarrying is often necessary until the obstacles to our sanctification are removed by our thorough consecration (Luke 11:13; 24:49). As they did, so we must do.

The second means of sanctification is God. Paul says, "God . . . sanctify you . . ." (I Thess. 5:23). Sanctification is the work of the triune God, but particularly the Holy Ghost is the agent and does the sanctifying. God the Father elects us unto sanctification (I Pet. 1:2). Jesus Christ the Son quickens us unto new life (Rom. 6:11). The Holy Spirit sanctifies us (Rom. 15:16). The abundant teaching of the Bible on sanctification is that the Holy Spirit must perform it. Therefore, we must understand the ministry of the Holy Spirit. A brief study of the work of the Holy Spirit as taught in Ephesians alone will show us that when we believe, we are sealed by the Holy Spirit (Eph. 1:13). If we do not obey the Holy Spirit, we grieve Him (Eph. 4:30). And we are to be filled with the Holy Spirit (Eph. 5:18,19).

The Holy Spirit uses the means of God's Word to convict, convert, warn, and induce to holiness. The Word of God gives all the objective standards of holy thoughts and acts. It, in conjunction with the ordinances of God, results in the sanctification of the soul.

Nevertheless, in the high priestly prayer of Christ, to which we have referred, He said, ". . . I sanctify myself . . ." (John 17:19). Jesus consecrated Himself, though He was already pure, holy, and absolutely sanctified, for the sake of His disciples and of the work which He was to do. In following His example, we too are to consecrate ourselves so as to be utterly separated and holy for the sake of God's people and God's work. This is an indispensable condition. Paul said, ". . . let us cleanse ourselves from all filthiness of the flesh and spirit, perfecting holiness in the fear of God" (II Cor. 7:1). Such self-sanctification, or separation from evil, or consecration unto God, or yieldedness bears an inestimable influence upon others for whom we are responsible.[7]

III. *The Manifestation of Sanctification*

Paul prayed in the text, ". . . your whole spirit and soul and body be preserved blameless unto the coming of our Lord Jesus Christ" (I Thess. 5:23). The realms of human nature affected by sanctification are the spirit, soul, and body or the whole man. These are to be holy. The very word "whole" modifying spirit is the Greek *holokleros* which is "ethically free from sin."[8] There are only two substances in the world, one is matter and the other is spirit. We have people who call themselves "materialists" and people who call themselves "idealists." These are monists, for they only believe in one substance. But Christianity is a dualism. It believes in matter and in spirit. Man is treated as body, soul, and spirit both in

the Old Testament (Gen. 2:7) and in the New Testament
(Heb. 4:12). A natural man, *psuxikos,* is contrasted to the
pneumatikos or spiritual man (I Cor. 2:14; 15:44-46). This
does not mean that man has three substances but that the soul
is used to embrace both spirit and soul sometimes and at other
times they are contrasted one with the other. "The spirit . . .
is the ruling faculty in man . . . through which he holds
communication with the unseen world." [9] It is God-consciousness. The soul is the seat of all affections and impulses and is
man's man-consciousness. The body links him to the material
world and is the instrument of his outward deeds. It is his
world-consciousness. Sanctification involves the whole man,
as is evinced by the words "holy" and "whole" and "blameless."

The result of sanctification upon man, therefore, is that he
becomes holy or blameless. This repetition of words to impress us with sanctification conveys the idea of faultlessness,
even though one of them may be ascribed to the spirit alone.
Whether one can live sinlessly or not depends upon one's
definition of sin. If sin is a voluntary transgression of the law,
we may be faultless. If sin involves ignorant transgression or
involuntary lack of conformity, then we cannot live without
sin. Let us reach for the blameless, holy state, even though it
may seem impossible of attainment. Let us not underestimate
the grace of God. Browning said, "Ah, but a man's reach
should exceed his grasp, or what's a heaven for?" [10]

Paul concludes by connecting this with the coming of the
Lord Jesus Christ. The doctrine of the coming and presence
of Christ in glory is never out of sight in this epistle. That
great event is here re-emphasized as he closes this work. It is
the desire of the Christian to be like Him when He comes and
to be pure as He is pure (I John 3:2,3; Rev. 22:12). This is
a mighty incentive to all believers to be holy when Christ
comes. When the believer shall be displayed as the redeemed,
as the son of God before the whole creation, which is the

meaning of "our adoption" (Rom. 8:23), then he will want to be holy and pure. Are we ready for this public acceptance of us as sons and our installation before the universe as God's heirs?

We are not without encouragement. Paul declared, "Faithful is he that calleth you, who also will do it" (I Thess. 5:24). God puts forward the standard, God creates the desire in us and God provides the means for us. He will not mock, disappoint, or frustrate us. God calls us now to sanctify ourselves by consecration, confession, and commitment that we may be holy both now and when He comes. God gives us the Holy Spirit to regenerate us, to fill us, to enable us to perform the work which He wants us to do. He said, "I will pray the Father, and he shall give you another Comforter . . ." (John 14:16). This Comforter is a divine advocate. This promise was fulfilled in His provision made on the day of Pentecost and His precept to us is to be filled with the Holy Spirit. What then will you do about your sanctification? ". . . work out your own salvation with fear and trembling. For it is God which worketh in you both to will and to do of his good pleasure" (Phil. 2:12,13).

XX

The Primary Responsibilities
of New Church Members

Brethren, pray for us. Greet all the brethren with an holy kiss. I charge you by the Lord that this epistle be read unto all the holy brethren. The grace of our Lord Jesus Christ be with you.

—I THESSALONIANS 5:25-28

BEAR IN MIND THAT THE PEOPLE TO WHOM ST. PAUL HAD written this epistle had been Christians but a very brief time. Their induction into the Christian church and its resultant fellowship was quite in contrast to their former life in the heathen community. They were converts of an evangelistic campaign that is thought by some to have lasted only three weeks and at most could not have lasted much longer than that. They had been Christians for only a matter of months at the longest, and their instruction had been of the most elementary sort.

The test of evangelism may well be centered on the permanence and the quality of life of its converts. To lead men to a decision to follow Christ is not enough unless it results in a total change of their lives. Decision is only the beginning of a Christian life. The validity of a conversion depends upon the regeneration of the whole disposition of one's nature. It must involve his understanding, his affections, and his volition. All else is but a temporary conversion. True conversion involves the entire man. Thus new converts must be directed into churches, into instruction classes, and into Christian service, which is essential for their stability. Without such fellowship, enlightenment and activity, new converts will soon backslide. There is a great casualty list among the converts of all evangelistic campaigns. People drift, stray, and fall back into their old ways of life because they have not been cared for by the church. Others become enmeshed in erroneous movements because their desire to do good has been perverted. Evangelism resulting in the loss of its converts may well result in more harm than good.

The travail of soul through which St. Paul passed until his converts were established is evidence of the importance he placed upon this matter. Earlier in this epistle he declared that they prayed night and day exceedingly that they might see the faces of their converts and perfect what was lacking in their faith (I Thess. 3:10). Similarly, Paul was so burdened over his Galatian converts that he said, "My little children, of whom I travail in birth again until Christ be formed in you, I desire to be present with you now" (Gal. 4:19,20). The Apostle had been compelled to depart very suddenly from Thessalonica, because of the riot which arose over preaching the gospel. The revival which had attended his ministry was suddenly interrupted and persecution followed and was maintained even after he departed. This was the cause of his intense burden over these converts. By his own testimony, he had tried "once and again" (I Thess. 2:18), to come unto them, but Satan hindered him. That hindrance in all probabilities was the persecution and opposition of his Jewish compatriots who had stirred up the riot in the beginning. As a substitute he had sent Timothy because he could stand separation from them no longer and could not bear to be in ignorance of their condition (I Thess. 3:1,2). Paul was determined that his evangelistic work should be followed up, if not by himself, then by someone else. The evaluation of a man's work in evangelism may well be his follow-up work, the attention which he gives to these converts after they have made a decision. There is a valid criticism that many churches take in members and then forget them or that evangelists get people to come forward to accept Christ and then no one follows them up. Whenever an evangelistic campaign is held, there is a great responsibility for those involved to follow up their converts that they do not stray, backslide, or become enmeshed in error.

The teaching which St. Paul so informally imparted in this epistle was intended to deal with the condition of these new converts. He presented the most simple, direct, courageous answers to the questions which they were asking and which had been relayed to him by Timothy. Hence, there is great value of this epistle to us. The topics we have used emphasize the basic nature of the epistle's teaching. Anyone who observes such teaching will immediately become different from non-Christians.

In these concluding verses of his epistle, St. Paul is stressing the reality of Christian life. Men who become Christians must seriously relate their Christian faith to all thought and life. One cannot live in a vacuum. He must constantly be asking the question, How does my being a Christian affect this relationship or that action? A new convert must begin to practice the presence of God, to take God into partnership with himself, to consider His will in all that he does. One may be a real person without sham, hypocrisy, and pretense and still be a true Christian. A new convert should seek such sincerity.

The Christian life entails certain responsibilities. One must know what to believe and how to live after he has made a committal and openly confessed Christ in baptism. The questions asked by these Thessalonian believers showed that they sincerely and intelligently sought to understand their responsibilities. The message of this first New Testament writing deals with the life of their converts in their pagan environment. The content of the epistle reveals the elevated quality of their lives which resulted from conversion. The epistle is therefore ended with these simple words requesting prayer, love, and Bible reading. It is almost an oversimplification of the responsibilities of a Christian, and yet it is almost exactly what we must tell our new converts when they embrace Christ. We urge them to pray, for that is a means of grace; to associate themselves with a church in order that they might have fellowship with Christians, to read their Bibles in order that God might speak to them and guide them, all of which is urged upon these Thessalonian converts by St. Paul.

I. *Pray for Your Ministers*

Paul declared, "Brethren, pray for us" (I Thess. 5:25). How much Paul had prayed for them and how much he was in constant prayer for all of his churches and converts is very evident from his constant affirmations of this practice in his epistles. This very epistle began with the words, "We give thanks to God always for you all, making mention of you in our prayers; remembering without ceasing your work of faith . . ." (I Thess. 1:2,3). Thus also he wrote to the Colossians (Col. 1:3), and to the Philippians (Phil. 1:3,4), and to the Ephesians (Eph. 1:15,16), declaring his practice of prayer. Ministers must pray for the sanctification of their people, both as a whole and by name when problems and particular needs arise. Ministers who do not pray for their congregations are only a semblance of what they should be. Robert Murray McCheyne was a great man of prayer who, though demitting this life early in youth, left a lengthening shadow over Scotland. During a journey to Palestine, his strength ebbed, but he neglected not his prayer life. "While the tent was being erected at the end of a day's arduous journey, he would lie down on the ground under some tree, completely exhausted by the long ride. After lying almost speechless for half an hour, when the palpitation of his heart somewhat abated, he would propose that his friend Andrew Bonar, who was also a member of the party, and he should pray together. Often, at the point of death in a foreign land, feeling his faculties going, one by one, with every reason to expect that he would soon be with his God, McCheyne devoted himself to prayer for his people. He wrote to them, 'When I got better, I used to creep out in the evenings about sunset. I often remembered you all then. I could not write, as my eyes and head were much affected; I could read but very little; I could speak very little, for I had hardly any voice; and so I had all my time to lay my people before God and pray for a blessing on them.' " [1]

The converse of ministers praying for their people is for people to pray for their ministers. Paul desired prayer for himself and his companions as servants of Christ, as ministers of the gospel, as missionaries of the cross, as teachers of the Word of God. Prayer must form a basic part of the Christian's life. A Christian cannot live without prayer. It is his very breath, it is the channel of divine blessing to his soul, it is his contact to the eternal and the invisible, and part of that prayer ought to be expressed on behalf of the ministers of the church, especially those who have brought and still bring spiritual blessing and life to the believers. When a convert prays for the minister who teaches and serves him, he is ultimately praying for blessing upon his own life.

It is of the Christian faith that prayer changes things. Prayer can release forces in this physical world and in the spiritual world. What blessings then may be prayed upon ministers. This I covet above all other blessings which could be bestowed by my congregation and friends, namely, an interest in their prayers. How much of protection from accident, from physical harm, from disease; how much of inspiration and spiritual power; how much of influence through open doors I owe to the prayers of God's people I shall never know until we get to glory, but I believe that such prayers have had a primary part in whatever usefulness I have known.

The ministry is dependent upon prayer. St. Paul was in particular need when he wrote this epistle. He had been beaten, he had been very greatly discouraged, and he had faced the satanic attacks through his fellow countrymen, and he knew that prayer would affect all of these realms. Paul often was in physical danger and needed the prayers of God's people for his deliverance. He could have died under any one of the five scourgings which he endured or the three beatings with rods, or the four shipwrecks, or at the hands of robbers, or through the hatred and plans of his own fellow country-men, but a divine providence superintended his life. In writing to the Romans (Rom. 15:30), he besought them for the sake of Christ and by the love of the Spirit that they would strive together with him in prayer that he might be delivered from them who did not believe in Judea and that he might ultimately come to Rome refreshed and ready to serve them. Paul had an intimation of the divine plans that he was to suf-fer, as he testified in Acts, saying, ". . . behold, I go bound in the spirit unto Jerusalem, not knowing the things that shall befall me there: save that the Holy Ghost witnesseth in every city, saying that bonds and afflictions abide me" (Acts 20:22, 23). The knowledge of these divine plans, however, was not held by St. Paul in a fatalistic way. He did not say, "I know that I must surely go to Rome, and therefore I have no need of any precaution or of any intercession; rather it was a lively, free acquaintance with the plans of the true personal God, which are fulfilled through the working together of the free actions of human beings." [2]

Paul was often in discouragement (II Cor. 1:3-10), and yet through the prayers of God's people, he was delivered from such discouragement and from the problems which beset him.

Paul often faced great spiritual battles when Satan attacked him, attempting to stifle the witness. This happened at Ephesus, at Corinth, at Thessalonica, and at Rome, but the prayers of God's people delivered him from such satanic activity.

The needs of ministers today are equal to those of the ministers of Paul's day. They have hindrances to their devotion, they have need of enlightenment and empowerment, they must be men of victory, of vision, of faith, and of courage. They must be used of God as soulwinners, as reformers, as teachers, and God's people should be praying for them for that purpose.

Our day is one of the most difficult days in which to serve the Lord Jesus Christ. There are physical dangers by flying through the air, by traveling on land and sea, there is the hostility of great atheistic forces and those engaged in the ministry of the Word, especially in travel and in foreign countries, stand in the need of our prayers.

There are many new currents of thought which would attack the minister's spiritual and intellectual life. He must be alert and awake to these currents of thought, but he must be kept from them by an intimate relationship to God.

The need of ministers for prayer is greater than for education, for material provision, for commendation or for human cooperation. Thus Paul says, "Brethren, pray for us" (I Thess. 5:25).

Ministers are transformed by prayer. I know of a case where a man was a minister of a great Presbyterian church and did not believe certain basic truths. His elders, instead of criticizing him or bringing him to trial, set their faces to God praying for him, and in a relatively short time the brother was brought around to a hearty embrace of these truths and became one of the most famous preachers of these particular truths in our generation. Just a few days ago I was told by an officer of a church where they had been having trouble with their pastor that the whole attitude in the church had changed.

They had had certain great problems about which to pray and the officers had been led to pray much about them. As a result, the whole attitude and outlook of the preacher had been changed so that now they had harmony, sweetness, and light where before there was conflict. I received a letter from a woman who had complained about the fact that her pastor had not been preaching the gospel or been interested in evangelism, so she testified how she and a group of other people had formed a cottage prayer meeting to pray for her minister, and her church, and her community. Before long the minister became interested, attended the prayer meeting, became taken up with evangelism and the whole attitude of the community had changed under his influence. God wrought by prayer.

When churches languish under failing ministers, they can be transformed by the prayers of the people. Great is our responsibility to pray for Christian workers, for missionaries, for teachers, for ministers that they fail not, that they fulfill their ministry, and that they find the power of God available for all the demands made upon them. Once again we say with St. Paul, "Brethren, pray for us" (*Ibid.*).

II. *Love Your Fellow Christians*

St. Paul said, "Greet all the brethren with an holy kiss" (I Thess. 5:26). The word for kiss in Scripture is *filema* and is derived from *filos*, meaning love. A kiss then is a token of love. It is not derived from *eros* meaning passionate love nor from *agapas* meaning divine love but from *filos*, the fondness of one person for another. Paul joins the word "holy" with the word "fondness" and thus unites the Christians' spiritual fondness one for another within the Christian church. Let us distinguish this from the kind of holiness which was ascribed to an individual like Rasputin who became a holy devil. The word holy can never be united with passion. It is said that there was a time when this accusation was made against the

Christians[3] and that thus the practice of the holy kiss was discontinued.

The word was used to describe the action of the woman who washed Jesus' feet and covered them with tokens of her fond gratitude for what He had done in forgiving her sins. The word is used to describe the wicked betrayal of Judas in the Garden of Gethsemane when he gave a token of intimacy in kissing Jesus. Evidently Jesus and the disciples had used this kiss of greeting, so that it would not be out of place for Judas to so greet Him in the garden. It was the witness of fellowship among believers, and it has been continued by the Russian church unto this day. We substituted shaking hands one with another in greeting, although women quite generally express their greeting with a kiss. Let that handshake and that greeting be sincere. If one feels not the heartiness of the greeting, let it not be expressed, for then it would take upon it the nature of a Judas kiss.

This symbol manifested the affectionate fellowship of Christians one for another. Such affection is emphasized in Scripture, especially in the teaching of Jesus. He declared, "This is my commandment, That ye love one another, as I have loved you" (John 15:12), and "By this shall all men know that ye are my disciples, if ye have love one to another" (John 13:35). In recalling Jesus' teaching, John declared, ". . . this is the message that ye heard from the beginning, that we should love one another. We know that we have passed from death unto life, because we love the brethren . . ." (I John 3:11,14). Love is the evidence of a transformed nature. It is not normal to human beings, but when a man has been transformed by God's grace and there is engendered in his heart a love for Christ, this also leads him to love others who love Christ and whom Christ loves. A critical, censorious attitude toward fellow Christians is evidence of an unregenerate heart. The full effect of such love upon society is beyond computation. It is Christian love, one for another, which has spanned the barriers that separate men and established true altruism in human relationships. It is love that leads men to identify themselves with others in need, to minister in the name of Christ, and to serve their fellow men.

Love of the brethren is a mark of the true church of Jesus Christ. It was said of the early Christians, "See how they love one another." Tradition tells us that when John was an aged man and was carried into his pulpit to preach, all he could say was, "Little children, love one another." By this test of Christian love for our fellow Christians, men truly will know that we are followers of the Lord Jesus Christ.

III. *Read Your Bible*

Paul said, "I charge you by the Lord that this epistle be read unto all the holy brethren" (I Thess. 5:27). St. Paul put these men who received his epistle under a Christian oath to read this epistle to all the members of the church at Thessalonica. Scripture is instructive for all people. It is a source of life for the believer. It is our heavenly manna, our food, the source of our strength. It is not for the mind only but for the soul, for in the Scripture God speaks to our souls. The Scripture is the written Word, just as Christ was the incarnate Word. They knew Christ by hearing Him, seeing Him, and handling Him. We can know Him through the Word of God as it is quickened by the Holy Spirit to reveal God to us.

The Word is the standard of our knowledge of the truth about the world, about God, about man, about sin, about salvation, and about Christian life. Christian doctrine is derived from the Word or the Scripture, a beginning of which was given in this epistle of St. Paul.

To the Scripture the Christian goes for succour in temptation, trial, doubt, uncertainty, and need. There is no situation in life in which the Scripture will not give us guidance. Paul intended that his writing should answer the problems of sex, of death, of work, of authority, of attitude among the brethren. That writing will still illumine our pathway.

Scripture is inspired and authoritative. This epistle was the first of thirteen epistles written by St. Paul. There is utterly no doubt about the authenticity of the first epistle to the Thessalonians. It is admitted to the canon of Scripture by all parties. When Paul ordered that it be read, he was initiating a practice that later became general. Seven of Paul's epistles are universally admitted to be genuine and authentic Scripture. Some questions are advanced about six of his epistles, but generally the church has even accepted these.

After the writing of I Thessalonians, Paul wrote his second epistle to Thessalonica, then the two letters to Corinth, then the letter to Galatia, then to Rome, then to Philemon, then to Colosse, then to Ephesus, then to Philippi, then the first epistle to Timothy, then the epistle to Titus, and then the second epistle to Timothy. All of them bear true Pauline marks and give us the great body of teaching for the church of Jesus Christ.

Full authority is claimed by St. Paul for his own writing in this very epistle, for he commended them that ". . . when ye received the word of God which ye heard of us, ye received it not as the word of men, but as it is in truth, the word of God, which effectually worketh also in you that believe" (I Thess. 2:13). Peter says of the writings of St. Paul, ". . . in which are some things hard to be understood, which they that are unlearned and unstable wrest, as they do also the other scriptures, unto their own destruction" (II Pet. 3:16).

Scripture is to be read by all believers. Paul said, ". . . read unto all the holy brethren" (I Thess. 5:27). The elders of the Thessalonian church were to read the Scripture publicly and also from house to house so that all the holy brethren could hear them. Public reading of the Scripture had to be sufficient then for the Bible was not complete and there were only copies which could be made by the laborious process of writing them out by hand. It had been very difficult to get Scriptures into the hands of the common people until the art of printing was invented, but a personal reading of the Scripture is now within the reach of every man. There is no excuse for our not studying it. Today the Bible is published by the tens of millions of copies every year, but there is a difference between it being the best seller and it being the best read book. We are entering an age when the deficiency of scriptural knowledge is such that even to refer to the Bible is not understood on the part of many people. A minister must explain his reference so that people can understand the story for they are not familiar with the background of Scripture. Yet Christian life must depend upon a knowledge of the Word.

New converts then must be urged to a private reading of the Bible for devotional study and for information as essential to the health of the soul as well as to the edification of the church. Converts will become established as they pray, as they have fellowship with other Christians and as they come to know the Word.

This basic epistle to the church is concluded with the words, "The grace of our Lord Jesus Christ be with you" (I Thess. 5:28). Grace is the source and sum of all other blessings, and it flows to us through the Lord Jesus Christ. One could wish no greater blessing upon anyone than the grace of God. Nevertheless, God's grace comes to the Christian through the means of grace, namely, through prayer, through church fellowship, and through the Word of God. Let every Christian be careful to observe these means of grace.

XXI

The Church in Tribulation

So that we ourselves glory in you in the churches of God for your patience and faith in all your persecutions and tribulations that ye endure.

—II THESSALONIANS 1:4

A FEW DAYS AGO A STUDENT AT WHEATON COLLEGE WROTE A letter asking, "Will the church go through the tribulation?" This subject is in the forefront of controversial thinking and writing at the present moment. My answer is, yes, and no, as we shall see.

You are a member of the church and you must pass through tribulation. The tribulation of a believer may be of many kinds, but it is inevitable. Sometimes it arises from marriage. Sometimes a person's tribulation arises from illness and from physical pain. Few of us are spared all pain through our entire lives and we must be ready for such tribulation. Sometimes tribulation comes from social or mental conditions. What nightmares the fearful, the psychotic, the ostracized have passed through in their lifetime.

Will you have patience in the tribulation which befalls you? Patience may be translated "heroic endurance." In conversing with a woman on the subject of tribulation, I received this response: "I am not made of that stuff, so I am glad I haven't been called on to suffer as the early Christians were." It was her opinion that she could not pass through that kind of suffering, but one cannot know in advance what patience or endurance he may have. God does not permit us to be tempted above what we are able. Experience proves that a special grace is given to us in accordance with our need. That was essentially true of the early Christians. Our tribulations are often the result of the freedom God has granted to us as men. That freedom implies the possibility of choosing contrary to God's will. That choice has been made by man who has revolted against God, has sinned, and has set in motion much suffering in the world.

It is faith which will enable you to meet such tribulation. When you give mental assent to the sovereignty of God, acknowledging His existence and that He has given freedom to man, for He feared not the results of that freedom, being able to overrule evil for good, you have the intellectual preparation for faith. In such a background, acceptance of tribulation as the result of sin working in all realms of human activity is rational. Such tribulation becomes a magnificent training ground for the development of character, and the man of faith receives from God's hand that which comes to him through the selfishness, impatience, jealousy, and hatred of men. The man of faith knows that someday God will strike in judgment, but now He withholds His wrath for the purpose of giving man a chance to repent and to receive forgiveness in Christ. Such faith that God is and rewards them that diligently seek Him is able to sustain one in tribulation.

I. *The Church Must Go Through Tribulation*

The biblical teaching declares that the church will suffer tribulation. Think of the persecutions of this Thessalonian church. It was born in the midst of persecution and tribulation. After the departure of Paul, which was caused by such persecutions, their sufferings were intensified and became so stringent that they confused them with the great tribulation to come before the great and terrible day of the Lord. The introduction to this Book in the Scofield Bible says: "The Thessalonian converts were 'shaken in mind' and 'troubled,' supposing . . . that the persecutions from which they were suffering were those of the 'great and terrible day of the Lord,' from which they had been taught to expect deliverance by 'the day of Christ, and our gathering together unto him'." The hostility and persecutions by the enemies of the gospel must have been very severe. This in fact was the reason for the second letter to the Thessalonians written within so short a time of the first letter.

Critical study leads us to believe that this second epistle to the Thessalonians was written by Paul and his companions, Timothy and Silas, from Corinth to Thessalonica within a few weeks, or at the most months, after he had written his first letter. Actually, there are the same writers, the same situation, the same church and the same time. (For critical questions, see the *International Critical Commentary* by Frame, and the *Moffatt Commentary* by Neil for a summary of critical thought of the last century.)

In this epistle Paul apparently is more formal than he was in the first epistle. Instead of bursting with joy over the faithfulness and love of the Thessalonian Christians, he now uses formal words such as "We are bound to thank God always for you, brethren, as it is meet" (II Thess. 1:3; 2:13). Some claim that there was a slight rift between St. Paul and the Thessalonian church, that the relations between them had become strained, that what was incipient when he put them under an oath to read his epistle to all the holy brethren was now in the open. Actually, instead of being overformalistic here, it was a recognition of an imperative to give thanks unto God for their abounding faith and love. The same kind of expression is used in Philippians 1:7 and it means "it is more than you deserve." [1] The great reason why some have thought that Paul did not write the second letter to the Thessalonians is that it defers the day of Christ until certain observable signs have taken place, whereas the first epistle implied the immediacy of that coming. When one understands the factions that were in this church, namely, the workers and the idlers, and that it was essential for Paul to impress upon these idlers that the coming might be deferred for a long time so that they would get to work, we have an understanding as to how he could have written both epistles. He also had to deal with another group which was disposed to receive teaching which would shake the church from its faith as though it were from St. Paul, although it possibly was a forgery. This accounts for the difference in emphasis.

The Thessalonian church may well be a pattern for other churches. As it was warned of the inevitability of tribulation and persecution which came to pass in fact, so the whole church is warned ". . . that we must through much tribulation enter into the kingdom of God" (Acts 14:22). In the apostolic era, such persecution was almost universal. Hence, Jesus said to His disciples, ". . . In the world ye shall have tribulation . . ." (John 16:33). Tribulation is to be expected when the entire life pattern of people becomes changed and they break with their cultural surroundings. How could it be otherwise? The people in contact with them most certainly will persecute them. Persecution is to be expected when the kingdom of darkness is shaken to its foundation, as it was through the preaching of those early apostles. Actually it was Christianity which overthrew pagan Rome. It planted a seed of culture which was diametrically opposed to the integrating principle of the Roman Empire and finally it so weakened the Empire that the Empire fell. This was the stronghold of paganism and emanating from it was the satanic opposition centered against these little cells of the church which were the foundations of a future Christian culture. It is to be ex-

pected that persecution will be a measure exercised against the
church all through its history, but we are not to expect it in
eras of great influence of the church with the intensity with
which a non-Christian culture would react to the Christian
message and way of life as in the first century.

The historic fact is that the church has been persecuted in
all of the great eras of its history. It was born in the midst of
persecution. The first persecution broke in Jerusalem when
the Sadducees rejected the message of the apostles and singled
out Stephen as a test case. He was condemned and stoned,
creating the incident which loosed the antipathy and hostility
of the Jews against the early church in Jerusalem. Thus the
Christians were scattered abroad from that Jerusalem concen-
tration.

Fortunately, Christianity was considered a subdivision of
Judaism for the first thirty-five years of its history. Judaism
had won a respect in the Roman Empire as an ancient national
religion and was tolerated by the Romans.[2] Hence, Christianity also was tolerated as a sect of the Jews until after St.
Paul's trial in Rome in probably 63 A.D. Following that, it
was recognized that Christianity was not a sect of Judaism
but was a new religion universal in its appeal and claim.
Therefore, the Roman emperors recognized that they could
not tolerate it as they could tolerate an ineffective pagan deity
or some non-evangelistic religion that was strictly national.
Thus there ensued a period of persecution which lasted from
64 A.D. to 313 A.D., during which some ten waves of persecution are identified, but seven major persons figure in the
decrees bringing about that persecution.[3]

The first was Nero. On July 19, the year 64 A.D., Nero
commanded Rome to be burned. Tacitus, the most respectable
historian connected with that era, lays the blame directly at
the door of Nero and exonerates the Christians.[4] Nevertheless,
the accusation was made that the Christians burned Rome
and since the Roman populace was indignant over this act

of vandalism and was ready to believe almost anything, it turned against the Christians and Nero caused many of them to be arrested and tried. There they freely confessed Christ, refused to worship the emperor, declared the doctrine which they believed and as a result were declared to be contrary to all men. Therefore, the Christians were rounded up and put through the most terrible period of suffering that human ingenuity could devise. They were inhumanly thrown to the beasts in the arena to satisfy the bloodthirsty desire for amusement of a debased populace. Young girls were gored by bulls. Strong men were tied to the stake, covered with oil or rosin and then burned alive while Nero drove his chariot through the Vatican gardens by the illumination of these burning persons.

From Nero to the time of Domitian, the Christians had some respite although they were considered an illicit sect. Then Domitian (81-96 A.D.) toward the close of his reign, also proscribed them, declaring them worthy of banishment and death. In this persecution many Christians died, others had their property confiscated and were exiled. Probably during this period John the Beloved was banished to Patmos, where he wrote the Book of Revelation. Evil persons everywhere denounced their enemies as Christians, especially if they were Christians, in order that they might have a part in the confiscation of their estates.

Trajan who reigned from 98 to 117 A.D. at first was favorably disposed toward the Christians, but when the issue arose in the Eastern Provinces and he received the request from Pliny for a decision as to what he should do about those who practiced this "depraved and immoderate superstition," he replied that they should not be sought out, but when accused and convicted, they should be punished.[5] Consequently, another wave of persecution broke over the Eastern Provinces of Rome. It was during this period that Ignatius was seized, sent to Rome in irons, and thrown to the beasts in the arena, where after a few moments nothing remained of him but a few bones.

The next great period of persecution came under Marcus Aurelius from 161 to 180. The Roman Empire was struck by catastrophes in the form of floods, earthquakes, and pestilences which gave rise to the belief that the Christians had caused this, and bloody persecutions were launched against them, especially in Gaul. There very famous martyrs became known and large numbers of Christians were put to death.

In the year 249 Decius became emperor and promulgated an edict for all men to return to pagan religion under the heaviest penalty. This became the signal for the widest, most cruel, and devastating persecution to that date. It spread over the whole Roman Empire and Christians everywhere paid for their confession with their lives. Following him, after three years, came Valerian who decreed the death penalty to all Christians. Then a period of respite occurred from the year 260 to the end of that century, but the pagan forces of the Roman Empire gathered their strength and struck under Diocletian in the year 303, which became the greatest and the final spasm of hatred of demonic powers against the Christian religion. Philip Schaff says, "All former persecutions of the faith were forgotten in the horror with which men looked back upon the last and greatest: The tenth wave . . . of that great storm obliterated all the traces that had been left by others." He goes on, "All the pains which iron and steel, fire and sword, rack and cross, wild beasts and beastly men could inflict, were employed to gain the useless end." [6] Finally, it was seen that Christianity could not be conquered by persecution and, under Constantine, it became a legalized religion.[7]

What occurred during these two-and-one-half centuries occurred again during the time of the Inquisition, this time under a professing church. The Protestants, or so-called heretics, were put to death by the tens of thousands in the most cruel ways that the human mind could invent, including auto-de-fes, slow burnings, the rack, crucifixion, decapitation, etc. Torquemada in Spain killed thousands. The Duke of Alva in the Netherlands put to death over 60,000 people in a few months. The Medici in France perpetrated the St. Bartholomew's Day massacre in which tens of thousands of Huguenots perished. The then so-called Christian church stopped at nothing to stamp out the revival of New Testament Christianity which was occurring in the name of Protestantism.

The persecutions did not end then. Our modern day has revealed that human nature is capable of producing the same persecutions and tribulations for the Christians. During the Nazi reign, Christians were put through all manner of tribulation when they would not submit unto the authority of the state. Pastors of Germany were incarcerated in labor camps and mistreated until death overtook them.[8] In Communist Russia millions of Christians were left to die by starvation by being denied food and shelter or were banished into Siberia. In present Communist China Christians are again being herded into camps, into prisons, and into places of execution. No, the church of Jesus Christ has not ceased to endure tribulation.

What is the expectation of the church for the future? Strange as it may seem, some Christians expect to escape all tribulation. They adopt the futurist interpretation of Revelation, which identifies the suffering of the saints under the anti-Christ with the suffering of the Jews after the church is taken to be with Christ (Rev. 13). Surely if these Thessalonians had identified their suffering with those sufferings of the tribulation before the great and notable day of the Lord come, as the introduction to the Scofield Bible declares, then Paul would have disabused them by informing them that the church was not to pass through and to suffer in the great tribulation to come. If it is not so to do, Paul was morally responsible to declare that teaching, but, rather than that, he gave them signs by which they would know when that notable day of the Lord should come. This certainly suggests to us that God has no pets among His children, and if He allows the church to suffer in one age, He may allow it to suffer in any age as well as at the end time. We have no guarantee that we will not suffer at the hands of men, but we have the guarantee that we will not suffer at the hands of God when His wrath is poured out at the end time. When Jesus described the great tribulation at the end time, He declared that it would have to be shortened for the elect's sake. We do not hold that these elect are identified with the Jews but that they are identified with the believers, the children of God, the members of the church. Therefore, we hold that the wrath of men under the anti-Christ may very well be poured out on the church of Jesus Christ at the end time (Matt. 24: 15-28).

II. *The Church Will be Delivered from the Wrath of God*

This epistle has in mind the coming of the Lord Jesus Christ. The reference to the day of Christ (II Thess. 2:2) is a reference to the day of the Lord Jesus Christ, which identifies what interpreters often divide, namely, the day of Christ and the day of the Lord. Some interpreters say that the day of Christ is the day in which He comes for His church and that the day of the Lord is when He returns for judgment. There is a difference of perspective in reference to the coming of our Lord Jesus Christ. One is the expectation by the church of its rapture or its being caught up to be together with Christ. The other is the expectation of judgment which falls upon the ungodly, but there is only one coming of our Lord Jesus Christ, not a whole series of comings. A widespread practice divides these two aspects of the coming as the topics of the two Books of Thessalonians. The coming of the Lord for His church is affirmed to be treated in I Thessalonians and the coming of the Lord in judgment to be treated in II Thessalonians. A seven-year period is placed in between these two during which time the anti-Christ appears, the great tribulation occurs, the Jews preach to the world, a multitude is saved, and then judgment begins. Such an interpretation could by no means be drawn from this second epistle to the Thessalonians. It is far more probable that the primary impression is that the day of the Lord Jesus Christ applies both to the gathering together to Him of the saints and to the coming of Christ in judgment.

Paul even identifies the events before the day of the Lord and our gathering together unto Him occurs. He speaks of "a falling away" (II Thess. 2:3). This is a repudiation of Christianity and of Christ by the professing church. Whether it could be partially identified in Paul's day or not we do not know, but certainly in our day such a falling away has occurred in what is called "modernistic Christianity," which repudiates every basic doctrine of the faith and is ". . . another gospel which is not another . . ." (Gal. 1:6,7).

Paul also says that this day will not come until the ". . . man of sin be revealed . . ." (II Thess. 2:3). This man of sin is anti-Christ. He must come before this end. The church, according to this Scripture, is not to be taken until he appears. Evidently the anti-Christ will appear while the church is still here and not after its gathering unto Christ.

Paul also points out that this day will not come until "he who now letteth will let, until he be taken out of the way. And then shall that Wicked be revealed . . ." (II Thess. 2:7,8). Some affirm that this is the Holy Spirit who will be taken away and that these events cannot occur until the Spirit is taken away. It appears to us rather absurd that God will do after the Holy Spirit is removed from earth what He was not able to do during the dispensation of Holy Spirit power. This we hold cannot refer to God's Holy Spirit. The early commentators thought that it applied to the Roman emperor,[9] but the meaning of this teaching is not altogether clear.

Another limiting circumstance is the "strong delusion" (II

Thess. 2:11) which God will send that they might believe a
lie "because they received not the love of the truth, that they
might be saved" (II Thess. 2:10). This has been identified by
some with the doctrine of evolution and by others with communism, but its identification is also questionable and may yet
be future in appearance.

These things will precede the revelation of the wicked one
". . . whom the Lord shall consume with the spirit of his
mouth, and shall destroy with the brightness of his coming:
even him, whose coming is after the working of Satan with
all power and signs and lying wonders" (II Thess. 2:8,9). The
divine judgment shall fall upon the anti-Christ and those
who believe his lies. They "shall be punished with everlasting
destruction from the presence of the Lord, and from the
glory of his power; when he shall come to be glorified in
his saints, and to be admired in all them that believe . . ."
(II Thess. 1:9,10). No believers will be caught in this out-
pouring of the divine wrath.

The church's comfort in reference to that future tribulation
rests in its expectation to be gathered together with Christ.
Paul opens this description of the anti-Christ by saying, "Now
we beseech you, brethren, by the coming of our Lord Jesus
Christ, and our gathering together unto Him, that ye be not
soon shaken in mind . . ." (II Thess. 2:1,2). It is very clear
from these two epistles that the believers are to be delivered
from God's wrath (I Thess. 1:10; 5:12; II Thess. 2:1). This
does not teach that the church shall escape the tribulation
under the anti-Christ. There is no word of Scripture that tells
us that we believers will be delivered from the wrath of men,
but we most certainly will be delivered from the wrath of
God. God did not save us to pour His wrath out upon us.

The destiny of the church is to be gathered together with
Christ, to be caught up into the heavenlies and to forever be
with the Lord (I Thess. 4:17; II Thess. 2:1). This includes
both the dead and the living saints, the dead to be resurrected

and the living to be transformed and together to be caught up with Christ in the clouds. At that time will come the celebration of the wedding feast of the Lamb. Herein the groom, which is Christ, and the bride, which is the church, will be united and will celebrate their union. The conjugal union of man and wife is used in Scripture as the figure of this mystical union betwixt Christ and His church which will be maintained forever (Eph. 5:25-27). Following this rapture and union with Christ, the church is to descend with Christ to judge the world. (This is the so-called mid-tribulation rapture.) Meanwhile, upon those who are on earth will be poured out the wrath of God described in this epistle, in the Book of Revelation and in many passages of the Old Testament. If the dead saints are to be resurrected and united with Christ in glory, there is no reason why the dead unbelievers should not also be resurrected and suffer this wrath of God, which will be poured out at the end time.

The conviction which enables the church to withstand persecution and tribulation is this expectation of God's coming. As for the Thessalonians, their persecution and their expectancy of the imminence of the Advent made them think that it was useless to attend to the things of a doomed world. Thus they gave up their work. This is a severe error, but it is not confined to the Thessalonians. It has appeared several times in church history and it is rearing its head today. I know of a high-school student in Boston who will not go on to college, despite the pleas of his parents, because he believes that our society is now doomed to another war and it is useless to study any farther.

The preachments of Paul were intended to counteract the two tendencies and to impart balance to these believers, so that the doctrine of the coming of Christ would sustain them in their tribulation.

We too may be persuaded that we will never suffer the wrath of God and that this conviction will be sufficient to enable us to endure the wrath of men. Polycarp, a student of John the Beloved and elder of the Ephesian Church, was born in 66 A.D. He was martyred in 155 A.D. in the most cruel fashion by being burned at the stake and yet the entire testimony given concerning his martyrdom is that he apparently felt no pain. God has a way of counteracting the evil intentions of men.

III. *The Church Will Manifest Her Witness in the Tribulation*

Paul rejoiced in their patience in tribulation, speaking of it as ". . . a manifest token of the righteous judgment of God, that ye may be counted worthy of the kingdom of God, for which ye also suffer" (II Thess. 1:5). In Christian teaching, a value is placed on suffering for the sake of the kingdom. We are told, ". . . if so be that we suffer with him, that we may be also glorified together (Rom. 8:17); that ". . . our light affliction, which is but for a moment, worketh for us a far more exceeding and eternal weight of glory (II Cor. 4: 17); and that "if we suffer, we shall also reign with him . . ." (II Tim. 2:12). Thus many of the early Christians sought what was called "the crown of the martyrs" or "a better resurrection." They had almost a morbid interest in dying for Christ's sake. Thus Ignatius, a father of the church, sincerely sought martyrdom and when he was apprehended, tried and condemned to death, he rejoiced that he was to receive the martyrs' crown. In 115 A.D., he was sent to Rome and thrown to the beasts, where within a few moments his entire body was consumed. Paul speaks of their being "counted worthy" (II Thess. 1:5) when under suffering for Christ. The apostles themselves when they suffered for Christ's sake at Jerusalem rejoiced that they were counted worthy to suffer shame for His sake (Acts 5:41). Thus the Christians in the periods of martyrdom of the church have always counted it a great honor to suffer for Christ's sake. Paganism could never break that spirit.

In the midst of this, God vindicated His righteousness to which Paul refers as ". . . a manifest token of the righteous judgment of God . . ." (II Thess. 1:5). When persecution came, they grew in faith and they abounded in charity. They enjoyed the fellowship of suffering. Paul had prayed that he might ". . . perfect that which was lacking in your faith" (I Thess. 3:10), and that they might ". . . increase and abound in love one toward another and toward all men . . ." (I Thess. 3:12), and now through their tribulation his prayer was answered, for their ". . . faith (grew) exceedingly . . ." (II Thess. 1:3), and ". . . the charity of every one of you all toward each other aboundeth." (*Ibid.*) This also is evidence that God strengthens His people for the demands which are laid upon them.

They had victory over external circumstances so as to become a boast unto all churches. What a witness was theirs in the midst of tribulation and persecution. If a newly elected church could meet tribulation thus, so can the church with a historical record of the martyrs and the confessors behind it. It need not fear such things as persecution or tribulation. It will not fail, even when Satan makes his last great attack at the close of this dispensation.

St. Peter wrote his first epistle about the time of the Neronian persecutions in Rome. Out of them he wrote these words: "Beloved, think it not strange concerning the fiery trial which is to try you, as though some strange thing happened unto you: but rejoice, inasmuch as ye are partakers of Christ's sufferings; that, when his glory shall be revealed, ye may be glad also with exceeding joy. If ye be reproached for the name of Christ, happy are ye; for the spirit of glory and of God resteth upon you: on their part he is evil spoken of, but on your part he is glorified. But let none of you suffer as a murderer, or as a thief, or as an evildoer, or as a busybody in other men's matters. Yet if any man suffer as a Christian, let him not be ashamed; but let him glorify God on this behalf" (I Peter 4:12-16).

XXII

The Triumph of the Church

When he shall come to be glorified in his saints, and to be admired in all them that believe (because our testimony among you was believed) in that day.

—II THESSALONIANS 1:10

EVERYONE WANTS TO BE ON THE WINNING SIDE. THIS IS TRUE in athletics. Recent bribery and corruption revelations in reference to college athletics have demonstrated what individuals as well as organizations will do to be on the winning side. Schools spend thousands upon thousands of dollars to turn out winning teams. They scour the country for prospective athletes who will enable them to be on the winning side.

People want to be on the winning side in politics and will often make great compromises in order to be there. It is a frustration to always be voting on the losing side, as some have done for nearly a quarter of a century in this country.

In economics people want to win out in the struggle of life, so that they can enjoy some of the good things of this world. They pursue happiness in the possession of certain material things. It is a natural desire to be on the winning side.

The destiny of the church of the Lord Jesus Christ is to win in the struggle in which it is engaged. It has a glorious future. Its triumph is secure. The church may be persecuted and under tribulation now, but it will not always be under persecution. These words concerning the triumph of the church were written by a persecuted man to a persecuted church, and yet his eye was not on the present, but on the future. The rule of this present world is under the prince of darkness, so that the righteous suffer. But that order will some day be reversed. The struggle of the church against evil is only a temporary struggle, and its victory is to be complete. This is the assurance which is given to a suffering church to sustain it in the midst of its trials.

Paul emphasized that the members of the church are made worthy of the kingdom by their suffering for Christ's sake. This prepares them more adequately to enter into the glory of the future kingdom. Hence, Paul urges them to relax, to rest, to wait in the faith that the denouement of the kingdom will bring the reward of the saints and the punishment of evil doers. Just as tribulation produces tautness, the experience urged here and described as "resting" is the relaxation of the bowstring after its use. Relax, for the settlement of the affairs of life does not come now. The sufferings of the church and of the Christian will be avenged by God. Let us take an eternal view and, with the sense of an historical perspective, relax even in the midst of tribulations and of suffering. The ultimate reward of the righteous and the punishment of evil doers is assured.

Many are the descriptions of the church's triumph contained in Scripture not the least of which is this passage in II Thessalonians. This is the description of Christ's kingdom when He comes in power and in glory. It is the climax to the history of the church of Jesus Christ. It is a concomitant of His coming in glory and majesty to set up His eternal kingdom.

At this time believers will be exhibited as the sons of God, the heirs of the kingdom, and the rulers of the world. When

Octavian was sixteen years of age, he was designated by Julius Caesar as his successor. At nineteen he was in command of an army and was away from Rome. At the hands of Brutus, Cassius, and other friends, Julius Caesar was assassinated. Octavian had not received the public adoption by Julius as his son and heir. Therefore, he had to fight his way to the sovereignty of the empire.[1] The old Roman practice of public adoption of one to become a successor and heir illustrates what will some day take place for the sons of God. They will be publicly declared God's heirs and will be vested with glory and sovereignty. This is referred to in our text.

Accompanying this great event will be the execution of judgment upon the wicked who have resisted God's authority, have persecuted God's church, and have disobeyed God's law. In the midst of their present tribulation, Paul urged them to lift their eyes unto the final outcome of the struggle of good and evil in the form of the triumph of the church.

I. *The Day of the Revelation of Jesus Christ*

This triumph of the church will occur ". . . when the Lord Jesus shall be revealed from heaven with his mighty angels, in flaming fire . . ." (II Thessalonians 1:7,8). This is a description of the second advent of Christ. He will come from heaven. John says, "And I saw heaven opened, and behold a white horse; and he that sat upon him was called Faithful and True, and in righteousness he doth judge and make war . . . And he hath on his vesture and on his thigh a name written, KING OF KINGS, AND LORD OF LORDS" (Rev. 19:11,16). The Lord Himself described this advent in the words, "For as the lightning cometh out of the east, and shineth even unto the west; so shall also the coming of the Son of man be . . . then shall appear the sign of the Son of man in heaven: and then shall all the tribes of the earth mourn, and they shall see the Son of man coming in the clouds of heaven with power and great glory" (Matt. 24:27,

30). Heaven is where Jesus is now at the right hand of the Father. Heaven is the place to which the spirits of redeemed men go at death. Heaven is the place from which Jesus will come in glory and power.

That advent will be attended by the angels. They are described as the angels "of his power" (II Thess. 1:7). The Authorized Version calls them "his mighty angels." The emphasis is on the ministers of the divine power. In this coming, the omnipotence of God is emphasized. The Lord Jesus said, "The Son of man shall send forth his angels, and they shall gather out of his kingdom all things that offend, and them which do iniquity; and shall cast them into a furnace of fire: there shall be wailing and gnashing of teeth. Then shall the righteous shine forth as the sun in the kingdom of their Father . . ." (Matt. 13:41-43). The angels attended every great step in the redemptive process and they will be in great evidence at the coming of Christ in glory.

Christ is described as coming "in flaming fire" (II Thess. 1:8). This first of all, according to interpreters, bespeaks His glory. When the angel of the Lord appeared unto Moses calling him to be the deliverer of Israel, it was in a flame of fire. The conversation ensuing demonstrated that this angel of Jehovah was God Himself or an appearance of the Lord Christ before the incarnation. In like manner He appeared unto Manoah and did wonderfully, for His name was Wonderful. In such glory He appeared unto His disciples on the Mount of Transfiguration. To this Peter later referred when he said, "For we have not followed cunningly devised fables, when we made known unto you the power and coming of our Lord Jesus Christ, but were eyewitnesses of his majesty. For he received from God the Father honour and glory. . . . And this voice which came from heaven, we heard, when we were with him in the holy mount" (II Pet. 1:16-18). That coming will be visible, glorious, personal, catastrophic, and final. It is the second advent of Christ.

Preceding this will occur the summons to His saints. We have seen in the first epistle to the Thessalonians that He shall descend from heaven with a shout, with the voice of a trumpet, and the dead in Christ will rise first and then they which are alive and remain unto the end shall be caught up together with Him in the clouds. This summons precedes the glorious manifestation unto the whole world. It is part of one great process which is called the second coming, but in order of events it occurs first. The saints are changed, transformed, glorified, and caught up together with Christ in the air (I Cor. 15:51,52). The order of the series of events which occur as concomitants of the second coming is debatable. The dispensationalists declare that seven years occur between the rapture of the church and the revelation of Christ in flaming fire to take vengeance upon those who know not God. In the interim, a great tribulation occurs and the anti-Christ is revealed. The historic creeds declare that the rapture and the revelation of Christ occur practically simultaneously. It seems from Scripture that some time must ensue between the gathering of the saints with Christ and the conclusion of the era in judgment of the wrath of God. There are certain events foretold in Scripture, such as the conversion of Israel, which must occur at that time. We ought not to be dogmatic about the time element in reference to this great event.

A suggestion is involved in the different words which are translated "coming" or "presence" of Christ. The first word is *parousia*, which means presence of one who is coming, hence, his advent. In the New Testament it refers to the visible return from heaven of Jesus to raise the dead. In a real sense we may say that Christ is present now and the *parousia* is so used, and yet it also refers to His ultimate coming. Some confine this to His coming for His church.

A second word is *apokalupsis*, which means a visible appearing. It is used of events by which things, or states, or persons hitherto withdrawn from view are made visible to all. It is a public manifestation. Peter declares that at His coming Christ's glory shall be revealed, and Paul declares that we wait ". . . for his Son from heaven . . ." (I Thess. 1:10), that is, His revelation.

A third word called *epiphaneia* which means appearing, not only that by which His saving presence and power appears in this generation, but also that illustrious return of Christ from heaven in glory (II Tim. 4:1-8; Titus 2:13). The words *epiphaneia* and *apokalupsis* are joined together in II Thessalonians 2:8, so that His visible appearing results in His actual presence in this means of judgment.

II. *The Day of Tribulation for the Ungodly*

Paul says He shall come "In flaming fire taking vengeance on them that know not God, and that obey not the gospel of our Lord Jesus Christ: who shall be punished with everlasting destruction from the presence of the Lord, and from the glory of his power" (II Thess. 1:8,9). This bespeaks judgment of certain individuals with punishment.

That judgment will occur at the coming of our Lord Jesus Christ is evident. The fact is that wicked men shall be judged, wrongs shall be righted, man shall suffer for his misdeeds. Moral reason demands this if we live in a moral universe. Revelation declares this (Rom. 2:16; Acts 17:31; Hebrews 9:27). That judgment will be determined by Christ, for all judgment is committed to Him. He describes Himself as sitting upon His throne and sitting in judgment upon all men.

The form of judgment will be in flaming fire. The phrase which describes the glory of Christ's coming is also applicable to the judgment which falls upon unbelieving men. Christ Himself spoke of a place where their worm dieth not and their fire is not quenched. Hence, this flaming fire refers both to the glory of Christ and to the mode of vengeance. The Old Testament descriptions of the day of the Lord, as in Isaiah 2 and 13, make evident that this judgment will be one of fire, (whether it is a figurative fire or a literal fire we cannot say).

The force of this enabled St. Paul to exhort them to love, to deeds of faith because of an ultimate vindication. All through Scripture the exhortation of the writers is to fret not because of evil doers (Psa. 37), to be not moved when the wicked flourish as the green bay tree (Psa. 73), and to be un-movable in righteousness in the light of our future glory. The end of the wicked is established. They walk now in slippery places. They will be judged (Psa. 1).

The classes to be judged are here described by St. Paul. They are those ". . . that know not God, and that obey not the gospel of our Lord Jesus Christ" (II Thess. 1:8). The first class consist of the heathen who have not heard the gospel but who reject the light of general revelation. That which may be known of God (Rom 1:21), they have rejected. The accusation of their own consciences (Rom. 2:14), they have quenched. The light which lighteth their hearts (John 1:5), they have refused. They are guilty before God and hence they know Him not. They shall be judged by God in accordance with the test which is given to them.

The second class consisted of the Jews and Gentiles who have heard the gospel and who refuse to obey it. They ". . . obey not the gospel . . ." (II Thess. 1:8). Whenever a man hears the gospel and he refuses it, he loses his opportunity for salvation. He awaits only the judgment of God. Evil doers may come from either class, those who know not God and those who obey not the gospel. They came from both classes in Thessalonica and they have come from both classes all through the history of our age.

The punishment of these persons in judgment was destruction from the presence of the Lord and from the glory of His power. Destruction does not mean annihilation, but it means being ruined for that for which they were made. An automobile may be destroyed without being annihilated. So a man may be destroyed as an object of the glory of God, but he is not annihilated. Hence, these are described as crying for the rocks to fall on them to hide them from the wrath of the Lamb. Their punishment is not to be remedial punishment as is evident from this Scripture, but they are to have everlasting destruction from the presence of the Lord. It gives no hope of reconciliation and restitution. Not all of God's punishments are remedial, although some are. There is to be a retributive justice when all chance is gone and when the judged will be forever lost.

Their judgment is described as separation from God (II Thess. 1:9). They will be God-forsaken. They will be away from the presence. This is a terrible punishment. It is to be banished from God forever and to endure the pains of remorse, of memory, and of positive punishment. They also shall witness a loss of glory. Having seen the glory manifested in the sons of God, they will have a full realization of the loss which has come to them through their unbelief.

III. *The Day of Reflection of the Glory of God in the Saints*

Paul declares that Christ is coming ". . . to be glorified in his saints, and to be admired in all them that believe . . ." (II Thess. 1:10). The saints shall share the glory and triumph of Christ. They will attend Him in His glorious advent. Jude declares He shall come with ten thousands of His saints, and when heaven opens and the Son of man comes forth as a rider on the white horse, He shall be attended by a great host wearing garments of white. The saints will share His power, His authority and His glory. They also will share in the judgment of angels who are reserved unto the judgment of that great day. Having been gathered together with Christ, having been glorified, having been united with Him, as the bride is to the bridegroom, they now will share in His authority and power.

Christ will come with them to be admired in them by the whole creation. Unless the Lord is glorified in us now, He can hardly be glorified in us when He comes. Therefore, the process which precedes glorification is regeneration, renewal, and transformation, so that we may reflect Christ, His mind, His Spirit, and His way of life in us.

When He comes to achieve sovereignty over the universe and to reign, we shall reign with Him (II Tim. 2:12). We shall be glorified with Him (Rom. 8:17). This is the promise which is given to those who suffer with Christ.

Christ shall come to be glorified in the saints. Here His power to save through conviction, through conversion, through changing lives, through producing new character and works of righteousness will be demonstrated and acknowledged. He will be glorified. If in the day of Christ's coming our converts will constitute our glory and crown of rejoicing (I Thess. 2:19), how much more will the purified, glorified, transformed church without spot or wrinkle glorify Christ's saving power (I Cor. 1:9). In that hour the saints will be made like unto Him. Having been predestined to be conformed to the Son of God (Rom. 8:29), we shall be like Him (I John 3:2). The Holy Spirit will have completed His work of transforming us from glory to glory into the image of Jesus Christ (II Cor. 3:18). That of which we have had the earnest in the presence of His Holy Spirit will have been completed in the redemption of our bodies (Rom. 8:23).

This is the consummation of the divine redemptive purpose to lead many sons into glory. The decrees of God embrace the process of creation, the permission of the fall, the incarnation, the redemption through calvary, and the restoration of these fallen but repentant sons into glory. They will share the being and the glory of God. The development of this process throughout history has been challenged at every step by Satan. He will challenge every step of it in our own lives through temptation, tribulation, and persecution, but there is victory for us. At the denouement of the kingdom of glory, those who believed, obeyed, suffered and were persecuted shall share in the glory of the kingdom.

All this is contingent upon the exercise of faith. Paul says, ". . . because our testimony among you was believed . . ." (II Thess. 1:10). This involves a decision. When the gospel was offered to them, they believed it with an active committal. When Christ comes, the difference between our being glorified with Him and admired or our being judged as those who obey not the gospel will depend upon our response to the gospel. When you are faced with the gospel, your eternal destiny is at stake in the response that you make.

The deeds which follow this decision will demonstrate our faithfulness. The heroic endurance of the Thessalonians was the result of their faith. Paul speaks of their faith and patience because of this expectancy of the coming of the Lord. Their vindication was not to take place in the day in which they lived, but in the day of the Lord Jesus. Then they would be declared worthy of the kingdom for which they had suffered and which they awaited.

Their destiny was determined by their attitude toward the testimony of the gospel. As it was then, so it is now. Do you believe? Will you share in the triumph of Christ? Are you a member of the militant, mighty, marching army of God's church? If you share not with His suffering now, you shall share not with His glory hereafter.

XXIII

Worthy of Membership in the Church of Christ

Wherefore also we pray always for you, that our God would count you worthy of this calling, and fulfil all the good pleasure of his goodness, and the work of faith with power: That the name of our Lord Jesus Christ may be glorified in you, and ye in him, according to the grace of our God and the Lord Jesus Christ.

—II THESSALONIANS 1:11,12

THE TEXT CONSTITUTES ONE OF THE INTERJECTED PRAYERS OF St. Paul which occur several times in this epistle. This prayer follows his teaching concerning the tribulation of the church and the triumph of the church. After dealing with these great truths, Paul demonstrated his interest in the present experience of Christian truth and blessing known by the Thessalonians by saying, "to this end" (II Thess. 1:11). His prayers were directed to the end that the Thessalonians might be prepared to share the triumph of Christ in that day because they had believed the testimony of the apostles when it was given. The next prayer of Paul in this epistle says, "Now our Lord Jesus Christ himself, and God, even our Father . . . comfort your hearts, and stablish you in every good word and work" (II

Thess. 2:16,17). His third prayer says, "And the Lord direct your hearts into the love of God, and into the patient waiting for Christ" (II Thess. 3:5), and his last prayer is, "Now the Lord of peace himself give you peace always by all means. The Lord be with you all" (II Thess. 3:16). The fact of the inevitable coming of judgment connected with the day of the Lord and the revelation of the Lord Jesus Christ stimulated these prayers of St. Paul. He knew that these Christians would come before the Lord in judgment, and his earnest solicitation was for their being acceptable in that day.

I. *Judgment of the Believer by God*

Paul prayed ". . . that our God would count you worthy of this calling . . ." (II Thess. 1:11). The verb *axiose* means to judge worthy and it implies a judgment. There is a great truth often overlooked by Christians, namely, that the church will be brought into judgment. This is thoroughly consistent with the biblical teaching that "there is therefore now no condemnation to them which are in Christ Jesus . . ." (Rom. 8:1). We are specifically told that ". . . the time is come that judgment must begin at the house of God . . ." (I Pet. 4:17). Christians as members of the church most certainly will be judged by God. We do not refer to the chastening which the Lord gives unto us now, but to the time when the Christian must stand before the judgment seat of Christ (II Cor. 5:9). In that judgment there most certainly will be condemnation to those who have done things worthy of condemnation. A Christian who lives on in sin is one who has a false hope and may even have a false confidence, so that he may not be a Christian at all. Those who live in sin (I John 3:9) will be revealed as mistaken, as having a false hope, as being deluded concerning their salvation.

The time of that judgment is explained by Paul as "in that day" (II Thess. 1:10). It is the dispensational view that we as Christians will be judged immediately following our death.

That is what is called *bema* or judgment seat of Christ. For many sound biblical scholars, it is questionable whether there is more than one judgment day. The day referred to here is the day of the revelation of the Lord Jesus Christ, and it is hard to believe that the reference to judgment of believers is not to that same day of the Lord. The deeds of our lives will reveal the faith of our souls. We shall not be judged for what happened before our conversion, but we most certainly will be judged for what happened after our conversion. Our works must reveal our faith and judgment will always be of works.

The test or the criterion of that judgment is "this calling" (II Thess. 1:11). What is your calling? It is the divine summons to repent, to believe, and to obey as children of God. It is referred to in the second chapter of this very epistle in the words, ". . . God hath from the beginning chosen you to salvation through sanctification of the Spirit and belief of the truth: whereunto he called you by our gospel, to the obtaining of the glory of our Lord Jesus Christ" (II Thess. 2:13, 14). Our calling is most certainly to walk worthy of being children of God in holiness and purity and service. How does that calling come? By the gospel of our Lord Jesus Christ. Those who hear and believe are effectually called. The Westminster Confession of Faith defines effectual calling as "the work of God's Spirit, whereby convincing us of our sin and misery, enlightening our minds in the knowledge of Christ, and renewing our wills, he doth persuade and enable us to embrace Jesus Christ, freely offered to us in the gospel." [1] Calling comes by God's Holy Spirit attesting the truth of the gospel in our hearts.

Wherein we have fulfilled this calling will be the essence of the test. Paul enjoins us to ". . . walk worthy of the vocation wherewith ye are called" (Eph. 4:1). The investigation at judgment will be made as to our worthiness of this great privilege and position. What a joy it will be to be declared worthy, to be justified by God not only because of what the

Lord Jesus Christ has done for us, but because we have
walked pleasing in His sight.

II. *Provision for the Believer by God*

Paul prayed that God would ". . . fulfill all the good
pleasure of his goodness, and the work of faith with power"
(II Thess. 1:11). The inner desire for goodness on the part of
the believer is described by the phrase "good pleasure of his
goodness." Holiness, virtue, and goodness should be the objectives for which we strive because of God's call. We must
endeavor to be like Christ, to be righteous, to be absolutely
good on earth. So many of us forget that the Beatitudes describe the character of a Christian. The hunger for such goodness should mark every Christian heart. The closer we get to
God the more we ought to aspire to such goodness and the
greater our deficiency ought to appear, but "Blessed are they
which do hunger and thirst after righteousness: for they shall
be filled" (Matt. 5:6). When such yearnings are absent in
self-satisfaction, we are indeed spiritually cold. The great
saints were those who ever sought to new heights of holiness.
Hope is held out for us that we might attain to a measure of
realization in this goal. By self-crucifixion, by seeking the
glory of Christ, by serving, we may find that we have marks
of achievement toward the goal of holiness. Because the
absolute perfection of goal seems impossible, it ought not to
frustrate us in the seeking of the goal.

When the inner desire for goodness is present, the outer
works of faith appear. Inevitably the inner spiritual condition
affects the outer manifestation of life. The springs of all
action are of faith, but the existence of faith is evidenced by
works. Such works can never justify, produce goodness, or
win merit, but they reveal the state of our faith. The great
heroes of the faith were always revealed by the works which
they performed. Each hero in the roster of Hebrews 11 is

described by some work of faith. Thus also our faith will reveal itself in works.

Paul adds that God will fulfill this inner desire for goodness and these works of faith in power. Thus God Himself is the source of fulfillment by filling His people with the Holy Spirit. Only the Spirit can bring a true satisfaction for these yearnings of heart and a strength to perform the labors of faith. Thus we work out our salvation according to Him who worketh in us to will and to do of God's good pleasure. God's Spirit is the means of this power. Universally through Scripture, power attended the ministry of the Holy Spirit. Thus if God is going to enable us to fulfill the yearning of our heart or the aspirations of our soul and also to perform the works of faith, it must be by being anointed with the Holy Spirit. Power belongeth unto God, and if the Holy Spirit is given unto us, then we may experience power as the children of God. God's power is thus available for all who will appropriate it by fulfilling the conditions of being filled with the Holy Spirit.

III. *The Witness of the Believer for God*

The result of this prayer by St. Paul is that "the name of our Lord Jesus Christ may be glorified in you, and ye in him . . ." (II Thess. 1:12). The consequence of yearning after holiness and of performing good works is to become more and more like Jesus Christ. An unconscious transformation into His image is wrought by the work of the Holy Spirit (II Cor. 3:18). The inward man becomes renewed by God's Holy Spirit so that his intentions, purposes, desires, affections, and disposition are changed (II Cor. 4:16; Eph. 4:22). God is glorified by our good works, and if we live in uninterrupted good works, we glorify our Father who is in heaven (Matt. 5:16; John 16:8). Men who see these good works recognize that the source of inspiration is God and they glorify Him.

Unless Christ is glorified in believers, He will not be glorified in this world. We are His portion or His inheritance. Thus we must glorify Him before men. There is a comparison here between the way we glorify Christ and the way Christ glorified the Father when He was on earth. In His high-priestly prayer He could say, "I have glorified thee on the earth . . . glorify thou me . . ." (John 17:4,5).

The reference of St. Paul is again lifted, however, to the day of the revelation of Jesus Christ. He is speaking about the coming of Christ in glory and our glorifying Him in that day, just as we have been glorifying Him now. That will be the day of the redemption of our bodies (Rom. 8:23; I John 3: 2,3). The return of the Lord Jesus will bring this glorification to all who have been worthy of their calling (II Thess. 1:8-10). "When he shall come to be glorified in his saints, and to be admired in all them that believe . . . in that day" (II Thess. 1:10). There is a direct relation between our glorifying Christ here by our works and our glory with Him in that day. Paul said that if ". . . we suffer with him . . . we may be also glorified together" (Rom. 8:17).

There is a combination of His glory and our glory in that day. The power of Christ to redeem will be exhibited and admired in all them that believe, and this will be to His glory, but it will be by means of glorifying His servants. What a demonstration of the triumph of the church that will be!

All such worthiness of membership in His redeemed church is of the grace of God. Paul said, ". . . according to the grace of our God and the Lord Jesus Christ" (II Thess. 1:12). Here is grace that is greater than all our sins. It is grace that is able to make us pure within. By this grace we shall be made like unto God Himself.

XXIV

Apostasy in the Church

Now we beseech you, brethren, by the coming of our Lord Jesus Christ, and by our gathering together unto him, that ye be not soon shaken in mind, or be troubled, neither by spirit, nor by word, nor by letter as from us, as that the day of Christ is at hand.

—II THESSALONIANS 2:1,2

THE TENDENCY OF THE CHURCH TO BE SHAKEN, MOVED, DIS- turbed, and deflected from its purpose and objective and to become discouraged by fears, tribulations and false expecta- tions is noted by the Apostle Paul. It was not confined to the Thessalonian Church. The church is easily shaken today.

The situation at Thessalonica calling for this second letter was due to their unbalanced interest in the second coming. Unauthorized teaching from some who professed to be apostles, either by their verbal preaching or by written letter or by supposed attestation of the Spirit of God in them, moved the church from its stability. There is not a little of such teaching today. Men profess authoritatively to tell the details concerning the second coming of Christ and thus pervert the faith of individuals. An unstable condition resulted in that church. If we believe that Christ is coming in a day, or a week, or a year, the question inevitably arises, Why should we build for the future? Recently, the sons of an elderly Christian gentleman wrote me urging me to intercede with him not to give all his money away on the ground that Christ was immediately coming. Since he is already well advanced in years and physically strong, they were afraid that he would not have sufficient substance to keep him during his advanced years. Motivated by the thought of the imminence of the coming of Christ, he was making large gifts of the substance which he possessed.

In dealing with these aberrations in the Thessalonian Church, Paul did not deny the second coming of Christ but affirmed it as the ground of their stability. He said, "Now we beseech you, brethren, by the coming of our Lord Jesus Christ, and by our gathering together unto him" (II Thess. 2:1). The coming of the Lord is the basic doctrine of these two epistles. The catching up, or gathering out, or rapture of the saints is here reaffirmed as concomitant with that coming of the Lord. Yet Paul was deeply concerned that they should rightly understand that coming and that rapture. Literally translated, he said, "I beseech you in behalf of the coming." He wanted them to understand its real meaning. His following teaching was upon this subject to clarify it and to remove all chance of becoming a means of instability for the church. Heed should be given by modern prophetic students to this exhortation lest overconcern with the second coming produce an instability in Christian conduct and attitude.

In clarifying the doctrine of the second coming, Paul foretold the precursors of that event. His emphasis was that they should not be shaken ". . . as that the day of Christ is at hand" (II Thess. 2:2). There is a very great danger of instability from overemphasis upon the imminence of the day of Christ. Deceptive measures have arisen as a result of this, and men have been shaken in their faith. No difference exists between the day of Christ and the day of the Lord. Some would translate this the day of the Lord and make it refer to the time of the vengeance of Christ rather than to His *parousia* or His gathering of His people unto Himself. A distinction between these two is read into this passage. It is simply not here. The reference is to the day of the Lord Jesus Christ. The meaning of day does not change from what it was in the first chapter and the tenth verse.

Therefore Paul delineates the events which must occur before that day of the Lord Jesus Christ comes. These are truly signs for which the church must look so that that day shall not take us unaware (I Thess. 5:4). That day shall not come except four things occur. There will be an apostasy or a falling away from the faith. There will be the appearance of the anti-Christ. There will be anarchy in government. There will be the advent of great and widespread delusion, which will be sent by God Himself. Here we will deal only with the first of these signs, namely, the apostasy.

I. *The Condition Called Apostasy*

Paul said, ". . . except there come a falling away first . . ." (II Thess. 2:3). The word apostasy may be defined as "a falling away, a defection." [1] If there is a falling away, there must be something from which one has apostatized. This implies a rejection of the content of Christianity as it was given to us in its incorporation papers, namely, the New Testament. The content of New Testament Christianity may easily be determined by reading these incorporation papers, namely, the New Testament. They declare that Christ was pre-existent, became incarnate, was uniquely divine, performed miracles, lived sinlessly, claimed to be equal with God, made atonement for our sins by shedding His blood, rose from the dead, and ascended to the right hand of the Father. There He exercises authority and power in His mediatorial kingdom. The content of such teaching concerning Christ is contained in I Corinthians 15:1-3. According to these papers, Christians are made by a committal of faith, a trust in the person of Christ which results in regeneration and a new life. The characteristics of such a life are given to us in the Beatitudes, which show the difference between a believer and the world. The church itself is a supernatural organism composed of such redeemed believers. It is not a club, or a society, or a reformation of the world; it is Christ's body, the redemptive agency of God in the world.

The Christians of the first century who wrote these books so understood Christianity as they had received it from the Lord Jesus Christ. If they were wrong, where will we find the true meaning of Christianity? Will we turn to tradition? Will we turn to some oral statement before the incorporation of the tradition in the New Testament writing? Will we go to history? There simply is no place to go if we abandon the content of the writings of the New Testament. The creeds of Christendom confirm this content of Christianity. Those ecumenical creeds are accepted by the church universal.

In spite of all this, four or five decades ago there was a widespread revolt against Christianity which repudiated this biblical content and produced a new content for Christianity. It consisted of a deliberate rejection of revealed truth by willful men who misled a whole generation of people while professing to be Christian teachers and leaders. In the March 12, 1952 *Christian Century*, a recent graduate of Union Theological Seminary, William Hordern, wrote an article entitled "Young Theologians Rebel." This article declares that a new revolt is on against the liberalism of the previous generation of theologians. The argument is that the last generation rebelled against biblical Christianity, but this generation is rebelling against modernism and is returning to orthodoxy.

We do not imply that reality of faith is inconsistent with holding some error concerning the truth, which position may be due to ignorance or deception. This is not a deliberate rejection of Christian truth and can be corrected, but apostasy

cannot be corrected. It awaits judgment. Concerning apostasy
the writer of the Book of Hebrews has said, "For it is impossible . . . if they shall fall away, to renew them again
unto repentance; seeing they crucify to themselves the Son
of God afresh, and put him to an open shame" (Heb. 6:4,6).
Such apostasy from the faith will bring divine judgment.

There are many texts in Scripture which describe apostasy.
Paul said, "For the time will come when they will not endure
sound doctrine; but after their own lusts shall they heap to
themselves teachers, having itching ears; and they shall turn
away their ears from the truth, and shall be turned unto
fables" (II Tim. 4:3). Peter declared, ". . . there shall be
false teachers among you, who privily shall bring in damna-
ble heresies, even denying the Lord that bought them, and
bring upon themselves swift destruction. And many shall follow their pernicious ways . . . These are wells without
water, clouds that are carried with a tempest; to whom the
mist of darkness is reserved for ever" (II Pet. 2:1,2,17). Jude
said, "For there are certain men crept in unawares . . . denying the only Lord God, and our Lord Jesus Christ" (Jude 4).
And Paul wrote to the Galatians, ". . . there be some that
trouble you, and would pervert the gospel of Christ. But
though we, or an angel from heaven, preach any other gospel
unto you than that which we have preached unto you, let him
be accursed" (Gal. 1:7,8). These individuals according to
Paul were ". . . false brethren unawares brought in . . ."
(Gal. 2:4).

Illustrations of such apostasy were given to us in the Scripture. The Jews hated, persecuted, and tried to put St. Paul to
death because they accused him of causing their brethren to
apostatize from Judaism. (Acts 21:21.) In a very real sense
Paul had apostatized from Judaism and the accusation was
correct. Among Paul's own followers was the case of Hy-
menaeus and Alexander who made shipwreck of the faith (I
Tim. 1:19,20), also Demas who forsook the faith, having

loved this present world. There were also the Judaizers who rejected the faith for another gospel and who did it deliberately. The entire controversy eventuating in the Jerusalem Council dealt with this problem (Acts 15; Gal. 2). The consequence of apostasy is judgment. The apostate has nothing to expect but the indignation and judgment of God.

Such apostasy will be displayed in the end time. St. Paul said, "in the last days" (II Tim. 3:1), and "the time will come" (II Tim. 4:3,4) when there will be a falling away. In the time preceding the coming of Christ, there will be a great falling away, a great revolt, a rebellion against Christian truth, against God's revelation. Inquiry may be made as to whether such apostasy exists in our own day. Each one must answer that for himself, but in some areas it is amazing how little Christianity may be found.

II. *The Content of Apostasy*

When Paul described this movement, he spoke of ". . . another gospel: which is not another . . ." (Gal. 1:6,7). Modernism is another gospel. It came about through the influence of evolutionary naturalism upon the thinking of men, theologians not escaping. This evolutionary naturalism was applied to the Scripture so as to make it represent the religious evolution of the Hebrew people and to remove it from being an infallible record of divine revelation imparted to the Hebrew people. Modernism was the result of the impact of the scientific method in theology. Men turned to induction, to discovery, to generalization from particulars, and they substituted this for the method of receiving divine revelation and thinking God's thoughts after Him. Consequently, they accommodated their views of religion to science. The supernatural was bowed out and everything was explained on the ground of naturalism. This viewpoint invaded the theological seminaries under the terminology of higher criticism, which rearranged the Books of the Bible to make them represent the narrative of the development of the Hebrew people from a primitive polytheism to an ethical monotheism. No Bible scholar rejects historical criticism, but a Bible-believing Christian rejects higher criticism in its attack upon the Scriptures. Through the seminaries, the pulpits of the church were affected and through the pulpits the people received this false gospel.

The theological content of this teaching dealt with every major doctrine in the Bible. The Bible itself became a mere record of the Hebrew search for God, a history of their evolution from polytheists to monotheists. If, then, an early Book of the Bible such as Deuteronomy describes them as being monotheistic, it must be very late, and if a later Book of the Bible described them as polytheistic, it must have been earlier, so the Bible should be rearranged. So speaks the modernist.

When the modernist approaches Christ, he interprets Him in the form of a natural birth out of wedlock, as mistaken in His teaching, as wrong in His claims about His deity and destiny, and as a mere man who made an impact upon His age which was interpreted in legendary clothing of miracles. They believe that He died as a martyr and that His body remains in the grave but that His influence lives on today.

The death of Christ upon the cross was not an atonement for our sins but was a noble example of one giving His life in sacrifice for the truth and exhibiting His love even unto death. It exercises a moral influence, but it does not propitiate deity.

The way of salvation for the modernist is to follow the example of Jesus and live a self-denying, sacrificial life of service. Thus he also will come to God. He will practice the presence of God as Jesus did, and he will thus come to know God. It is not the doctrine of reconciliation through the God-man as the mediator between God and man and the only redeemer of God's elect.

Christian character is made by education, by habit-formation, by response to environment under controls and not by any supernatural birth. The possibility of the new birth is totally denied by the modernist.

The church is not the body of the Lord Jesus Christ, the redemptive agency of God in the world, but it is the vanguard of daring souls in the social revolution. The great work of the church is to reform society through the social gospel.

The second coming of Christ according to the modernist is merely a remnant of Jewish apocalypticism joined with certain mythological content and has no literal application at all. It was simply a symbol of the triumph of Christian truth.

Following the introduction of modernism, a great ecclesiastical battle was waged in the Christian church. At the turn of the century it was still possible to have trials of clergymen who denied the basic teaching of Christianity. But modernism made such headway through the schools and the pulpits of the land by the beginning of the twentieth century that it was impossible to hold a trial of a man who was guilty of heresy. One great church leader declared in the forties, when he was moderator of one of the leading Protestant denominations, that twenty-five years before he had talked of leaving the church because his theology was so contrary to that held and taught by the church. He had, however, stayed in and twenty-five years later holding the same views, he was honored with the leading position in his denomination, which reveals the change in conviction in that denomination. The control of ecclesiastical machinery and funds is in the hands of the modernist. The battle was lost by the Bible-believing Christians in the twenties and modernism has ridden high ever since. Orthodoxy continued only in isolated churches and in small ecclesiastical movements.

Today there is a new modernism. It is a revolt against liberalism's naturalism, unitarianism, and accommodation to science. William Hordern says, "One of my friends told me how shocked his minister-father was to learn that his son believed there was some religious value and truth in the Garden of Eden stories. The father, at considerable risk to his ecclesiastical position, had thrown these stories out the front window. It was dismaying to see his son dragging them back through the door." [2] This revival of what is called orthodoxy in varying degrees has been going on in most theological seminaries for several years. It is the effect of a teaching of Karl Barth and Emil Brunner, the advocates of what is called neo-orthodoxy. Through them the old liberalism with its belief in inevitable progress and the goodness of man has been totally discredited. Recently, I received a letter from a Congregational pastor in Connecticut who has been amazed at the way in which the neo-orthodox individuals are taking the pulpits of former liberals, and he raised the question, If they are truly orthodox, why have they not repented and confessed their previous unbelief? This so-called neo-orthodoxy is still a repudiation of biblical Christianity. It is still liberalism. Hordern says, "The battle against fundamentalism gave to liberalism a thrilling task that appealed to young theologians thirty years ago. Today there is seldom such a battle. We would have to look a long time today to find a Protestant congregation that cared one way or another whether its minister believed in the Virgin Birth." [3] The so-called new orthodoxy, which is really modernism, declares that the Bible is the Word of God and yet it is not the Word of God, that Christ is God and yet He is not God. It has affirmed sin, but it has not gone on to redemption. Hordern declares, "Some of the leaders of our movement to orthodoxy sometimes seem to know only one of the Christian doctrines—original sin. They seem not to have heard of redemption." [4] No, the new orthodoxy is not orthodoxy at all. It is still a form of modernism.

III. *The Consequences of Apostasy*

When apostasy comes into the church, the church takes the avenue of retreat from victory. Its zeal, fervor, and enthusiasm leak out from its message. It substitutes the social gospel of left-wing reformation and socialism for the redemptive gospel of the Lord Jesus Christ which is able to transform souls. Men are left without God and without salvation. There can be no evangelism with such unbelief. Consequently, for twenty-five years until recently, the church has been left without primary evangelists and great evangelistic movements.

In education the Sunday-school literature became nature-centered, history-centered or child-centered. Christ was given a secondary place. Biblical doctrine was removed altogether and Sunday schools were emptied by the thousands. Millions of pupils dropped out of the Sunday schools, so that in 1950 we had far fewer students in our Sunday schools than we had several decades before.

In missions the nerve was cut by the eclectic theology. There was no absolutism, no doctrine of heaven or hell or of salvation. Hence, there was no use in going to the heathen in order to convert them. The only answer that the modernists had was to take the good out of every religion, to exchange that good and treat all men as on an equal level. How far this is from biblical Christianity may quickly be seen.

The milk-and-water Christianity of a God without justice, of an atonement without the cross, of judgment without hell left men prey to the isms of the day. New England is a great illustration of this. Once historic Christianity commanded the great centers of New England. Today historic Christianity is a pitiful minority in this great area. The isms have taken over. Another illustration is Hawaii. There was a day when the Congregational biblical missionaries went to Hawaii, evangelized the islands, and won the population to Christ, which resulted in their transformation. But then at the close of the century modernism moved in. The note of authority, of zeal, of enthusiasm leaked out of the church and, as a result, the isms took over. Today Mormonism, Buddhism, and sacerdotalism command the islands. Hence, the leaders of the churches in the islands recognize that the only answer to their problem is a return to biblical Christianity.

The church through this unbelief was utterly impotent to face the great problems of society such as immorality, delinquency, drunkenness, dishonesty, and violence. Good men and women do not come about by chance but by convictions based upon great truths. The truths have been abandoned for a generation and the character of men and women is crumbling. The moral fiber of this nation needs to be renewed. God demands repentance, confession of wrong, faith, and obedience to His gospel and law if a change is to come into the lives of men.

In this great apostasy from New Testament Christianity, we could see a sign which would warrant us in believing that Christ's coming may not be far away. There has always been some measure of apostasy and at times that apostasy has been great, but not as it has been in these fifty years. The alternative is revival in us and in the nation. There must be a preaching of and an acceptance of the biblical Christ who alone can save and satisfy the souls of men. The antidote is the gospel preached and obeyed in the power of the Spirit. On this we stand where we stood in the midst of the conflict twenty-five years ago—on the rock of God's Word, the revelation of the gospel of Jesus Christ.

XXV

The Warning to the Church—Anti-Christ

. . . that day shall not come, except there come a falling away first, and that man of sin be revealed, the son of perdition; who opposeth and exalteth himself above all that is called God, or that is worshipped; so that he as God sitteth in the temple of God, shewing himself that he is God.

—II THESSALONIANS 2:3,4

ASSURANCE WAS GIVEN TO THE THESSALONIAN CHURCH THAT the day of the Lord Jesus Christ would not come until certain signs were fulfilled. Paul introduces this by saying, ". . . that day shall not come, except. . . ." These words are understood from the previous reference to the day of the Lord Jesus Christ and the hiatus is natural. The day means the day of the *parousia* or the coming of Christ for His church (I Thess. 4:16,17). It is also the day of His revelation or *apocalypsis* when He shall come to take vengeance on them that know not God (II Thess. 1:8), and it may well be called the day of His glorification in His saints (II Thess. 1:10). The nearness of that day of the Lord Jesus Christ can be known by certain signs. In the interim, the church should not be troubled until the signs are fulfilled. These signs include the apostasy or the falling away from biblical Christianity, the anarchy in government which will permit the appearance of the anti-Christ, and the appearance of the anti-Christ himself.

Already in Paul's day the mystery of iniquity was at work. The spirit of evil, of lawlessness, of revolt, of wickedness was already present and working in the world. There were definite evidences of the presence and activity of evil in that age, as there will be in every age. Nevertheless, the denouement of the mystery of iniquity depends upon a restraining power, which is described both in the neuter and in the masculine as he and that which restrains. The nature of that restraining power is a question deserving our keenest study. When the restraining power is removed, the mystery of iniquity will be revealed in the person of the anti-Christ.

I. *The Picture of the Anti-Christ*

Paul describes the anti-Christ as a man, a human being, not some angelic power or impersonal force or movement, but an incarnation of satanic cunning and human wickedness in an individual person who has the characteristics of the devil himself. The word anti-Christ describes any anti-Christian system of thinking, but such systems will reach their apotheosis in an individual expressing the anti-Christian teaching and tendency. The major attribute of the anti-Christ will be lawlessness, so that he is known as the man of lawlessness. There is an analogy in all lawless men, who are forerunners of the anti-Christ. The spirit of lawlessness is abroad today. There never was a time when lawlessness, wickedness, and corruption had pervaded the United States government, so that politicians and law-enforcement officers are connected with criminals and gangsters as they are today.[1]

The anti-Christ is a Messianic counterfeit, the devil's caricature of the true Messiah. He is called by St. Paul "the son of perdition" (II Thess. 2:3), who challenges and usurps divine prerogatives but who is a doomed person, a son of destruction. As the pseudo-Messiah, he will incarnate all that is blasphemous and impious. Every false Messiah of the past is only a harbinger of this individual, for he will surpass them all before his separation from God occurs to which he is doomed. One should note that Judas was called "the son of perdition" (John 17:12), and there may be some connection here. This individual is hidden but will be revealed, from whence we know not.

He is described as setting himself against God and all that is worshiped. A preliminary figure who suggests this character is described in Daniel 11:36 which St. Paul here quotes, namely, Antiochus Epiphanes who in 176-164 B.C. profaned the temple by setting up an altar to Zeus in the holy place, by worshiping the god of Roman force, and by forcing Greek paganism on Jewry. That he is a type of the coming anti-Christ is evident from Paul's description of him in this verse. It is quite possible that Caligula's attempt to set up a statue of himself in the temple at Jerusalem, which was so shocking to the monotheistic Jews, was in Paul's mind. It was only a short time after this that Nero claimed to be divine and launched his hideous practices. The question of the end-time meaning is still open. Already the spirit of such self-deification and anti-theism is found in man. Man has been deified and God has been humanized in the generation in which we live.

This impious individual will substitute himself for God. Paul said, ". . . he . . . sitteth in the temple of God, shewing himself that he is God" (II Thess. 2:4). The temple is not the Jerusalem structure (ieros), but the spiritual temple (naos). I do not look for the rebuilding of the temple in Jerusalem and the re-establishing of the sacrifices. The trait referred to here is the setting forth of one's self as the vicar of God, as the vicegerent of God assuming the rights of God. The forerunners of this individual were found in the Prince of Tyre (Ez. 28:2) and in Lucifer (Isa. 14:13,14). All who oppose and substitute themselves for God will be brought down to hell. It is true that this activity is approximated by the papal system in which its leader assumes divine honors and this has led many interpreters to assume that the papal system is anti-Christ.

This individual is to be motivated by Satan. Paul says, ". . . whose coming is after the working of Satan . . ." (II Thess. 2:9). Satan will be his father, as God was the father of the Lord Jesus. This means that there can be no identification of the anti-Christ with Satan. A series of supernatural persons is described as opposing the Trinity. We find this in Revelation 12 and 13. The dragon, or devil, stands opposed to God. The anti-Christ, or beast, stands opposed to Christ. The false prophet, or second beast, stands opposed to the Holy Spirit. The beast gets his authority and power from Satan. Thus the spirit of Satan will activate him, as Christ was filled and activated with the Spirit of God. Paul here includes the attributes of both beasts of Revelation 13 in his description of this supernatural individual.

The powers of the anti-Christ are described as ". . . with all power and signs and lying wonders, and with all deceivableness of unrighteousness . . ." (II Thess. 2:9,10). The Lord Jesus did "miracles and wonders and signs" (Acts 2:22) when He was here upon earth. Thus also Satan will do signs and lying wonders (Rev. 13:13,14). The Scriptures agree that this will be a supernatural person in the powers which he exercises and they will counterfeit many of the miracles which the Lord did when He was here on earth. All miracles are not of God. There are four great periods of miracles given to us in the Scripture. First, at the inauguration of God's revelation through Moses; second, at the preservation of the true religion under Elijah and Elisha; third, at the authentication of the New Testament revelation through the apostles; fourth, at the end time under anti-Christ, who will simulate the true religion. We do not accept an individual because of miracles, but we test his miracles by their moral quality (John 14:22 ff.).

This individual is to master men by guile instead of force.

He is to work as an angel of light. He will substitute error for
the truth, pleasure for purity and indulgence for discipline.
This aspect of his work is comparable to that of the false
prophet (Rev. 13:13 ff.).

Men shall fall into his power because they resisted the
truth. Says Paul, ". . . because they received not the love of
the truth, that they might be saved" (II Thess. 2:10). Responsibility for their blindness, their lack of discernment of
the truth and error, their captivity to sin rests upon men
themselves, not upon the predestination of God. Because they
would not have God in their minds, God gave them up. This
is the philosophy of history and it will be epitomized at the
end time. The rejection of light leads one to darkness and to
death. Walking in the light leads to salvation. The results to
these men is that they will perish. They are doomed. They
could have been saved, but they elected a fate with anti-
Christ, with Satan, and with the false prophet in hell.

The punishment of anti-Christ is declared. Paul says, ". . .
whom the Lord shall consume with the spirit of his mouth,
and shall destroy with the brightness of his coming" (II Thess.
2:8). His will be a short reign. The suggestion is that he will
be revealed and destroyed at approximately the same time.
Some have interpreted Daniel's three-and-a-half-years or
times, times and half a time and the forty-two months of
Revelation to be a year per day and thus to extend over 1260
years, to be an extended length of time. However, the suggestion in Scripture is not that long.

His will be a sudden end. It will occur at the coming of
Christ. Two words are joined describing this appearing of
Christ in this verse which are used separately throughout the
Scripture. One is *epiphania* and the other *parousia*. It describes
the personal advent of the Lord in glory. When He comes, by
His word (the spirit of His mouth), He will consume this
evil personage (cf. Rev. 19:11 ff.). It will be a great spiritual
victory for Christ and it will be attended by destruction of

the anti-Christ. He will not be annihilated, but he will be separated from God. There is a supernatural judgment that will fall. He will be judged along with Satan in the lake of fire or the second death forever (cf. Rev. 19:20; 20:10).

II. *The Power Which Restrains*

In the midst of this description, St. Paul tells us there is something which withholds the mystery of iniquity. He says, ". . . what withholdeth . . ." (II Thess. 2:6). The fact that something or someone restrains the mystery of lawlessness from culminating in the man of lawlessness is evident. There is that which now restrains. There is some great power which hinders the revelation of the man of sin. What is that power? It was identified to the Thessalonians. Paul said, ". . . ye know . . ." (*Ibid.*). These Thessalonians knew the identity of that power or person. It may be either, for both the neuter and the masculine are used to describe it. Paul told them when he was with them (II Thess. 2:5), and now he only recalled what it was to their memory. Why was he so secretive about it? Was it identified with someone or something which he dared not mention for fear of antagonizing them and bringing on a persecution of the Christians? How we wish he had informed us so as to settle these subsequent controversies as to the identification of this power. Nevertheless, he will be revealed ". . . in his time" (II Thess. 2:6). There will be a time when all shall behold the revelation of the man of sin. When shall that time be? Did the New Testament Christians see it? Did the medieval church see it? Are we seeing it in our day? Is it yet future? Whatever we may think of it, it is an appointed time. In the first epistle Paul refers to it as ". . . the times and the seasons . . ." (I Thess. 5:1).

The forces identified with this power have been various. First there was the Roman Empire. The Roman Empire had hindered the Jews from killing Paul several times. It preserved order. It was the magistrate of God. Paul was a Roman citizen and he appealed to the laws and the courts of Rome. Hence the neuter for the empire may have been used and the masculine for the emperor may have been used. Since St. Paul believed that the empire would fall, this might explain the cryptic reference to his verbal teaching, for to put in writing that Rome would fall would open the Christians to the charge of sedition and to subsequent persecution. The early fathers from Tertullian on believed this was the meaning of "what withholdeth" (*Ibid.*).

Modern dispensationalists declare that this refers to the Holy Spirit in the church. One dispensationalist says, "I have put this question (Do you know what restrains the full manifestation of evil?) to Christian audiences many times and I have never failed to get the answer. Yes, it is the Holy Spirit who restrains. This is exactly what we are told in Isaiah 59:19, 'When the enemy shall come in like a flood, the Spirit of the Lord shall lift up a standard against him' or as it has been translated, 'The Spirit of the Lord shall restrain him.' The Holy Spirit is in the world working in and through the church of God; He indwells every believer individually and the church collectively; therefore, as long as the church of God is in the world, the anti-Christ will not be revealed." [2] Therefore, say the dispensationalists, when the church is raptured or taken out of the world, then the mystery of iniquity can culminate in the person of the anti-Christ.

The difficulty here arises in that it makes so much necessary after the removal of the Holy Spirit and the church in the rapture. Hence, the dispensationalist places the conversion of the Jews, the evangelization of the world, the tribulation, and other events in the interim between the rapture of the church and the beginning of the judgment on the ungodly. It also would remove this manifestation of the man of sin as a sign of the day of the Lord Jesus Christ, for that manifestation would not take place until after the church is gone. We have a duty to reconcile the question of why Paul was so cryptic about this if it referred to the Holy Spirit and the church.

The most acceptable view is that this refers to the Holy Spirit working in common grace through civil government. When civil government collapses and there is a breakdown of restraining law, the result is lawlessness. Civil government was instituted of God (Gen. 9). Its purpose is expressed as ministering the will of God (Rom. 13), and the Roman Empire was part of that civil government. This interpretation alone fulfills the requirement. The precursors of such a breakdown of civil authority are evident on every hand in the world today. They threaten our national and international life.

The future may well be a time of anarchy out of which will emerge the man of sin. Christians ought everywhere to pray for government, to support the powers that be, to work for sound government in the earth. It is the attempt of communism to overthrow all such government and to establish anarchy that the world dictatorship of Moscow may be established.

III. *The Possible Identification of the Man of Sin*

There are several interpretations of the man of sin. The first is called mythological that tells us that the anti-Christ is not to be identified with a person, but is essentially a myth representing a great principle or system of falsehood, having various manifestations, forms of working, and degrees exemplified by different movements in history. The antagonism between good and evil is expressed in the form of conflict between God and the dragon, between Christ and anti-Christ, between the Holy Spirit and the false prophet, and in the end God overcomes and righteousness is triumphant. This is the mythological presentation and interpretation of the man of sin.

The historical interpretation was accepted by the early fathers, who sought him in a particular person to be identified. Some hit upon Nero, some upon Domitian, some upon a king to appear after the breakup of the Roman Empire who would resemble Antiochus Epiphanes and some on others. The reformers identified the anti-Christ with the papal system expressed in the Vicar of Christ. The arrogance, the error, the persecutions practiced by the papal system led them to this conclusion. Recent writers have sought him in individuals like Mussolini, Hitler, Stalin, Lenin, or someone to be revealed in the near future. Such identification has wrought infinite confusion in the minds of Christians in reference to the second coming of Christ and its antecedents.

The religious interpretation says that anti-Christ exists in every form of anti-Christian teaching and action in the world. At one time it is Jewish, at another time it is Roman, at another time it is papal, at another time it is German, at another time it is Russian, at another time it is Chinese in its manifestations. The advent of anti-Christ as a person embodying and incarnating the blasphemy, arrogance, lawlessness, and wickedness will appear before the end time, but these other events prepare us and at the same time comfort us in the sense that we may expect Christ to avenge the elect.

Those who follow anti-Christ and voluntarily give allegiance to Him in a lesser or greater form will be blinded with strong delusion, so that they will believe error and be damned, and those who would not receive the truth shall find that their delusion will cause them to embrace and follow anti-Christ when he appears. This is the law of spiritual retribution. God hardens us as we harden ourselves. Doom awaits the anti-Christ and all those who take their position with him.

XXVI

Consolation for the Church

Now our Lord Jesus Christ himself, and God, even our Father, which hath loved us, and hath given us everlasting consolation and good hope through grace, comfort your hearts, and stablish you in every good word and work.

—II THESSALONIANS 2:16,17

THE BLESSING OF CONSOLATION IN THE DARK PROSPECT OF end-time apostasy, anti-Christian persecution, and human anarchy is here presented by St. Paul. Paul has described the judgments, the holocaust, the catastrophe, and the suffering preliminary to the second coming of the Lord Jesus Christ (II Thess. 2:1-12). Eschatology is an awe-inspiring study. We should avoid lightness and any offhand manner of treating it. Christ's coming is the blessed hope of the church, but terrible events will precede it. Sometimes we are impressed with the blithe curiosity of Christians in approaching prophetic study. Some people even seem to take pleasure in the severity of these antecedents of the second coming, thinking that the saints will escape all this.

Those to whom Paul was writing constituted a little flock saved out of heathenism, persecuted in tribulation, struggling

with the problems of its own group in which aberrations of
conduct and creed occurred and who needed some real consolation and encouragement. They needed to be told that God
is not only powerful and stern, but that He is gentle and
tender. They needed to be reassured that God is like a mother
who broods over her children, who knows their sorrows and
cares, and who presents wonderful comfort. The picture of
Jesus weeping over Jerusalem and comparing Himself to a
hen who would have gathered her chickens under her wings
is a proper picture of God. Overemphasis upon the sternness
of God has sometimes led branches of Christendom to seek
for motherhood and tenderness in elevating Mary to a mediator between Christ and men.

Light, hope, and confidence emanate from this text in contrast to the gloomy picture preceding these words. It reminds
me of a section in the Hawaiian Archipelago, where a little
town of Koale gets rain a part of every day and sometimes
all during the day. Mountains are near at hand and trade
winds blow the clouds up against these mountains, so that
they release their rain over the little town of Koale and over
six hundred inches or more than fifty feet of rain fall on that
little town each year. At almost any time of the year anyone
driving through that section enters into clouds, lightning, and
great storms. Yet fifteen or twenty miles farther on to the
south of the Island of Kauai is the beautiful section of
Waimea, profuse with poinsettias, lilies, orchids all in bloom
and with fragrance and perfume filling the air in the beauty
and warmth of the sun. Such is the transition as we pass from
the first part of this chapter to this text. Now we move out
of the great holocaust, out of the events of the end time into
the consoling ministry of God to those who suffer.

This section is introduced by the address, ". . . brethren
beloved of the Lord . . ." (II Thess. 2:13). Paul spoke not
only to Thessalonian believers, but to Christians everywhere
and of all times, just as Christ prayed not only for His dis-

ciples, but for them also which shall believe on Him through the word of the disciples (John 17:20). You and I are included in the beloved because we have been born of God and included in the family of God through receiving and believing the truth. Paul declares that the believers possess the affection of Christ. They are beloved of the Lord, which is shown by His self-emptying, His identification with us, and His substitution for us on the cross. In opening his Epistle to the Thessalonians, he declared that the election of the brethren flowed from the divine love (I Thess. 1:5). Like Jesus, Paul thought that this relationship of love should be applied to believers. Paul had a sincere affection for the Thessalonians and they had a sincere affection for him. The experience of such love will allow us to say and do nothing to hurt one another and will impel us to understand, to help, to console, and to support the brethren. Love becomes the limiting or restraining motive and also the constraining motive. The teaching of I Corinthians must be applied to our Christian relationship.

The section opens, ". . . we are bound to give thanks alway to God for you . . ." (II Thess. 2:13). This is no mere form, but a real motion on the part of St. Paul. He is optimistic as well as realistic. Paul could deal with these realities of evil, the mystery of iniquity, the facts of judgment and hell just so long. Then his basic hopefulness, confidence, and optimism burst forth. This is a mark of the true Christian. He cannot stay in the slough of despond overlong. Joy, hope, faith, and power must exude and express themselves in our lives. If God exists, then let us live like He does.

An object lesson in optimism was the very existence of this flock of faithful believers in an age like the Roman Age. It was a day of wickedness, brutality, force, and atheism. Men were lovers of pleasure more than lovers of God. Yet here was a cell, a colony, a flock which foretold a new era. That such a flock existed at all was a testimony and witness to the power of God. It was an harbinger of what was to come. When these cells multiplied over the whole Roman Empire, the Christian movement was destined to conquer Rome.

Over against those who ". . . received not the love of the truth, that they might be saved . . . who believed not the truth, but had pleasure in unrighteousness . . ." (II Thess. 2:10,12) were these who were beloved of God. Those were doomed to perish; these were saved for eternity. The turning point between the two was their attitude to the truth. The Bible declares that rejecting the Gospel leads to hardness, blindness, and doom under the law of retribution of God, whereas receiving the Gospel leads to light, grace, and salvation. The responsibility is correctly placed on man. Salvation is of God. Reprobation is of man. "He, that being often reproved hardeneth his neck, shall suddenly be destroyed, and that without remedy" (Prov. 29:1). Thus Pharaoh hardened his heart and God confirmed that hardening (Ex. 11-13).

The tragedy of the condition of these people is that God sent them ". . . strong delusion, that they should believe a lie" (II Thess. 2:11). They followed false prophets and thus in the end time false prophets will lead to the anti-Christ. The refusal to open one's heart to the truth of the Gospel leaves one prey to moral delusion, which is a judicial infatuation with error. This passage may well explain many isms which exist in a Christian nation today.

I. *The Source of Consolation*

The origin of this consolation is ". . . God (who) hath from the beginning chosen you . . ." (II Thess. 2:13). The time of that choice is declared to be from the beginning. This does not mean the firstfruits of all missionary converts, but it is a reference to the eternal purpose of God to save a people for His glory (cf. Rom. 8:28-30; John 17:1-12; John 6:37-40; Eph. 1:4). Hence this reference take us back into the pre-earthly ages or to eternity. It was the time when the triune God made the covenant of redemption, established the decree, and accomplished the indwelling works of deity. As yet there was no creation and no world. It was then that God elected.

The motive is here declared to be love. The love of God determined Him to take a people into His own nature, position and glory. The attributes of divine wisdom, or of divine justice, or of divine power would never have accounted for redemption. The Bible ascribes this to God's love. Hence, God loved us before the world was. God has decreed that there will be a redeemed people who will be exalted above the angels to become partakers of the divine nature. God's grace is love in action redeeming unworthy man.

The divine decree is described with the words, "hath . . . chosen" (II Thess. 2:13). The choice is based on love to the end that we might know Him and be saved. That some kind of predestination is here taught is unequivocal. Paul does not enter into a discussion of predestination and freedom, but he uses predestination to dignify the position of this little flock in a world which was opposed to them. What majesty to know that God hath loved us before the foundation of the world.

An illustration of this exists in the experience of Christ at the Last Supper, where John says, "Jesus knowing that the Father had given all things into his hands, and that he was come from God, and went to God; he riseth from supper, and laid aside his garments; and took a towel, and girded himself. After that he poureth water into a bason, and began to wash the disciples' feet . . ." (John 13:3-5). Christ was able to do a great many things in humiliation because He knew whence He came and whither He went. Thus the little flock could endure persecution and its suffering because it knew of its origin and its destiny.

The means of this choice by God of the beloved is ". . . through sanctification . . . and belief of the truth . . ." (II Thess. 2:13). There is an interrelation of the work of God's Spirit and of the human spirit in salvation. It is not an arbi-

trary decree which is followed by human submission auto-
matically or all would respond, since it is God's will that
every man shall come to the knowledge of the truth, but it
depends upon our response to God's Spirit. It is the unanimous
testimony of Scripture that no one is saved without the work
of the Holy Spirit. The Holy Spirit convicts us of sin, moves
our hearts so that we may understand the Gospel, enables us
to embrace Christ in faith, and regenerates our nature. Without the Holy Spirit, preaching is vain. Paul declares, ". . . ye
are justified in the name of the Lord Jesus, and by the Spirit
of our God" (I Cor. 6:11) and Peter declared that we are
"Elect according to the foreknowledge of God the Father,
through sanctification of the Spirit . . ." (I Pet. 1:2). The
question of whether this work of the Holy Spirit is universal
or particular has divided men into two great groups called
Calvinists and Arminians. Whichever system you embrace,
be assured that it is an error to rush or hurry the profession
of faith by persons who are unconvicted by the Spirit. Such
action results in a shallow view of Christian experience and
life.

The importance of faith and obedience is stressed as a means
of such election. Paul speaks of ". . . belief of the truth" (II
Thess. 2:13). Regeneration depends upon faith. God's Spirit
does not work apart from faith. Faith even has a part in sanctification, which is the means of our being chosen. For all
practical purposes we may say that if a man believes the truth
and obeys the Gospel, he is elect of God and he may exercise
confidence in that fact. Destiny depends upon human response. Let us not overemphasize election to the detriment of
human responsibility. Otherwise the invitations, admonitions,
and exhortations of the Bible must be relegated to obscurity.

The end for which God chooses us is ". . . salvation . . .
whereunto he called you by our gospel . . ." (II Thess.
2:13,14). Calling "is the work of God's Spirit, whereby convincing us of our sin and misery, enlightening our minds in

the knowledge of Christ, and renewing our wills, He doth persuade and enable us to embrace Christ, so freely offered us in the Gospel." [1] It is the Holy Spirit who calls us by the Gospel. This calling eventuates in salvation, forgiveness, eternal life, and inheritance with God, and it manifests itself in Christian life here and now. Thus this text presents the doctrine of the Trinity. God plans or elects. Christ is redeemer and Lord. The Holy Spirit is the sanctifier. This passage contains a profound theology which is a precursor of the creeds of Christendom.

II. *The Nature of the Consolation*

Everlasting consolation is age-lasting consolation which means for this world during its whole extent. Such a firm trust in God's sovereignty has inspired the most heroic deeds on the part of martyrs, teachers, reformers, and confessors throughout the ages. All the reformers were predestinarian. Dr. Bainton of Yale tells us in his biography of Luther that Luther sometimes considered man as an ass or a donkey driven by God or driven by the devil. At other times Luther was not sure whether God was amusing Himself with a puppet show. At other times Luther came to the place where he cried out on behalf of human freedom, responsibility, and decision, and apparently he came to the conclusion that God in prevenient grace sent influences of the Holy Spirit into the hearts of men and women, convicting and enlightening them, so that they were able to respond in faith and evangelical obedience. In some ways Luther was even more predestinarian than Calvin. The Reformers withstood evil, launched great projects, and met opposition with the statement, "The will of the Lord be done." It is a great comfort that when we have done everything possible, we can leave the issue to God. This is not fatalism, but trust.

In meditating on the death of her husband, Mrs. Peter Marshall tells how Peter had narrowly missed death on many occasions. Once when he was walking through the moors of Scotland on an inky black night, he suddenly fell to his knees. Reaching out his hands ahead of him, he found that nothing was there. He had stumbled to the edge of a great gorge hundreds of feet deep, and if he had taken another step, he would have been hurtled out to his death. Something had preserved him. Another time he was out walking with a friend. An automobile accident occurred and the friend walking by his side was killed, but he was saved. On another occasion he missed his airplane for an engagement and the airplane crashed killing all who took it, but he was saved. Then when he was forty-six years of age, God suddenly took him out of the midst of a great ministry by a heart attack. Mrs. Marshall, in writing about the death of her husband, was comforted and strengthened because she believed God had a plan. She said that this was God's plan. God had a plan for this man. All this was embraced in the plan and He spared him until his work was done.[2] The acceptance of the Christian theology of God's eternal love, of His call, of His salvation, and of ultimate glory is the greatest source of comfort to the common man in the struggles of life that there is.

But God hath not only given us everlasting consolation, but also good hope. Hope applies to the world to come. He who pursues hope is one who has a foretaste of his future salvation. Paul declares, "For we are saved by hope: but hope that is seen is not hope: for what a man seeth, why doth he yet hope for? But if we hope for that we see not, then do we with patience wait for it" (Rom. 8:24,25). Christian assurance depends upon spiritual experience which makes us possessors of hope. ". . . being justified by faith, we have . . . hope: and hope maketh not ashamed . . ." (Rom. 5:1,4,5). Christian assurance was the great doctrine of the evangelical revival as presented by John Wesley and it may be the common experience of people today. A synonym for hope is ". . . the obtaining of the glory of our Lord Jesus Christ" (II Thess.

2:14). This means a full sharing of Christ's glory to come. We may possess that glory now even though its manifestation will be to come (cf. John 17; II Cor. 5:18; II Thess. 1:10; Rom. 8:23).

The everlasting consolation and good hope are through grace. God is favorably disposed toward us, as is evidenced by what He has done for us in giving Christ and salvation through Christ. God's favor is available to all in this era of grace. This is the "acceptable year" as contrasted with "the day of vengeance" (Isa. 61:2). It is this grace which is contrasted in the epistle with the dreadful things that will precede the coming of the day of the Lord. Today is the day of salvation. This is the day of opportunity, of evangelism, of revival, of missions. The mystery of iniquity is now intensifying and the mystery of godliness is intensifying. Both are developing simultaneously, preceding the end time. God's grace is not only extended to us, but it should be manifested through us. The scriptural statement, ". . . great grace was upon them all" (Acts 4:33), speaks of love, liberality, righteousness, and good works. The evidence of this among Christians is a great comfort.

III. *The Fruit of Consolation*

Consolation brings comfort and, Paul says, ". . . God . . . comfort your hearts . . ." (II Thess. 2:16,17). God's name is the ". . . God of all comfort" (II Cor. 1:3). God stands to us in the position of comforter. This is the work and the name of the Holy Spirit. He is called the Comforter, or the Paraclete. The need for comfort is universal. No man goes very far in life without it. We become hurt, tempted, buffeted, bereaved, and wounded, and our bruised hearts need to be bound up with the comfort of God. Consideration of the amount of suffering that comes to men ought to withhold us from inflicting any needless wounds upon the hearts of our fellows. Yet in the midst of such bruises, the Christian has the knowledge that there is no suffering which God cannot comfort.

> Come, ye disconsolate, where'er ye languish;
> Come to the mercyseat, fervently kneel;
> Here bring your wounded hearts, here tell your anguish;
> Earth hath no sorrow that heaven cannot heal.

Spiritual consolation also brings strength. Paul said, ". . . God . . . stablish you in every good word and work" (II Thess. 2:16,17). Just as Paul had sent Timothy to strengthen and establish them by a fuller knowledge of the truth and by Christian experience, he now commends them to God (cf. I Thess. 3:2). Here we see an analogy to the benediction given by Paul in the Roman Epistle. "Now to him that is of power to stablish you according to my gospel . . . be glory through Jesus Christ for ever" (Rom. 16:25,27). The knowledge and the consideration of the destiny of believers and the means to effectuate it strengthens the believer in word and deed. Our attestation to such establishment is in the quality of our words and our work. The tongue is called "the glory of man" (cf. Psa. 16:9; Acts 2:26). The words that proceed from one's tongue must attest his righteousness. Our works are the result of our hands being turned to God's program of mercy, righteousness, and truth. Thus the thoughts of our minds and the deeds of our bodies will be devoted to His will.

Hence, consolation brings stability. Paul says, ". . . stand fast, and hold the traditions which ye have been taught, whether by word, or our epistle" (II Thess. 2:15). The early apostolic teaching was verbal and constituted an oral tradition involving rules of conduct and sayings of the Lord Jesus (cf. I Cor. 15:1-5; I Cor. 11:23). These oral traditions were eliminated when the Bible was written. The written word displaced the oral word. Those who would exalt oral tradition above the Bible have a very fallible authority today, for such traditions became corrupted. All oral tradition should be brought into harmony with the written Word. The knowledge of God's revelation as contained in the Word is the ground of all stability and strength in the believer's life. The mind which finds the source of its authority in the Bible is settled in its direction and also in its criterion of action.

Thus Paul ends the doctrinal section of II Thessalonians on a high note of victory, power, and grace. If these were the only two epistles we had in the Bible, we would know from them the way of salvation. They cast God's light upon our pathway. No matter how evil conditions may get, we may derive comfort, strength, and stability from God's purpose, Spirit, and Word as contained in these Thessalonian epistles.

XXVII

Freedom for the Word

Finally, brethren, pray for us, that the word of the Lord may have free course, and be glorified, even as it is with you.
—II THESSALONIANS 3:1

IN PAUL'S EPISTLES, THE WORD FINALLY MARKS THE TRANSI-
tion to the practical phase of his writing. In this epistle his
concluding remarks deal with the rule of conduct, with separation from unruly brethren, with the attitude toward work,
and with inner peace of heart and mind.

He begins with the request for prayer for the advance of
the Word of God. The Word is equivalent to the gospel
which was committed once and for all to the saints. In some
instances Paul equates the Word with his own commandments
concerning their conduct, but, for the most part, we are to
understand by it the content of the gospel of the Lord Jesus
Christ.

Prayer is the Christian's commodity in trade. It is as natural
to him as music is to the musician, as wool, iron or lumber is
to the trader, and as essays to the literateur. Paul requested a
share in their prayers. Does anyone ever think about you as a
person of prayer? Does anyone covet your prayers? Does
anyone request them? Are you producing anything in the

spiritual realm? As a Christian, is prayer your commodity in trade?

The purpose of Paul's prayer was the advance of the cause of Christ, not only in Thessalonica, but also in Corinth. He said, ". . . pray for us, that the word of the Lord may have free course, and be glorified, even as it is with you" (II Thess. 3:1). It is prayer which makes the going forth of the gospel prosper. R. A. Torrey says, "When I started around the world in 1901, I sent out five thousand letters to people whom I had learned knew how to pray, asking them if they would pray for Mr. Alexander and me every day as we went around the world. One of the hardest tasks I ever had in my life was signing those letters, signing my name five thousand times, but it paid, for soon letters came back by the thousands from these persons saying that they would pray for us every day. When Mr. Alexander and I reached Melbourne, Australia, ten thousand people had taken it up and were praying for us every day, and when we reached England no less than forty thousand people were praying for us every day. Who could not preach under such circumstances, and is it any wonder that the marvelous results followed that did follow?" [1] The picture Paul gives us is the Word of God speeding on in ever new conquests, victories and triumphs. He uses the words, ". . . have free course and be glorified . . ." (II Thess. 3:1). Lightfoot translates it as "have a triumphant career." [2] A sense of independence is communicated to the Word or to the gospel in this instance. It is pictured as moving over the countryside apart from the missionary, yea, even beyond his effort. Here we see the inherent power of the Word as God's speech, His message, His voice which awakens, summons, and renews the spiritual nature of man. In the narrative of the creation, we read, "And God said . . ." (Gen. 1:3), and then we read the description of the enormous things which took place at the voice of God. God is speaking today in His gospel and that gospel has power, but the sweep of such power is never known to occur except it is attended by prayer for its progress. Thus Paul petitioned these people to pray for the triumphant career of the Word.

Certainly it is not out of order for us to plead for such daily prayer on the part of Christians for the progress of God's Word in the farthest corner of the world. Oh that the Word of God might run, might prosper, might sweep triumphantly over our cities. Would that we might hear its thunder, see its lightning, hear its warning, feel its comfort, experience its strength, and know its protection. This would be a triumphant career of the Word.

Oh that the saints who have experienced the power of the Word would be burdened for America. What difference would then attend the preaching of the Gospel? What trophies would be claimed by the cross! What transformation would take place in the character and life of our people!

Oh that we would saturate the preaching of the Word by our missionaries with such prayer that the Word would sweep all opposition before it, that the results would glorify the gospel, and that triumph after triumph would be experienced. Such is by no means beyond the bounds of possibility according to the teaching of this text.

I. *Prosperity for the Word in Having an Open Door*

Apparently the Word of the Lord is having free course and is being glorified in America today. We think of the great campaigns which are being held all over this nation. In some areas it almost seems to be the popular thing to go to church, to attend the evangelistic campaigns, and to gather in great gospel rallies. Billy Graham has addressed a congregation of between fifty- and one-hundred-thousand people many times in the last five years and such meetings are not uncommon, although perhaps not of such proportions, in many areas of the country today. Sometimes a thousand to fifteen-hundred people will make profession of faith in one great meeting. An era which many had declared was gone forever has returned. It is the era of mass evangelism. People had said that we must now resort to personal calling, to individual enlistment, to hand-picking of the fruit for we were drawing nigh unto the end of the age, and yet greater meetings for the advancement of the gospel are being held today than ever before. As this wide hearing is being given by radio so that one gospel preacher can address as many as fifteen million by television, by screen, by mass meetings, by newspapers, and by magazine, let us rejoice that the Word of God is speeding over our land today. We ought not to have a false optimism because of this, for much of the churchgoing and many of those who listen to the gospel do not respond affirmatively to its message, but insofar as the interest is there, we thoroughly rejoice. The gospel is having a triumphant career.

Yet all do not believe, for as Paul said in this text, ". . . all men have not faith" (II Thess. 3:2). There are areas of the world which are being closed to the gospel. How sad that China which only so recently was calling for missionaries, evangelists, teachers, colporteurs, and Christian workers has now driven all such foreign workers from her shores and is systematically attempting by communistic methods to wash from the minds of Chinese Christians all their Christian convictions and faith. Our own missionaries returning from China tell of the methods used by these Communists to indoctrinate Christians with communistic doctrines, then to force them by imprisonment, and finally to make them face death if they do not apostatize from the faith. A satanic persecution is being carried on against the Word of the Lord and all who adhere to it in areas of the earth. Christians are suffering because of their loyalty to the Word of God and to faith.

The activity of the Word in such areas will be due only to the prayers of God's people. When Paul was in prison he said, ". . . the word of God is not bound" (II Tim. 2:9). He could be bound, Christians can be bound, but the Word cannot be bound. Then if Christians will be faithful in their prayer, it can transcend every barrier, even as it went into the palace of Caesar in Paul's own day when he was in prison.

Antipathy to the Word or the gospel is to be expected in every age. Those who do not believe, who are not of faith, who do not have spiritual understanding cannot grasp the activity of those who do. They neither accept the faith nor do they believe.

The second phase of Paul's request was that the brethren would pray "that we may be delivered from unreasonable and wicked men . . ." (II Thess. 3:2). Such individuals thwart the Word of God wherever it is possible. This was true in the first century of the Christian era, it has happened throughout the ages, and it is happening today. When Dr. Charles E. Fuller was recently to hold his meeting in the auditorium in Altoona, Pennsylvania, the enemies of the gospel attempted to have his contract canceled. When that was impossible, those who had contributed the chairs to the auditorium had trucks move up just before the meeting and removed every chair from the auditorium. That is opposition on a local scale. The refusal of denominations to let well-trained ministers who graduate from evangelical seminaries which are not denominational serve in churches that are without pastors exhibits another phase of such opposition. It was known in the days of Wesley and Whitefield when they were forbidden the use of the Anglican pulpit and it is widespread today. The ridicule which is put upon the authoritarian view of the Bible by many of the liberal so-called Christians of our day is yet another way of thwarting the Word of God.

In May, 1952, the Evangelical Confederation of Colombia published a list of persecutions which had taken place against the Protestant Christians in that nation over a period of ten weeks, beginning with December 1, 1951. These included beatings, imprisonments, destruction of property, confiscation of Bibles, and even the taking of life. Persecution is by no means ended in those areas, where unreasonable and wicked men hold forth in political or ecclesiastical control.

The teaching of God's Word stirs the hostility of men who are "bigoted" [3] or "out of place" [4] or "outrageous." [5] Apparently, Paul considered these men out of reach of the gospel, beyond the pale of hope. Instead of asking that they should pray for those men to be converted, he prayed that he might be delivered from them. Rather than be faced by the demands of God's Word, such men will do almost anything to hinder or stop its circulation.

II. *Prosper in Being Believed by Many*

The Word of God may have free course in the hearts of men and women by being believed. The wonder of a true revival is not due to methods, but it is due to the Word of the Lord. There is a difference between relying on fleshly methods to reach the masses with the gospel and depending upon the Word of the Lord. The spiritual way is to preach the Word, to pray that the Word may have free course, and to depend upon the power of the Spirit to use the Word.

In the Book of Acts, there are several descriptions of such triumphant sweeps of the Word of God in areas evangelized. One was at Jerusalem during the time of the persecution waged by Herod. There we read, "But the word of God grew and multiplied" (Acts 12:24). The persecution was not sufficient to stop the advance of the Word of God. The servants of the Lord might be killed, but the Word swept on. Again, when St. Paul was preaching at Pisidian Antioch and there was keen opposition among certain elements of the people, we read, "And when the Gentiles heard this, they were glad, and glorified the word of the Lord: and as many as were ordained to eternal life believed. And the word of the Lord was published throughout all the region" (Acts 13: 48,49). Likewise, in Ephesus a great revival occurred as a result of the ministry of the apostles. They had preached in

the School of Tyrannus for the space of two years, so that all
who dwelt in Asia heard the Word of the Lord Jesus, and
in Ephesus many who believed came and confessed and
showed their deeds, and then we read, "So mightily grew
the word of God and prevailed" (Acts 19:20). The result of
this prevailing of the Word of God was that the whole population turned away from the worship of Diana and the silver-
smiths who made idols to her were thrown out of work.

This power of the Word is described and designated in
numerous ways in the New Testament. We read, "They
preached the word" (Acts 8:25), and "They heard the word"
(Acts 10:44), and "They received the word" (Acts 8:14),
and "The Holy Ghost fell on all them which heard the
word" (Acts 10:44). The growth of the church was always
connected with the Word of the Lord.

What should we preach today to witness such a sweep or
triumphant career of the Word of the Lord? Should we seek
a new gospel of social improvement, of morality, of character
achievement, of legislation, of pacificism, or of human improvement? The answer is no. We need a renewed declaration
of the love of God embracing weak and sinful men; of the
punishment and pain of sin; of forgiveness and righteousness
through the cross; of abundant life both now and of life forever; of peace, joy, and love in believing. This is the gospel
which men's hearts need in every age.

We ought to preach a hearing and an obeying of the Word
for ourselves before we can authoritatively communicate it
to others. Probably in this lies the hindrance to the power of
our modern church. We have treated the Word as something
extraneous to our own lives. God is speaking to us, to the
church, to the world, but men are not hearing the voice of
God.

Has the Word freedom in your life? Are you among those
who have faith, who believe, who hear, and who receive
God's Word? Have you submitted your mind and heart to

its authority? If so, you may rejoice at its message of salvation, you may live at peace with God and yourself, and you may know His direction in all that you do.

Are you among those who are out of place or "have not faith" (II Thess. 3:2), or hostile to righteousness, or thwarting the Word of God? If so, the consequences are not only hardness of heart now, which may be described as perverse or unreasonable, but they are eternal in the loss to your soul.

Are you among those who corrupt the Word of God (II Cor. 2:17), or who handle the Word of God deceitfully (II Cor. 4:2), thus perverting souls with error, or with false comfort, or with direction in mischievous ways? Paul said, "But though we, or an angel from heaven, preach any other gospel unto you than that which we have preached unto you, let him be accursed" (Gal. 1:8). Certainty, strength, and direction come to those who make the Word of God their rule of action.

III. *Prosper in Obedience to the Word*

The Word has free course when we are ready to obey it. The Presbyterian standards declare it to be "the rule of faith and life." [6] Therefore, we are to live according to it—it is our rule of life. Obeying the Bible is serious business. It may cost preferment, popularity, position, but we choose it whatever the cost. It means that we are to seek first the kingdom of God and His righteousness. He who seeks the righteousness of God in self and in society is living according to God's Word. Then whatever health, happiness, and prosperity comes to him is in consistency with the Word of God and the plan of God.

The rule of faith demands that we serve our fellow men. This was the standard of greatness according to Jesus. He contrasted it with the way of the heathen, who expected men to serve them and to wait upon them, but it should not be so among His disciples. Therefore He set them the example that

". . . the Son of man came not to be ministered unto, but to minister, and to give his life a ransom for many" (Matt. 20:28). He who is aware of a child's sense of ego will note that the reluctance to serve and the desire to be waited upon merely reflects this feeling and attitude of the natural man.

Taking the Bible as the rule of faith means that we will sanctify every relationship of life and will live it in accordance with the will of God. Whether we work, whether we worship, whether we play, whether we relax, we will do it to the glory of God and maintain an obedience to His Word.

Thus it is time for those of us who are believers to learn the principles of ethical conduct which are to be applied in all situations according to God's Word. One Christian movement stressed four tests for all action; namely, absolute love, absolute truth, absolute honesty, and absolute purity. While they are not perfect, they at least suggest to us that there are principles of Christian conduct. Mr. H. J. Taylor, chairman of the board of the Club Aluminum Company of America, worked out four rules of business conduct to be applied by every person who worked for him in every phase of the business under his control. He did it on the basis of Christian principles.

Let the Word rule in every situation of life. It is remarkable how the Bible has principles which can govern us. He who follows those principles will have the consciousness of being directed by God. He who has recourse to the Word will have provided for him a constitution of Christian living. Therefore, turn to it, study it, apply it, and obey it. The revival of soul, of church, of righteousness will come as the Word sweeps triumphantly over all.

In accordance with this petition of St. Paul, our church has professed to accept and to obey the Word as the infallible rule of faith and practice. Therefore our lives must be under the control of the Word. Let that be our determination.

Mr. Franklin D. Roosevelt introduced the fireside chats of

the presidents of the United States to the people. In an un-obstructed way, the president could speak to millions of people and sweep the nation by his will or his voice. On the contrary, the Voice of America, which propagandizes the satellite states of the Communist orbit, is often jammed by powerful stations within the borders of Russia itself. These two experiences illustrate what may happen to the Word of God. The channels may be clear so that the Word will have free course and be glorified, or the channels may be jammed by obstruction, hatred, and thwarting on the part of evil and perverse men. Only as the Word of God has free course in our hearts, in our homes, in our society will we have the prosperity of the Lord.

XXVIII

God's Work in the Believer

*But the Lord is faithful, who shall stablish you, and keep
you from evil. . . . And the Lord direct your hearts into the
love of God, and into the patient waiting for Christ.*

—II THESSALONIANS 3:3,5

HERE WE HAVE GOD'S WORK IN THE BELIEVER. PAUL FOUNDS
that work upon the faithfulness of God, for God is faithful.
This great truth is declared again and again in Scripture. In
I Corinthians 1:9 we read, "God is faithful, by whom ye were
called unto the fellowship of his Son Jesus Christ our Lord."
And in I Corinthians 1:8 we read, "Who shall also confirm
you unto the end, that ye may be blameless in the day of our
Lord Jesus Christ." When God calls us, He is also faithful to
keep us.

In I Corinthians 10:13 we read, ". . . God is faithful, who
will not suffer you to be tempted above that ye are able; but
will with the temptation also make a way to escape, that ye
may be able to bear it." It is introduced with the words, "God
is faithful."

In I Thessalonians 5:24 we have the words, "Faithful is he
that calleth you, who also will do it." They follow the teach-

ing that God will preserve us blameless unto the coming of our Lord Jesus Christ.

In the second epistle to Timothy, chapter two, verse thirteen, it says, "If we believe not, yet he abideth faithful: he cannot deny himself." God will be faithful to His promises in spite of us.

Then, in I John 1:9, we read, "If we confess our sins, he is faithful and just to forgive us our sins, and to cleanse us from all unrighteousness." The Bible makes it very plain that God is faithful.

Now, the contrast is drawn between the previous statements in this epistle and this declaration for Paul said, ". . . all men have not faith" (II Thess. 3:2). Here, of course, we have reference to the unbelief and the unfaithfulness of ungodly men, but in contrast to that, God Himself is faithful. It is of His own nature, it is an attribute of His own being, and on the ground of the Divine faithfulness Paul postulates His work within the believer.

That faithfulness of God is also displayed in nature. The very principle of the conformity of nature is the basis of modern science, the principle of Heisenberg notwithstanding, namely, the discontinuity of nature within itself. All science is based upon the conformity of nature to law; that must be based upon some inherent principle that holds these things together, such as the being of God Himself.

Now the Scripture declares that. It says, "While the earth remaineth, seedtime and harvest, and cold and heat, and summer and winter, and day and night shall not cease" (Gen. 8:22). Oftentimes when the Lord declares His own faithfulness, He says, as in the case of His promise to David, "His seed shall endure for ever, and his throne as the sun before me" (Psa. 89:36). God bases this faithfulness upon the way in which He fulfills the provisions of nature. That great hymn that we so often sing in prayer meeting expresses that. " 'Great is Thy faithfulness,' O God my Father, There is no shadow of turning with Thee." As we sing that, we often postulate in our minds the great faithfulness of God unto the believer in all of His attributes and actions.

We depend upon that as believers. When the Lord promises to us salvation, if we will meet certain conditions, we believe in His faithfulness: ". . . that whosoever shall call on the name of the Lord shall be saved" (Acts 2:21). Well, if that were true in one day and were not true in another, our evangelistic work would be very difficult. Or, if the Lord made a promise with us concerning prayer and concerning His keeping power and it were true one day and not true another, it would be very difficult. But the promises of God are yea and amen; we may depend upon them; we may believe what He says; and if we come to an individual who is distressed over the problem of sin, over the guilt of wrongdoing and we declare that God is faithful, that He will forgive us if we confess those sins and turn unto Jesus Christ, we are acting upon the faithfulness of God.

Only yesterday it was my privilege to so declare the gospel unto a troubled soul and to see the peace that came into that face and countenance when that troubled soul came to trust Jesus Christ as Saviour and Lord. We can do that on the ground of God's faithfulness.

We also may postulate and believe that the Lord will be faithful to all of the prophetic movement of Scripture, as He has declared that ". . . the earth shall be filled with the knowledge of the glory of the Lord, as the waters cover the sea" (Hab. 2:14); that ". . . The kingdoms of this world are become the kingdoms of our Lord, and of his Christ" (Rev. 11:15); that ". . . there shall be no more death, neither sorrow, nor crying, neither shall there be any more pain . . ." (Rev. 21:4) in that kingdom; that the day will come when our outward body, which is perishing day by day, is renewed and is made like unto His own glorious body; that we shall enter into a kingdom with a renewed earth and a renewed heaven and we shall know the power of His redemption. Yes, we believe that we can trust that great promise of God. He is faithful.

Now, on the faithfulness of God, Paul declared the Lord's works in the believer, and he listed four of them in these three verses of II Thessalonians 3:3-5.

First of all, he said that the Lord would do the work of establishing the believer; then, that the Lord would keep the believer from evil; then, that the Lord would enable the believer to fulfill His commandments; and last, that the Lord would direct the believer into the love of God and the patience of Jesus Christ. Here are then declared by Paul four works which God is eminently faithful in doing for you.

I. *The Work of Stabilizing the Believer*

Is it not strange that so many of us who profess His holy name are unstable in being established in the faith?

Is it not strange that the holy loathing which we had for sin in the hour of our pardon departs from us when the blandishments of the world and the attractions of temptation reappear dressed up in some new garb, or when we find ourselves in the presence of those who have no sympathy for our profession of Christian faith. When that happens, we find that even as Christians we are unstable, that it is easy to sin, that we are prone to wander, prone to leave the God we love, that it is easy to walk in the ways of disobedience and into a return to the thralldom of sin. This is instability.

Now Paul prayed for them and declared unto them that God would establish them, establish their hearts, their experience, their faith, their testimony, their witness, their lives in all that they did. God knows that we need that establishment in the Christian faith. "A double minded man is unstable in all his ways" (James 1:8). Double-mindedness means that we look first to the right and then to the left, and we consider two objectives and not one. Instead of being single-minded, instead of having a direct purpose, we are torn between the two, and such an individual, declares James, the brother of the Lord, is an unstable man.

If that is a description of you, if you are torn between a desire to worship the Lord and a desire to indulge in the things that you love to do, if you are torn between a desire for holiness and a desire for things which you know to be contrary to God's will, that is to be double-minded.

There is a picture of that in the Bible. When the Lord came to His disciples in the midst of the night season as they were rowing across the Lake of Gennesaret, where a storm had engulfed them, He came walking on the water, and Peter and the other disciples were simply amazed. Peter said, ". . . Lord, if it be thou, bid me come unto thee on the water" (Matt. 14:28). And Jesus told him to come. Peter climbed out of that boat and started to walk to Jesus on the water, and then it says, "But when he saw the wind boisterous, he was afraid; and beginning to sink, he cried, saying, Lord save me" (Matt. 14:30). He was double-minded. While he walked, while he saw the Lord, while he was engrossed in the glory and the power and the dominion and the Person of Christ, he was able to have victory. When he looked at the circumstances round about him, he began to sink. And thus we are.

We see the problems pressing us economically, we wonder about the people who prosper in an ungodly way, we become double-minded about the honesty and integrity of our souls. We see these people who enjoy the pleasures of sin for a season, maybe in lust, or licentiousness, or other ways in the world, and we become double-minded for a moment. When we do, we are unstable in all of our ways.

How wonderful it was that God could take that man Peter, whose name was Simon, which could be translated "double-minded" or "unstable" and make him into a rock. That is exactly what Paul wanted to happen to those believers. He wanted God to establish them so that whether it was summer or winter, springtime or harvest, whether it was hot or cold, whether in an easy place or a difficult place or wherever it was, that they would be established in God and in God's righteousness. So he prayed for them, that God would establish them.

How is that stability brought about? Well, we think it is brought about by the ministry of God's Holy Spirit, whom Christ gives unto the believer and who is able to enable him to perform God's will within the heart, when the individual doesn't do it in his own strength or cannot do it in his own strength. Does this mean that there must come some second blessing for us beyond what we had as Christians? Not necessarily, but it does mean that we must recognize our weakness and our foibles, our temptations, our besetting sins, our tendency and proneness to walk in the ways that are contrary to God. Paul acknowledges that. Look at the Book of Romans, the great treatise on theology. There Paul dealt first of all in the initial five chapters with our sins that we commit, and our justification from them, and our being declared righteous in the sight of God. Then in Romans 5:13 and following, he began to deal with our heart condition. When we are prone to wander, when we want to continue in sin that grace might abound, when we want to do the things of the flesh, he said that then we are to reckon ourselves as dead unto sin, we are to be joined with the resurrected Christ, we are to have the Holy Spirit dwell within us, quickening our bodies, mortifying our physical deeds, guiding us, helping us, and assisting us in God's way. You see, Paul took cognizance of this reality, of the proneness of the believer to be unstable, and if he did it theologically, then surely we ought to recognize it in experience, and that it is necessary for us to yield unto that indwelling Spirit of the living God, so that our surrender to Him by our constant obedience to Him, by our acknowledging of the position as a bondslave unto Jesus Christ will enable us to have God work out His salvation within us with

His power. That is why Paul says, ". . . work out your own salvation with fear and trembling. For it is God which worketh in you both to will and to do of his good pleasure" (Phil. 2:12,13). What I cannot do, you cannot do, and no believer can do in himself, God can do through the gift and the ministry of His Holy Spirit in us.

Is it any wonder, then, that on the basis of the faithfulness of God, Paul should exhort them that they might be established, that God should establish them, in the faith and in their Christian practice?

Some of you are going to need that exhortation. Some of you are going to be in places where you will waver, where you will hesitate, where you may even go so far as to deny the name of your Lord Jesus Christ. Simply remember that God is still faithful and that in those hard circumstances, in those incongruous situations, He will keep you and establish you according to the gospel of our Lord Jesus Christ.

II. *The Work of Preserving the Believer*

Then Paul said, ". . . and keep you from evil" (II Thess. 3:3). Now this preservation of the believer from evil is something for which the Lord Himself instructed us to pray, but it is also one of the points of that system of doctrine called Calvinism, the final point, the preservation of the believer. It is postulated upon Christian truths, divine revelation, for God says that "He that believeth on the Son hath everlasting life: and he that believeth not the Son shall not see life; but the wrath of God abideth on him" (John 3:36). God also says, "My sheep hear my voice, and I know them, and they follow me; and I give unto them eternal life; and they shall never perish, neither shall any man pluck them out of my hand. My Father, which gave them me, is greater than all; and no man is able to pluck them out of my Father's hand. I and my Father are one" (John 10:27-30). Security is given unto those who are in the keeping of the Lord Jesus Christ as His own sheep. He is able, abundantly able, to keep them in every exigency, in every evil that shall arise. Now I suppose when He said, ". . . keep you from evil" (II Thess. 3:3), and He used this in the masculine sense, He was thinking of the evil one from whom all tribulation, temptation and trials arise, and they will beset our footsteps as sure as we are children of God; but the triumph, the ultimate overcoming is assured for those who are God's own for He will keep us from evil.

Is that not what He said in the Lord's Prayer, ". . . pray ye . . . lead us not into temptation, but deliver us from evil . . ." (Matt. 6:9,13). The Lord knew how easy it was to be led into temptation. He was tempted in all points, like as we are. When we examine the life that He lived and see all the aspects of temptation that came to Him, we recognize that we too shall be in that kind of temptation, and when we pass through it, let us remember that there is a power, the power of a Mediator, of a High Priest, of One who is forever after the order of Melchisedec and is in the presence of the Father, who prays for us, who understands, who knows, who sympathizes, who can really know the problems when we bring them unto Him in prayer and will succor us, will help us, will sustain us in that hour of that temptation and of that sin.

You take this temptation to grow angry. How general, how prevalent, how universal it is when the provocative things of life come. Now, it is true that the Lord Jesus grew angry, according to Scripture. He cleansed the temple and scourged the inmates. He upbraided them ruthlessly and fearlessly because of their hypocrisy and their sin. But, you know, the whole description in the four Gospels shows unto us that when He was reviled, when He was abused, He reviled not again, and when prodded, He answered not. He was as a sheep led to the slaughter. Consequently, though there were times when in His Messianic office He stepped up and He exercised that righteous indignation before God, yet He never indulged in any littleness and pettiness, which you find so constant and so universal among us who name the name of Christ. I say, He promises to keep us from evil. He knows, for He was tempted and He was tried in these points. If we come to Him about them, He will help us in our troubles. For, remember, He was not made after the order of the angels, but He took on Him the nature of the sons of Abraham, the nature of the sons of men that He might be a faithful and a merciful high priest and that He might be able to minister to us in all of our needs. Now He will keep you. Be not afraid wherever you go, whatever you do; He is able to keep you, He is able to make a way of escape from sin, He is faithful, He will deliver you from the evil one in such an hour.

III. *God's Work of Enabling the Believer*

And then Paul says, "And we have confidence in the Lord touching you, that ye both do and will do the things which we command you" (II Thess. 3:4). There were certain commandments that Paul had just made and some he was going to make. One that he had just made was that they should pray the Word of God would have freedom, that it would run from Corinth to Rome, and from Rome to Spain, and then back to Ephesus and all over; that it would progress and prosper in those days, and he wanted them to be faithful when he commanded them in praying for the prosperity of the advance of the progress of the Word of God. But he also commanded them here to work. He assured them that if any man did not work, he would not eat.

Then he commanded them that they should also separate themselves from certain ungodly believers or people who were not obedient to the commandments of God. And he referred to the commandments God has given us in His Word, and He expects us to keep those commandments and fulfill those commandments. And don't you believe for a moment any teaching that the Ten Commandments of the Lord do not have control over you today. We have a great propensity to talk about dishonesty in the high places of politics, but we forget about dishonesty in our own individual lives. We have a great propensity to talk about stealing in capitalism, but not stealing when it comes down to the little things of daily life. We have a great propensity to talk about violence when it deals with war and with the great social problems of lynching and such as that, but when it comes to the little things of violence, we are not willing to face those same problems in our own lives. Beloved, these Ten Commandments stand as a criterion of righteousness for you and for me before God. They are an absolute standard and we must remember that His Holy Spirit should be transforming us into the likeness of that standard. That is the plumbline that drops down to tell us whether we are righteous or unrighteous, whether we are obedient or disobedient, whether we are like God or not like God, because God gave us that standard of righteousness to make us know the difference between right and wrong. The commandments are there, but we have to pray as Augustine prayed, "God give me grace to do what Thou commandest me to do." [1] Only God can enable us.

Now Paul did not say that we have confidence in you. He said, "And we have confidence in the Lord touching you, that ye both do and will do the things which we command you" (II Thess. 3:4). It is only as God is within us; it is only as we are enjoying literal union with Him; it is only as by our faith we are united with the resurrected and living Christ and have His abundant life in us that we will be able to fulfill those commandments of our Lord. That is all. We cannot do them in our own strength. We shall surely fail.

So the Lord tells us that we are to live righteously and fulfill His commandment.

IV. *God's Work of Directing Our Hearts*

Now we come to that last great advice, which is in the form of a prayer, one of his four prayers in the second epistle.

He says, "The Lord direct your hearts into the love of God, and into the patient waiting for Christ" (II Thess. 3:5). It is a picture of God being in control by taking somebody under His supervision and leading him along the way. How beautiful. God directs your heart. God controls your heart. He holds the control of your affections. Now when the word "heart" is used here, it is not only affections, because the word "heart" in the New Testament involves the will and the mind and the affections—the whole man. The whole man is in the control of the Lord. The Lord direct your hearts into this holy character and living.

How wonderful that God has that superintending control over us as we move along. But, remember, He can't exercise that superintending control over us unless, as willing bond-slaves, as obedient servants, we are willing to accept guidance and leadership along the way. If we habituate the old places of sin, if we surround ourselves with the old temptations and companions thereof, we cannot be guided of the Lord.

I think of a young man whom we have known here who fell into temptation and bad companionship and had to be taken under the reform authorities and sent off to a reform school. Then he was under good behavior there. He listened to exhortation and teaching there, but the minute he was released and went back again to his home, he fell into the same old practices because he fell in with the same companions and the same habits, and he went down again into trouble.

Be careful of that. If we are going to be guided of the Lord, we have to follow where God leads, and the Lord will direct our hearts in two things, into the love of God and into the patient endurance of Christ. Now that is not God's love for us. It is perfectly true in Scripture that God loves us, that He made His divine overtures to us, that He exhibited His love all through history in the prophets and in the apostles and in the Person of Christ, and finally in Calvary; all these He has done in His good providences to us. Yet, this is not God's love to us. This is the return of our love unto God, and the prayer is that our hearts might be directed into the love of God, where we would live that life, loving God with all our hearts, and with all our minds, and with all our souls. It is an ideal, but how far below the ideal we fall. That we might love Him! That we might be lifted up into the fulfillment of the law, for love is the fulfilling of the law! God direct your heart into the love of God.

Now, it says, ". . . and into the patient waiting for Christ" (II Thess. 3:5). The emphasis of the epistle on the Second Coming is here felt on the translators for the word is not "patient waiting," it is "patient endurance." It is a different word altogether from waiting for someone to come; it is an endurance like unto an example. The literal translation is "into the patient endurance which is like that of Christ." Ah, Christ is our criterion; Christ is our pattern. As He endured the cross, despising the shame and is set down at the right hand of God, so He also becomes our pattern for endurance. He endured the contradictions of sinful men, and we are to endure it too. Yes, we are to look for His coming, that is the truth of the epistle, but it is not of this passage. It is that the Lord is going to direct our hearts into the love of God, and that means fulfilling His commandments, and then into the patient endurance, the patient fulfillment of the example of Christ in facing the line of duty no matter what that line of duty demands of us.

Now, you see, this was Paul's prayer for them. We saw their prayer for him, ". . . brethren, pray for us . . ." (II Thess. 3:1), and how he was strengthened in his knowledge that the Word of God was going to spread abroad because they were praying for him as he preached it. But here he was making a prayer for them. I think that was the kind of prayer that our high priest, the Lord Jesus Christ, prays for us. He is praying that we be established, established in righteousness, established in grace, that we will be strong in the Lord in the midst of all of the temptations and trials that come. He is praying that we will be kept from the evil one as He prayed in his high priestly prayer of John seventeen, Father ". . . keep them from the evil" (John 17:15). He is praying for us that God would empower us and enable us to stand, to fulfill His commandments, and He is praying that God would direct us ". . . into the love of God . . ." (II Thess. 3:5) and into the endurance of the line of duty as the Lord Jesus did.

My friends, if somewhere along the line there is a deficiency, if we have not been living like this, then let us join our prayers with His. Let us ask God to do these works in our hearts: the work of establishing us, the work of maintaining and preserving, the work of enabling us, the work of directing or guiding us into the kind of life He wants us to live. This is God's work in the heart of the believer.

XXIX

Christian Doctrine of Separation

Now we command you, brethren, in the name of our Lord Jesus Christ, that ye withdraw yourselves from every brother that walketh disorderly, and not after the tradition which ye received of us.

—II THESSALONIANS 3:6

IN A THOROUGH STUDY OF THESE VERSES OF SCRIPTURE, WE find that the predominant doctrine is that of separation, the church teaching on separation. It is illustrated by the condition of a brother or a group of individuals in the Thessalonian church who walked disorderly and who would not work. So we want to address ourselves, first of all, to the formal questions and then we will take up the material questions following that.

The rise of this particular problem of separation among believers has plagued the church for many centuries, but it is recurring in our own day. We are having a new emphasis upon the question of separation. The problem is this: Should a believer who is in a congregation where there are undisciplined unbelievers or who is in a denomination whose leadership is controlled by unbelievers, leave that denomination, or what should he do about it?

That is a very important problem and it is facing a great many people today because there is a serious invasion of the Christian churches and denominations by unbelief; or it may be called by the name of a party of Christianity, but when it is analyzed, it is soon seen to be no Christianity at all for it will not accept the very basic teachings of the Christian faith. I suppose I might suggest one for you, namely, the deity of the Lord Jesus Christ.

Now it is precisely on the person and the work of Christ that the Christian church is established and yet in the so-called Christian church of our day there are many people who do not accept the deity of our Lord Jesus Christ and who do not accept the biblical teaching of the work of Jesus Christ. They call themselves by the name Christian, they say that they con- stitute a party in the Christian church, but actually they are unbelievers who have come into the Christian church for some ulterior motive. In the early church they would not have been permitted to have been present at all. It was against such privily-brought-in false brethren that St. Paul waged his strongest contest and had the church been vigilant through the years, this would not of course have occurred. But it does exist.

So the question exists for many, many serious-minded be- lieving people. What shall we do about it? Shall we contend against these unbelievers who are now in our churches and often in positions of great power, or shall we just quietly and unobtrusively withdraw from the church, giving up the buildings, the endowments, the great name and heritage of that particular local congregation or that denomination? Or should these adopt something which they call Christianity but is not Christianity at all when it is judged by either the history of the church, the creed of the church, or the incorporation papers of the church?

Now, of course, those believers who have withdrawn from such denominations and such churches are within their rights.

They most certainly have a biblical ground for it if they so wish to do.

We do not hold, however, that they have a biblical ground for sitting in condemnation upon those who do not so withdraw from their churches. It is important for us that we look into this question now which is involved in the doctrine of separation. What exactly shall we do in conjunction with such situations which arise in the world today? Shall we join with those who withdraw, or shall we sit in judgment upon others, or what shall be the doctrine of our attitude?

Well, we certainly have to judge ourselves according to the Bible. If we are to be Bible-believing Christians and the Scripture becomes our standard of authority, it is essential for us then not to look at the practice of others, not to look alone at what some denomination or church may claim, but to look at the Bible and see what the Bible says. Therefore, I wish to point out to you now the church doctrine of separation, then to point out the discipline of an individual member on the ground of that biblical doctrine, and then the directions which stem from that for our own conduct and aspect of life.

I. The Church Doctrine of Separation

This is based upon the biblical doctrine of the church. Unless we understand the nature of the church, we will never know how we should withdraw ourselves or separate ourselves from those who are not in the church.

In this text we have some interesting words. We have a word there, "withdraw," which actually means striking a sail or drawing in your sails. It is a nautical term and often used for that purpose in which a man wants to avoid a reef or a shoal and he gives it a wide berth. Well, the analogy here is that we should restrict ourselves, draw in and withdraw, so that we do not get caught in trouble, that we give a wide berth unto that which is a source of trouble.

Then there is another word which is a very interesting one. It is the word for disorderly and actually means one who does not hold his post, one who is not loyal to his responsibility of life, one who does not fulfill the task which is actually his task. The statement is ". . . withdraw yourselves . . ." (II Thess. 3:6), or give a wide berth to this individual who does not stand at his post, who does not really fulfill his responsibility in this life, as far as doctrine, conduct, and activity are concerned.

Look then, if you will, at this church doctrine of separation. It is grounded now upon the church doctrine or the biblical doctrine of the church. When we look into the Bible for that teaching, we find two kinds of churches—the universal church, the great church of the Lord Jesus Christ, and the local church. This universal church is the ecumenical church, the catholic church, the church which constitutes His body. And there are certain marks of that universal church. The first mark of it would be its apostolicity, that means its continuity from the days of the apostles unto now. I do not think for one moment that that would necessitate an organizational continuity. It means a spiritual continuity, for the church of Jesus Christ universal is a spiritual entity. It is the body of Christ into which every believing man is baptized by the Spirit. So there must be a continuous spiritual organism with unity from the time of the apostles unto now. Then, also, there is purity, for that is a mark of the church. It is a holy, universal, catholic church and there must be a semblance of purity of holiness which is attached to that church. If it is ungodly, if it has repudiated the purity of doctrine, it of course ceases to be such a church. But purity is a mark of it. Also, there is the mark of unity. That unity means that it is one. It is marked as the body of Christ in which there are no divisions.

Well, you say, we look for such a church on earth but we do not find such a church. Yet such a church does exist. It is the universal, spiritual body of Christ made up of those who are born of God, who are members of His church, who are the saints of the household of faith, who are called the people of God. These are names for them in Scripture. Now that simply means this, that there is what we might call an intangible, spiritual body of Christ. It is not identified and coterminous with any organization as such which exists. Let me give an illustration. Rome which has existed from very early times but which was not sovereign in the church until about the fourth century and, in some respects, not until the ninth century has a continuity, but as far as purity of doctrine is concerned from biblical standards, it does not have purity. Therefore, though there are many believing Christians in Rome which we would acknowledge immediately, those of us who want to be biblical Christians cannot belong to the Roman church. We acknowledge that there are Christians within, but we ourselves find that we cannot belong unto an organization which does not retain purity of doctrine and practice according to biblical standards.

There is also the World Council of Churches that exists today, made up of probably two hundred fifty different groups from all over the world. And in that group there are men, some who are predominant leaders of the group, who are far disassociated from biblical Christianity. We could name them if it is necessary so to do. Now, though we say that there are probably millions of believing Christians in the World Council of Churches, yet for Bible-believing Christians to take their standard according to God's Word, they find that they cannot unite with that movement or organization.

Now then, if that is the universal church and if we admit that it crosses all denominational lines and all groups, even the lines of Rome and orthodoxy, and all denominations, we say that we belong to that as believers when we are born into the body of Christ, and we would not exclude ourselves from fellowship or anyone else from fellowship with us who belongs to the body of Christ, to the saints of God, to the household of faith, to the people of God. We are one in Christ Jesus.

There is another thing in the Bible beside that universal church and that is its counterpart—the local church. It has a specific organization. There is in the Bible, in Matthew sixteen, the grounds of the universal church and in Ephesians we have the encyclical epistle addressed to the universal church. In Matthew eighteen we have the local church composed of an organization with officers and elders and leaders, and we have in Corinthians the epistle addressed to the local church, dealing with the disciplines of that local church. In the Book of Acts we find different individual local churches.

Now those local churches have the responsibility of discipline. They admit and they exclude. They admit those who make their profession of faith on the ground of Christian doctrine and experience. They exclude on the ground of heresy or aberration of conduct. That is the right of the local church. Unfortunately, too many of our local churches have utterly lost all semblance of what may be called discipline. The local church which is a true Christian church according to the Bible is a church which has the mark of the preaching of God's Word, the worship in the sacraments, and also Christian action founded upon that Word. Of course that cannot be concerned and that cannot be fulfilled in the church universal, which is the spiritual body of Christ. It must be done in the local, organized, individual church congregation.

Here the lines begin to be drawn. They are drawn in the local congregation, not in the church universal, and whenever any individual church sets itself up as identical with the universal church, it is guilty of schism because it divides itself from the other brethren, and it separates itself from those which have also the right to be called the children of God.

It may be exclusive on the local grounds, but it cannot be exclusive on its universal grounds.

Where then, you say, do the denominations enter? That is a very interesting question. They are hybrid. They are neither the universal church nor are they the local church. All we can say of a denomination is that a denomination is the projection of the local church in a voluntary association with other local churches on like exclusive grounds so as to project a national or maybe even an international organization. That, however, cannot be identified with the church of Jesus Christ universal and it is wrong so to speak of that kind of church.

There are some people who talk about an invisible church and the visible organized church. They speak about the invisible church as the church which we have equated with the universal, catholic, holy church of Jesus Christ. They say we do not know who is in that church and, therefore, it is invisible. But there is no such thing in Scripture as an invisible church. The Scripture talks about the visible church, but it is the universal church, the church which is composed of born-again, believing people, the people of God in all groups everywhere, and spiritually they are one since the day of Pentecost. The Scripture also talks about a very definite local church, which some people equate with the visible church and which we have described to you as being an exclusive organization on the grounds of certain requirements and the exercise of discipline. So we cannot accept what is called an invisible and a visible church.

It is only on that ground that some people speak of having a totally pure church. Now, beloved, when you read the New Testament epistles written unto these churches, you will find that there is no such thing as a pure local church. Take, for instance, the church at Corinth. Was it pure? Paul addressed them as the ". . . sanctified in Christ Jesus . . ." (I Cor. 1:2). He called them the "brethren" (I Cor. 1:10). He acknowledged that they had the communion, the sacraments, the preaching of the Word, and all such things, but they were not pure. They had incest, they had divisions, they had drunkenness, they had immorality, they had all kinds of problems in that local church. Was it a pure church at Galatia? I think not. Paul speaks there about brethren that were privily brought in and about those who were heretics there. And so we might go on in the Colossian and other epistles of the New Testament. We may hold before us the illusion, if we please, of a pure local church, but that becomes utterly impossible as the epistles of the New Testament declare and as the history of the church declares. Every time individuals try to erect an absolutely pure individual church and separate themselves from the brethren, we multiply denominations ad infinitum, and God knows that we have enough of them in the United States now, between 250 and 275, depending on their size.

However, the question then arises, Does that mean that we shall remain constantly in fellowship with people who are not Christian people? That brings up the problem of separation in a detailed way.

There are three kinds of separation in the Bible. First of all, there is the separation from the world. The church is in the world but not of the world. The world is not to be in the church and the church is not to be identified with the world. We must serve Christ. It makes a clear line of distinction between the church and the world. Those who are to be in the church are the people of God, they are to be the born-again ones, they are to be the saints, the saved ones, not those put on a pedestal and elevated by beatification, by being canonized. A saint is one who is saved by the blood of Jesus Christ and is sanctified by the Holy Spirit and is joined by other believers into the church of Jesus Christ, and we in that group are divided from the world.

II. *Discipline of a Church Member*

But now, mark you, and the teaching comes from I Corinthians 5, we are told that we are going to be in the world. Paul says that God is going to judge the world. We are not going to judge the world. God judges the people who are in the world, and He says that in the world there are fornicators, and adulterers, and thieves, and violent men, and all kinds of individuals, and we have to live in the world and rub shoulders with those people in the world. On the basis of common grace, we must get along with them. But, said St. Paul to the Corinthian church, you must not take them into your church. And, he said, in the local church if there is a fornicator, and there was in that Corinthian church, you are to warn this man and admonish him and, if he does not repent and reform, you are to expel that man from your church, for it is wrong to have an idolator or to have a fornicator or an adulterer in the church of Jesus Christ. And that individual must be disciplined, according to St. Paul, in the local church.

Then he tells us also that the local church is to separate itself from idolatry. In II Corinthians 6:14-17, he says that idolatry has no communion with Christ, nor darkness with light, and that we are to come out from among them. Now that never in any sense means that the Christians were to come out of the Corinthian church. They were to come out of the world and the Corinthian church was to be separated from the world, not from the brethren, not from one another in any sense of that particular way. We were then, according to St. Paul, to be in the church but separated from unbelief which is in the world and from the practices therein.

Now it is on this ground that St. Paul begins to deal with these disorderly brethren at Thessalonica. Some of them would not work. Some of them because they believed that the second coming of Christ was imminent said that their brethren had enough money to keep them until such a time. Why then should they work? Paul then went into this problem in great detail. He pointed out that according to the Christian ethic involved the people are to walk orderly in this world, that they are to stand by their tasks, their responsibility, their duty; that they are to preach or that they are to fulfill and perform that before God and not merely before men. So he pointed out to them that if any man did not work, that man should not eat.

I wish that St. Paul had had the problem before him of forced employment in a modern industrial society. I wish that he had had before him also such things as the closed shop, that would shut men out from work when they want to work, and some of these other problems which are involved in modern industrial society. He did not have them before him, and the only way they can be solved today along Christian lines is to take the great principles of Scripture and apply them unto those problems. But I would say this, that the Scripture goes this far. It disassociates the Christian viewpoint of work from the heathen Greek viewpoint that looked on it as something ignoble and to be done only by slaves. It also disassociates itself from the Jewish viewpoint, although it absorbs it in part. The Jewish viewpoint was that there is a dignity to any kind of labor that was performed for the benefit of the community. Witness the practice of Jesus. He was the carpenter. Witness the practice of Paul, who undoubtedly was born in a very wealthy family and yet he was a tentmaker and practiced his trade. The Christian viewpoint is this: It builds upon the dignity of labor, but it also says that every Christian should look upon work as a responsibility and as a privilege, and that every man should be gainfully employed in some way in the world. Now that does not mean that he necessarily has to earn money if he does not need money, but it does mean that an individual who can contribute to the well-being of society simply as a Christian has that responsibility before God so to do. A Christian is not to sit in idleness, to be a loafer, to be ungainfully employed in his activity and time, in fact, Paul goes so far as to point out in his writings that this is a source of much mischief. He uses a play on words here in which he says that those who are not busy become busybodies, those who are not about their own business are working about everybody's business. They go round about working busily, but in the affairs of somebody else. Therefore, the Christian standard is that we should be gainfully, creatively employed. Take that in the analogy of Scripture and there are certain exceptions that have to be made. Paul makes them for widows, you know, who are a certain age and widows indeed, and for others as well.

I would like to pause here and inject a word about the Communist attack on this thing. Communism takes this statement by St. Paul, and perhaps he got it from someone else for some think that it came out of ancient Judaism, and communism accepts that: ". . . if any would not work, neither should he eat" (II Thess. 3:10). So, communism says, we will strike at the roots of modern poverty; we will remove all of the profit motive and we will let all of the profits of interest and of industry and of rents flow into the government, and the government then will use them for the benefit of the common people. But, says communism, it is a serious crime if a man will not work. Thus the Communists in agreement with Christian teaching on this say that an individual who will not work shall not eat and so, in a controlled society, communism denies him a bread card, denies him a passport, denies him the privileges of life, and that individual is left to starve if he is not put in a labor camp under forced labor to work for the state. For, says communism, there shall be no loafers, there shall be none of this idleness in our society. Men shall work according to their ability and they shall receive according to their need. Where communism says that it is an offense against society, according to Paul, this kind of idle life is an offense against God. St. Paul says that where you have that kind of individual, you should admonish him, warn him as a brother, but, if he continues after being warned, then disassociate yourself from him and exercise discipline on him in the church of Jesus Christ.

I suggest to you that there are many people, so-called Christian people, in this day, who need also to study this out of the Scripture.

A young man said to me, "I know you work hard, but a lot of preachers are living on other people, aren't they?" And I said, "Well, maybe I am too. I don't know. But let me point out to you a few things in Scripture, won't you?" And I took him to a few passages of Scripture where St. Paul said, "Do ye not know that they which minister about holy things live of the things of the temple? and they which wait at the altar are partakers with the altar? Even so hath the Lord ordained that they which preach the gospel should live of the gospel. But I have used none of these things: neither have I written these things, that it should be so done unto me: for it were better for me to die, than that any man should make my glorying void" (I Cor. 9:13-15). He said that he forewent his privilege for an example unto them that nobody could point at him and say that he had lived by the free gifts of other men. He has the right to do it, but God bless the man who is able to go beyond that and support himself at the same time as preaching the gospel, as did St. Paul.

III. *Directions for Church Separation*

What are the directions? Well, mark you this. First of all, the direction is that we are to be very careful in separating ourselves from others that we do not set up some shibboleth, that we do not do it on the basis of personality, that we do not do it on some ulterior motive and thus erect partitions that have already been broken down.

Certainly in the local congregation we are to be very careful that we maintain the purity of doctrine, that we maintain purity of conduct, that we maintain the purity of our sacraments. And we are to be very careful to take heed that the spirit by which we do these things is the spirit of love, the spirit of the Lord Jesus Christ, lest we hurt one another. Let us treat each other as brethren in the household of faith.

If I were to summarize it all, I would do exactly what Paul did on other occasions and that would be to say, "Be ye followers of me, even as I also am of Christ" (I Cor. 11:1).

XXX

God's Gift to the Church of Abiding Peace

Now the Lord of peace himself give you peace always by all means. . . .

—II THESSALONIANS 3:16

THIS TEXT IS A CONCLUSION TO A GREAT EPISTLE. WE ARE surprised how these first epistles of the New Testament, written to an infant church, throbbing with new-found life but facing serious problems, reflect the questions of present-day churches. As we conclude our study of the epistles of the Thessalonians, we have a sense of having shared the experience of primitive Christianity with all its riches of grace, its buoyancy of life, its perplexity amid the problems of adjustment to a heathen community, and its doctrinal immaturity in the light of the second coming of Christ with concomitant events. The preachings of St. Paul were addressed to these particular problems and should impart some degree of enthusiasm to us as they did to these early Christians. Ours should be a serious attempt to adjust our lives to first-century Christian standards.

At this point Paul was signing off his communications with the Thessalonian church, "The salutation of Paul with mine own hand, which is the token in every epistle: so I write" (II Thess. 3:17).

This personal attestation was occasioned by the questioning of the authenticity of Paul's epistles and by the possibility of non-genuine epistles being passed off as Pauline. Some think that the Galatian epistle was written between the two Thessalonian epistles but, with this exception, these were the two first epistles written by St. Paul. At the conclusion of the first epistle, he charged the brethren that the epistle should be read unto all the holy brethren, possibly inferring thereby that it should be in the church and also in various homes. In the second epistle he urges them to ". . . be not soon shaken in mind, or be troubled, neither by spirit, nor by word, nor by letter as from us . . ." (II Thess. 2:2). It is thought by some that spurious epistles purporting to come in the name of St. Paul had moved the Thessalonian Christians from their stability.

The practice initiated here by St. Paul of taking the pen from the amanuensis and signing off with his own name and salutation was repeated in Colossians 4:18 and I Corinthians 16:21. The Galatian epistle was probably written by Paul himself in large letters.

The authenticity of the Pauline letters has been the object of great and sincere scholarship in the last century. The question asked is: Were these and the so-called Pauline letters genuine? Every conceivable argument against them has been examined and the preponderant weight is in favor of their authenticity. The only Books seriously brought in question now are two of the pastoral epistles, and even they are most widely accepted.

The outcome of such research by scholarship has been a corroboration of the early church acceptance of and obedience to these epistles as Pauline and as deserving a place in the scriptural canon.

After signing off, Paul concludes by sending grace to all

of his converts. "The grace of our Lord Jesus Christ be with you all" (II Thess. 3:18). His epistles open and close with the sending of the grace of God. All that occurs within the Christian experience must be of grace which is derived from the favorable attitude of God who is reconciled by the blood of Calvary. Christian life begins and ends with grace. This grace is extended to all, even to those brethren who needed discipline as well as to the faithful and mature believers of Thessalonica.

Such establishment in grace or in the spiritual presence of God can compensate for the absence of the founder and teacher of the churches, namely, Paul. He desired to be with them (I Thess. 3:10) in order to perfect their Christian experience and learning, but he was hindered. Therefore he wished for them the grace of God to keep them from falling and to solve their problems.

In summarizing all his teaching to this Thessalonian church, he exalts the Lord Jesus Christ. The grace which he sends is of the Lord Jesus Christ, for He is the greatest manifestation of grace given to the world. The presence which he invokes is that of the Lord Jesus Christ, and God is known in Him. And the peace for which he prays is derived from the Lord Jesus Christ who is ". . . the Lord of peace . . ." (II Thess. 3:16). Thus the benediction of peace really closes the epistle with the exception of his attestation of genuineness of writing. This peace is the great gift to the church. Every member should enjoy the peace of God in all three aspects of its meaning.

I. *Abiding at Peace with God*

Spiritual conflict is the basis of our soul's condition of unrest. The unregenerate are not at peace with God. "But the wicked are like the troubled sea, when it cannot rest, whose waters cast up mire and dirt. There is no peace, saith my God, to the wicked" (Isa. 57:20,21). Our nature is at enmity to God. It neither obeys the divine law nor can it obey the law, but, by the blood of the cross, Christ ". . . abolished in his flesh the enmity, even the law of commandments contained in ordinances . . ." (Eph. 2:15). Whereas we were aliens and strangers from the promises of God and from the common-wealth of Israel, we are made nigh by the blood of the cross. Whereas we were in revolt, doing our own will rather than God's will, we come to a point of submission (Isa. 53:6; Rom. 3:10,11). While in this unregenerate state, the conflict with the law of God produced unrest of soul.

For such unregenerate people, there is a universal longing for peace, yet it is sought independently of God. Sometimes it is sought in very ignoble ways—through abandoning duty, through seeking selfish indulgence, through human love, through self-expression in fame, power, wealth, and security, or through deliberate rejection of the divine will. Sometimes it is sought in noble ways through sacrifice, service, intellec-tual achievement, in creativity. The search of the soul for rest by means of activity goes on and on until such rest is found.

Unrest tortures the souls of men, driving them ever on and on and on until it is resolved in Christ. Most of us have read the legend of the wandering Jew, which is grounded on the legend of a Jew who faced Jesus stumbling under His cross and said to Him, "Go on! Go on!" and the reply came to him, "Thou shalt go on till the end of time." Thus the story is written about the wanderings of this desolate Jew, ever seeking rest and finding none. It was Augustine who said that the soul is restless until it rests in God.

Peace with God is the result of reconciliation through the blood of the cross. The enmity which we have experienced has been removed by that cross. The holiness of God which has been in action against sin and is called wrath has been satis-fied, and the enmity between God and man has been re-moved (Rom. 6:26). Christ died ". . . that he might recon-cile both unto God in one body by the cross, having slain the enmity thereby" (Eph. 2:16). The entrance to a justified state of righteousness or acceptability in the sight of God is through faith in Jesus Christ. This faith unites us with Him so that we hold a new position before God which terminates the conflict of enmity we had with Him. Hence, the believer enjoys the rest which remains to the people of God. Unbelief alone can keep us from entering that rest which has been offered us in Jesus Christ.

Peace is thus a characteristic of a true member of the church of Christ. One who is born again or made a member of the body of Christ by the baptism of the Spirit has entered into this rest. He may continue in it as long as he walks worthy of God (II Thess. 1:12). Being worthy of God and being worthy of the Lord Jesus Christ are equated in these epistles. No rest exists for a believer who is disobedient to the Spirit and who thus grieves God. Paul prays that these believers might be sanctified by the God of peace. There is a conjunction of sanctification and of the God of peace (I Thess. 5:23). Perfect peace depends upon the nature of a sanctified life as described in this chapter.

II. *Abiding in the Peace of God*

The peace of God is a description of the state of experience of a Christian heart and mind. The Lord Jesus said, "Peace I leave with you, my peace I give unto you: not as the world giveth, give I unto you . . ." (John 14:27). We speak of the sweet peace which is the gift of God's love. That peace is the same peace which Christ had in the midst of His trial, His anxieties, sufferings, indignation, and disappointments, and it is the gift of God. Happy is the man who enjoys such peace. Paul speaks of ". . . the peace of God, which passeth all understanding . . ." (Phil. 4:7). This is different from peace with God. Peace with God is a cessation of conflict or enmity which occurs through the reconciliation at Calvary. The peace of God is the gift of God which is a state of the Christian heart. Paul says, ". . . let the peace of God rule in your hearts . . ." (Col. 3:15). This depends upon faith in the sovereignty of God, that He is able to make all things work together for good for those who love Him (Rom. 8:28). It is impossible to enjoy peace in a world of caprice or one bound by inexorable law. Peace comes from faith in an omnipotent and good God. It is only in such a world that we can resign ourselves to His will. Such resignation becomes the secret of peace. Then we are able to trust our cause unto God, trusting that He will avenge us rather than taking vengeance into our own hands (Rom. 12:19). Our conduct will derive from such inner peace of soul.

There is a distinction in the kinds of anxiety which are discussed in Scripture and which are contrasted with peace. In Philippians 2:20, Paul commends Timothy for having a "care for your state," and in Philippians 4:6, he declares "be careful for nothing." The same word, *merimnao*, which means to have a care, is used in both cases. In the first case there is an expression of strong approval of Timothy for caring for the churches. In the second place there is strong disapproval or condemnation in the care of things of life. The secret of the reconciliation of these two uses of the same word in the same epistle is in the kind of care of which Paul is speaking. First is godly care, of which the Apostle speaks, the second is sinful care. It is possible for us to have a temporary loss of peace through many incidents which may arise. This is a sorry condition for a Christian and yet we must admit that it is possible. Here we have the promise of peace always. Paul said, "Now the Lord of peace himself give you peace always, by all means . . ." (II Thess. 3:16). Is such permanent peace possible? If so, it can only be through Christ and through the grace of God. Many are the problems which affect our state of peace. Paul said, ". . . by all means" (*Ibid.*)—in conflict, in persecution, in bereavement, in discipline, in trouble—it is possible to maintain the peace of God always and in every way.

Paul makes it clear that Christ is the source of this peace. He is ". . . the Lord of peace . . ." (*Ibid.*). It is interesting here that Paul equates Christ with God. In Romans 15:8 he says, "the God of peace fill you with all peace." Here he speaks of Christ as the Lord of peace. Likewise in the first epistle, the fifth chapter, the twenty-third verse, he speaks of the "God of peace." Thus it is only through the Lord Jesus Christ that the peace of God is given unto our souls. He exhibited such peace in His own life and He can bestow it upon others. The emphasis of St. Paul is upon the Lord as the condition of peace. If He is with us, what need we fear? He can so control our wills, our fears, and our desires as to produce peace. Those who are in Christ Jesus by mystical union may have equanimity of life. If you long for the peace of God, seek it through the Lord Jesus Christ.

III. *Abiding in Peace with the Brethren*

Paul said, "If it be possible, as much as lieth in you, live peaceably with all men" (Rom. 12:18). The connection of this emphasis upon peace with our brethren and the conflict in the church of Thessalonica over disorderly brethren is very clear. The impression is irresistible that the consideration of the trouble (II Thess. 3:6-15) led him to pray this prayer for their peace, but it is impossible to confine it to this lowest level of human relationships as we have seen. It refers also to that glorious truth of justification by faith whereby we have peace with God and to the gift of God of peace in the human soul. The inference is that peace with God and of God eventuates in peace with our fellow men. It is hard to live at peace with men unless one is at peace in his own soul and with his God.

Such peace, then, is the consequence of committing our all to Jesus Christ. The Psalmist says, "Great peace have they which love thy law; and nothing shall offend them" (Psa. 119:165). And the Lord Jesus said, "Blessed are the peacemakers . . ." (Matt. 5:9). There can be no doubt that a premium is placed upon living at peace with our brethren as far as the Christian ethic is concerned.

Therefore it is the Christian duty to seek peace in all relationships of life. A Christian in the labor movement will not seek labor conflict and upheaval, but will seek understanding and peace. The Christian in the family relationships will not constantly be causing trouble, but will be seeking peace. He will sacrifice many of his own desires and his own interests for the sake of peace. The Christian in understanding or in taking leadership in the nations will work for peace. To do anything else is an anomaly as far as a Christian is concerned. We are not to sacrifice our principle, nor the truth, nor a national sovereignty in seeking peace, but we must be interested in it. Unfortunately, there is a vacuum in Christian leadership in these matters. When we recognize, as did Bishop Berggrav in speaking after the last war, that the Bible is the only basis of peace, then we need not be fatalists, but we may go ahead and attempt to introduce a measure of peace.

The first text emphasizes the abiding nature of peace, whether of God, or with God, or with our fellow men. This shall be ". . . always by all means" (II Thess. 3:16). This peace is your possession. Expect it, experience it, exhibit it. This is your heritage in the church in God. Peace be with you.

REFERENCES

CHAPTER I

[1] Dod, Marcus, *An Introduction to the New Testament*, Thomas Whitaker; p. 161: Godet, F., *Studies on the Epistles*, New York, N.Y., E. P. Dutton & Company; p. 9.
[2] Davis, John D., *A Dictionary of the Bible*, Philadelphia, Pa , The West minster Press, 1925; p. 773.
[3] Dods, *op. cit.;* p. 152.
[4] Neil, William, *The Moffatt New Testament Commentary: Thessalonians*, London, Hodder & Stoughton, 1950; p. 78.
[5] Davis, *op. cit.;* p. 661.
[6] Erdman, Charles R., *The Epistle of Paul to the Thessalonians*, Philadelphia, Pa.; p. 11.
[7] Lightfoot, J. B., *Notes on Epistles of St. Paul*, New York, N.Y., Macmillan & Company, 1895; p. 13.
[8] Godet, *op. cit.;* p. 4.

CHAPTER II

[1] Porritt, Arthur, *John Henry Jowett*, London, Hodder & Stoughton, 1924; pp. 217-219.
[2] Lightfoot, *op. cit.;* p. 6.
[3] *Ibid.*, p. 9.
[4] *Ibid.*, p. 10.
[5] *Ibid.*
[6] Neil, *op. cit.;* p. 42.

CHAPTER III

[1] Cf. Unger, M. F., *Biblical Demonology*, Wheaton, Ill., Van Kampen Press; McCasland, S. V., *The Finger of God*, New York, N.Y., 1952.
[2] Neil, *op. cit.;* p. 25.
[3] Phillips, J. B., *Letters to Young Churches*, New York, N.Y., The Macmillan Company, 1950; p. 133.
[4] Neil, *op. cit.;* pp. 29, 30.
[5] *Ibid.*, p. 31.
[6] Lightfoot, *op. cit.;* p. 16.
[7] Olshausen, Herman, *Commentary on St. Paul's Epistle to Thessalonians*, T. & T. Clark; p. 406.

[8] Neil, *op. cit.;* p. 19.
[9] Eadie, *Commentary on Thessalonians;* p. 47.
[10] MacLaren, Alexander, *Expositions of Holy Scriptures,* Grand Rapids, Mich., Wm. B. Eerdman's Publishing Company, 1944; Vol. XIV, pp. 164-170.

CHAPTER IV

[1] Thayer, *Greek-English Lexicon of the New Testament,* New York, N.Y., Harper & Brothers, 1896; p. 6.
[2] Neil, *op. cit.;* p. 32.
[3] Lightfoot, *op. cit.;* p. 17.

CHAPTER IX

[1] Bainton, Roland, *Here I Stand,* Nashville, Tenn., Abingdon-Cokesbury Press, 1950; p. 21.
[2] *Ibid.,* p. 42.
[3] *Ibid.*
[4] *Ibid.,* pp. 42, 43.
[5] *Ibid.,* p. 43.
[6] *Ibid.,* p. 44.
[7] *Ibid.,* pp. 193, 194.
[8] *Ibid.,* p. 27.
[9] *Ibid.,* p. 181.

CHAPTER XII

[1] Thayer, *op. cit.*
[2] Phillips, *op. cit.;* p. 136.
[3] Neil, *op. cit.;* p. 79.
[4] Phillips, *op. cit.*

CHAPTER XIII

[1] Thayer, *op. cit.;* p. 281.
[2] Phillips, *op. cit.*
[3] Trueblood, Elton, *The Life We Prize,* New York, N.Y., Harper & Brothers, 1951; p. 121.
[4] *Ibid.,* p. 129.

CHAPTER XIV

[1] Lightfoot, *op. cit.;* p. 63.
[2] *Ibid.,* p. 62.
[3] Neil, *op. cit.;* 91.
[4] Lightfoot, *op. cit.;* p. 67.

Chapter XV

[1] Lightfoot, *op. cit.*; p. 70.
[2] *Ibid.*
[3] *Ibid.*
[4] *Ibid.*
[5] Neil, *op. cit.*; p. 108.
[6] *Ibid.*, p. 109.
[7] Scofield Bible, p. 1212.
[8] Ironside, Harry A., *Addresses on the First and Second Epistles of Thessalonians*, Loizeaux Brothers, 1947; p. 56.
[9] Neil, *op. cit.*; p. 110.
[10] Phillips, *op. cit.*; p. 137.

Chapter XVI

[1] Trueblood, Elton, *Signs of Hope*, New York, N.Y., Harper & Brothers; p. 55.
[2] Thomas, Ivor, *The Socialist Tragedy*, New York, N.Y., The Macmillan Company, 1951; p. 167.
[3] The Westminster Shorter Catechism, question 31.
[4] Phillips, *op. cit.*; p. 137.
[5] MacLaren, *op. cit.*; pp. 205, 206.

Chapter XVII

[1] Olshausen, Herman, *Biblical Commentary on St. Paul's Epistles to the Galatians, Ephesians, Colossians, and Thessalonians*, T. & T. Clark, 1851; p. 450.
[2] Lightfoot, *op. cit.*; p. 76.
[3] MacLaren, *op. cit.*; p. 212.
[4] *A Service Book*, p. 140.

Chapter XVIII

[1] Thayer, *op. cit.*
[2] Phillips, *op. cit.*
[3] Neil, *op. cit.*; p. 123.
[4] *Ibid.*, p. 124.
[5] Neil, *op. cit.*; p. 125.

Chapter XIX

[1] Thayer, *op. cit.*; p. 6.
[2] Lightfoot, *op. cit.*; p. 87.
[3] Miley, John, *Systematic Theology*, Eaton & Mains, Vol. II; p. 354.
[4] *Ibid.*, p. 357.
[5] *Ibid.*, pp. 364, 365.
[6] The Westminster Shorter Catechism, question thirty-five.

[7] Cf. White, Alexander, *Lord Teach Us to Pray*, New York, N.Y., Doubleday Doran & Company, 1929; p. 221 ff.

[8] Thayer, *op. cit.*; p. 443.

[9] Lightfoot, *op. cit.*; p. 89.

[10] Browning, Robert, "Andrea Del Sarto," *Browning's Complete Poems*, Boston, Mass., Houghton Mifflin Company, 1895; p. 346.

CHAPTER XX

[1] Bonar, Andrew A., *Memoirs of McCheyne*, Introduction, Chicago, Ill., Moody Press, 1951; p. 25.

[2] Olshausen, Herman, *Commentary on St. Paul's Epistle to the Romans*, T. & T. Clark; p. 424.

[3] Neil, *op. cit.*; p. 136.

CHAPTER XXI

[1] Neil, *op. cit.*; p. 141.

[2] Bruce, F. F., *The Spreading Flame*, Grand Rapids, Mich., Wm. B. Eerdman's Publishing Company, 1953; Part II, p. 12-15.

[3] *Ibid.*, pp. 29-44.

[4] *Ibid.*, Part I, pp. 162-163.

[5] *Ibid.*, Part II, pp. 21-23.

[6] Schaff, Phillip, *History of the Christian Church*, New York, N.Y., Charles Scribners Sons, 1924; Vol. II, p. 64.

[7] Bruce, *op. cit.*; Part III, pp. 11-19.

[8] Stein, Leo, *I Was in Hell with Niemoeller*, New York, N.Y., Fleming H. Revell Company, 1942.

[9] Bruce, *op. cit.*; Part III, p. 17.

CHAPTER XXII

[1] Buchan, John, *Augustus*, Boston, Mass., Houghton Mifflin Company, 1937; pp. 24-51.

CHAPTER XXIII

[1] The Westminster Shorter Catechism, question 31.

CHAPTER XXIV

[1] Thayer, *op. cit.*; p. 67.

[2] *Christian Century*, March 12, 1952.

[3] *Ibid.*

[4] *Ibid.*

CHAPTER XXV

[1] Tobey, Charles W., *Return to Morality*, New York, N.Y., Doubleday, 1951; p. 67.

[2] Ironside, *op. cit.*; p. 99.

Chapter XXVI

[1] The Westminster Shorter Catechism, question 31.
[2] Marshall, Catherine, *A Man Called Peter*, New York, N.Y., McGraw Hill Company, Inc., 1951.

Chapter XXVII

[1] Torrey, R. A., *The Holy Spirit*, New York, N.Y., Fleming H. Revell Company, 1927; pp. 25, 26.
[2] Lightfoot, *op. cit.*; p. 124.
[3] Phillips, *op. cit.*; p. 141.
[4] Neil, *op. cit.*; p. 188.
[5] Lightfoot, *op. cit.*; p. 124.
[6] The Constitution of the Presbyterian Church in the U.S.A. (1888), p. 11.

Chapter XXVIII

[1] Augustine, Saint, *Confessions*.